ARISTOPHANES

THE COMEDIES OF ARISTOPHANES: VOL. 3

Clouds

with an Introduction, Translation and Notes by

Alan H. Sommerstein

Aris & Phillips is an imprint of
Oxbow Books

First published 1982. Second edition 1984. Third edition 1991.
Revised reprint with addenda & bibliography 2007.

ISBN 0-85668-210-1
ISBN 978-0-85668-210-0

A CIP record for this book is available from the British Library

The LaserGreek font used in the addenda is available from Linguist's Software Inc.
P.O. Box 580, Edmonds, WA 98020-0580 USA tel (425) 775-1130 www.linguistsoftware.com

Printed in Great Britain
by CPI Antony Rowe, Eastbourne

Contents

PREFACE

This third volume of *The Comedies of Aristophanes* follows the pattern of its two predecessors, except that in citing poetic fragments, where a modern edition has become standard I no longer normally give a parallel reference to an older one. For the principles followed in compiling the critical apparatus, the reader is referred to page 20 of the first volume (*Acharnians*); I here repeat my grateful acknowledgement of the help provided by Sir Kenneth Dover, while emphasizing that I am wholly responsible for any errors or shortcomings. I am also happy to thank Jeffrey Henderson and Giuseppe Mastromarco for their continuing assistance and encouragement.

But my greatest debt of gratitude this time must be to the medical, nursing and auxiliary staff of University Hospital, Nottingham, but for whom I very much doubt if this volume would ever have been completed. It would not be appropriate to dedicate to them an edition of a play in which all scientific activity is condemned as useless and anti-social; that tribute must await a better occasion. Let me for the time being merely put on record my thanks for the wonderful treatment (in every sense of those words) that I received at their hands when I needed it in 1980 and 1981.

Alan H. Sommerstein
Nottingham, November 1981

PREFACE UPDATE

This new edition includes addenda (pp. vi–xxvii), references to which are indicated by an asterisk in the margin of the text. The addenda are based on those published in my edition of *Wealth* in this series (2001), but with further additions and updates.

I have also added a bibliography, the lack of which was one of the main weaknesses of the original edition.

Alan H. Sommerstein
Nottingham, February 2007

Addenda

Introductory Note

p.2   *apparently intending to produce it again:* that the author of the Hypothesis cited on p.4 is right to assert this (whether or not he was doing so on the basis of any firm information) is carefully and convincingly argued by M. Revermann, *Comic Business* (Oxford, 2006) 326–332. He suspects that the revised script may not have gone into circulation until after (perhaps long after) Ar.'s death, but was preserved archivally by his family; fourth-century references to the text of *Clouds* may all, for all we know, be to the 423 version.

p.2   *it was placed third and last:* the failure of *Clouds* is convincingly explained by M. Hose, *Drama* 3 (1995) 27–50, as being due to its sharp deviation from the normal patterns of contemporary comedy, which Hose describes, on the basis of Ar.'s other plays of the 420s, as embodying the triumph of a representative of the Athenian ideal over a flawed reality. In *Clouds* no-one represents the Athenian ideal, and the dénouement is typically *tragic*.

p.2 n.1   Against the attempt by E.C. Kopff, *AJP* 111 (1990) 318–329, to downdate the revision to c.414, see J.J. Henderson in R.M. Rosen and J.J. Farrell ed. *Nomodeiktes: Greek Studies in Honor of Martin Ostwald* (Ann Arbor, 1993) 591–601. I have argued in P. Thiercy and M. Menu ed. *Aristophane: la langue, la scène, la cité* (Bari, 1997) 276 n.22 that the new parabasis, which assumes (534–6) that mention of Electra will call Aeschylus to mind rather than Sophocles or Euripides, must have been written between Dionysia 419 and Dionysia 417 and most likely in the first twelve of those twenty-four months.

p.2 n.3   Eupolis' *Baptai* does not directly give a *terminus ante quem* for the revision of *Clouds*, since it is probably responding not to *Clouds* but to *Anagyrus* (Ar. fr. 58 K-A).

p.2 n.4   On the portrayal of intellectuals in comedy, see B. Zimmermann (and discussants) in *EH* 38 (1993) 255–286; O. Imperio in A.M. Belardinelli et al., *Tessere* (Bari, 1998) 43–130; and C. Carey in F.D. Harvey and J. Wilkins ed. *The Rivals of Aristophanes* (London/Swansea, 2000) 419–436. Carey notes (pp.427–431) that there is little sign that Old Comic dramatists other than Aristophanes took much interest in the major rationalist thinkers of their day, other than Socrates and to some extent Protagoras, and that they, and presumably their audiences, seem to have been more interested in the allegedly parasitic role of intellectuals in society (cf. *Clouds* 331–4) than in their innovative ideas. This "avoidance of sustained engagement with the intellectual content of contemporary thought by [other] comic poets suggests that Aristophanes was taking a calculated risk in offering his audience [in *Clouds*] a play with so much intellectual meat. ... *Clouds* may have failed in part because it was too much concerned with ideas in which the audience had little interest." (Carey *op.cit.* 431).

p.3   *their dupe Strepsiades:* A. Grilli, *Inganni d'autore: due studi sulla funzione del protagonista nel teatro di Aristofane* (Pisa, 1992) contains a valuable discussion of the presentation of Strepsiades in *Clouds*. He regards Strepsiades, not Socrates, as the centre of interest in the play, holding that the immorality of the sophists, being axiomatic in Old Comedy, is not so much asserted as assumed. Strepsiades differs from all normal Aristophanic heroes (1) in his weakness, passivity, and ineffectiveness, and (2) in explicitly accepting the immorality of his own project; once this begins to become apparent (from somewhere between 73 and 98–99), there are only two subsequent scenes in which he regains some heroic traits, viz. the creditor-scene and the (new) ending.

p.3   *the unfair image of Socrates created by comedy:* Guidorizzi on 223ff, analysing Ar.'s image of Socrates, sees it as having been compounded from five elements: the priest of an exotic mystery religion (see comm. on 140); a Pythagorean ascetic (cf. A. Willi, *The Languages of Aristophanes* (Oxford, 2003) 113–6); an atheistic scientist; a sophist teaching grammar; and, to an uncertain extent, the real Socrates. To these one should surely add, as a sixth element, a teacher of rhetoric (such as Antiphon); Willi *op.cit.* 105–114 adds a seventh, a semi-divine sage like Empedocles.

p.3   *this prejudice is more dangerous to him:* the "indictment" brought against Socrates by this "first set of accusers", which he states twice *in extenso* (Apol. 18b, 19b–c) each time with a reference to comedy (18d, 19c), contains precisely the main elements of the portrayal of Socrates in *Clouds* ("studying things below the earth and in the sky, and making the weaker argument into the stronger, and instructing other people in these same things", 19b–c tr. M.C. Stokes) with the exception of his rejection of the traditional gods in favour of the Clouds and other novel deities, which for obvious reasons it does not suit the Platonic Socrates to highlight at this stage of his defence.

p.4   *revised in details:* better "partly revised"; see R.K. Fisher, *Aristophanes' Clouds: Purpose and Technique* (Amsterdam, 1984) 23 n.16.

p.4 n.10   I.C. Storey, *AJP* 114 (1993) 71–84, seeks to identify other elements in the surviving text which belong to 423 rather than later. His conclusion is that except as noted by the ancient commentators, revision had not progressed far and the play was a long way from being ready for restaging. In Thiercy & Menu ed. *Aristophane* 269–282, I argue that in the original play Strepsiades was not present during the *agōn*; that 1105–14 were inserted as part of the revision; and (in agreement with Storey) that outside the sections now represented by 518–562, 886–948, 1105–1115 and 1437–end there were few, if any, substantial changes (only one fragment of the first *Clouds*, viz. Ar. fr. 392, seems to come from outside these sections, and that may be wrongly attributed). For other recent views on the extent and nature of the revision, see H. Tarrant, *Arctos* 25 (1991) 157–181; MacDowell 134–149 (whose reconstruction of the original ending ignores the attested presence in the first *Clouds* of part of what is now line 1417); and A. Casanova, *Prometheus* 26 (2000) 19–34.

Note on the Text

p.5 n.1   Another papyrus not cited in the apparatus is Π65 (Rainer Papyrus III 20), a fragment of a commentary on *Clouds* 186–211, incorporating a few words of the text.

Table of Sigla

An ostracon of the first century BC in the Bodleian Library (*OBodl* I 279) has been shown by N. Litinas, *ZPE* 141 (2002) 103–5, to contain, in a very corrupt form (only one, or at most two, of the eight words are correct), the second half of *Clouds* 974 and the first half of 975; it is cited below as Ⅎ. Litinas thinks the text may well be (part of) a schoolboy's exercise.

A recent pair of articles by C.M. Mazzucchi, *Aevum* 77 (2003) 263–275 and 78 (2004) 411–440, dates K to 1180–86, which would place it alongside R, V, and perhaps Md1 as a rare representative of the tradition as it was before the 1204 sack of Constantinople.
U should be dated "late 13th": L. Battezzato, *Prometheus* 22 (1996) 29–34, has shown that it was produced in the same environment, and probably close to the same time, as Φ (Laurentianus *conv. soppr.* 66), whose date is now known (see K. Matthiessen, *Scriptorium* 36 (1982) 255–8) to be 1291.

Text and Translation

1–18   Since at 18 *pai* "boy" is the second, not first, word in the sentence, it is *not* being used to call the slave's attention, and therefore, as Thiercy has seen, he must be on stage from the start. Presumably he is asleep (cf. 5); Strepsiades must therefore wake him up with a nudge or kick before speaking to him. His first words to the slave should be rendered "Light a lamp, boy, ...".

35   K.J. Dover, *The Greeks and their Legacy: Collected Papers, Vol. II* (Oxford, 1989) 265, points out that V3 has the true reading in its text (doubtless an emendation made with the help of the scholia).

53–55   Lucian, *On Mourning* 17, shows that Greek *spathân* "weave closely, be extravagant" could also mean, in the middle voice (*spathâsthai*), "spend oneself sexually", and J.J. Henderson, *The Maculate Muse*[2] (New York, 1991) 171–2 sees here a play on this sense: Strepsiades' wife is being extravagant *both* with his money *and* with his sexual energies. This provides a much-needed punch-line (trans. e.g. "You're squandering my resources"); but in order to make it work, the business of displaying the cloak must be so managed as to draw attention not only, or even mainly, to the garment (under which Strepsiades has no doubt been sleeping, or trying to sleep), but to the flaccid phallus that is revealed when the garment is lifted up.

142   In the first hardcover printing this line (ἥκω μαθητὴς εἰς τὸ φροντιστήριον) was accidentally omitted from the text.

172–3   For "gazing open-mouthed at the sky" read "gazing up open-mouthed", and for "eaves" read "ceiling", for the following reasons: (1) "ceiling" (or "roof as viewed from within") is the normal (though not the invariable) meaning of Greek *orophē*; (2) geckos do walk upside down on ceilings (see e.g. H.S. Ngor and R. Warner, *Surviving the Killing Fields: The Cambodian Odyssey of Haing S. Ngor* (London, 1988) 421); (3) a person who went outside to look up at the moon would not stand directly under the eaves of a house; (4) this is how Plato seems to have interpreted the passage, to judge by *Rep.* 7.529a–b where the phrases "decorations on a ceiling" and "gazing up open-mouthed" (*anō kekhēnōs*, the same words used here) appear within a few lines of each other in a discussion of the study of astronomy. Until the end of 172 the story sounds like a little-altered version of that of Thales and the well (see comm.); then, as in 179, the scene suddenly changes, as it turns out that Socrates is conducting his astronomical investigations *indoors* (the preferred space of these pale-faced thinkers). Possibly we are to understand that he is so intent on his thoughts that he has forgotten it is the ceiling, not the sky, above him. The point of "in the dark" is that in a dimly-lit ancient room at night, with any lamp placed relatively low, a small animal high up would be very hard to see (especially if one's mind was elsewhere!).

178   The best solution for this crux (see comm.) may well lie in Guidorizzi's suggestion (in his commentary) of a lacuna (presumably after 178).

226   For "wicker cage" read "cheese-rack"; D. Ambrosino, *MCr* 19/20 (1984/5) 51–69, has argued convincingly (i) that this is what Greek *tarros* means here and (ii) that in view of 232–4 it is significant that fresh cheeses were put on racks *to dry out*. Socrates, it may thus be supposed, is standing on a four-cornered rack of stiff wickerwork which hangs by four cords from the hook of the stage crane. (Ambrosino places him on a rack *which stands on the stage-house roof*; but he would then need to go briefly offstage in order to get down to ground level, and 237–9 gives him no time to do so – contrast *Wasps* 155–168, *Lys.* 884–9.)

275–328   For a novel suggestion on the entrance of the chorus see now P. von Möllendorff in E. Pöhlmann et al. *Studien zur Bühnendichtung und zum Theaterbau der Antike* (Frankfurt, 1995) 147–151, who proposes (adapting to *Clouds* a suggestion made in relation to *Peace* by P. Thiercy, *Aristophane: fiction et dramaturgie* (Paris, 1986) 127–8) that the actual entrance of the chorus is made, not via a wing-entrance (*eisodos*), but *coming down through the audience area*. This ingenious suggestion, however, is rejected by Revermann, *Comic Business* 199–202, on the narrow but sufficient grounds that πλάγιαι (325) shows that the chorus entered from the side. His own solution is designed to draw attention to "the incongruity between the laws of nature, which require clouds to be above ground level ... , and the laws of the theatre, which needs a chorus of clouds to sing and dance in the orchestra". The clouds sing within the *skene*, then move into position to enter via the *eisodos*; then, from 323, "by means of gesture Socrates marks the final part of the journey from the northern border of Attica, at the audience's back [n.b.], while the clouds are not yet visible to them. As Socrates is speaking lines [324–5], his finger, still lifted up, slowly moves towards one side, while Strepsiades, who is eagerly following the finger, keeps staring up into the sky. Only now, perhaps, do the *choreutai* start to move onstage – with Strepsiades still looking for them in the sky until Socrates redirects him".

327   For "unless you've got styes the size of pumpkins" read "unless your eyes are running bottlefuls of rheum"; the *kolokuntē* is the white-

flowered bottle-gourd, *Lagenaria vulgaris*, the husk of whose fruit made a handy container for various liquids. Cf. J.L. Heller, *ICS* 10 (1985) 111.

337   If we read διερᾶς (Reisig) and assume that it is here used as a noun meaning "water, sea" (as its synonym ὑγρά often is: cf. *Wasps* 678, *Iliad* 24.341) we can omit the comma after this word and create a single phrase which may be rendered "the crook-taloned air-floating birds of the airy sea" (so Thiercy): not a very elegant phrase, but it's not meant to be!

340   Read λέξον νύν μοι (K^s: probably a variant rather than a supplement), since δή is more likely to be a gloss on νυν than vice versa (this gloss is often added to remind readers that this is the particle νυν and not the temporal adverb νῦν).

385   For "who do you expect to believe that?" read "what reason is there for believing that?"; see D.M. MacDowell, *CR* 33 (1983) 175.

398   For "the age of Cronus" read "the Cronia" (see Addenda to comm. *ad loc.*).

411–427   F.W. Fritzsche, *De fabulis ab Aristophane retractatis III* (Rostock, 1851) 6–7 suggested transposing 423–6 to stand between 411 and 412, which gives a much smoother sequence of thought: having completed his demonstration that the Clouds are the cause of natural phenomena traditionally attributed to Zeus, Socrates asks Strepsiades whether he will henceforth regard them (with Chaos and the Tongue) as the only gods (423–4), and on Strepsiades' assenting to this (425–6) the Clouds invite him to become their pupil if he can accept their discipline (412–9), he assures them he can (420–2), and they then ask him what he wants him to do for him (427–8). The displacement of 423–6 will have been due to the near-homoeoteleuton between 411 and 426 causing the four lines to be omitted, later to be restored to the text in the wrong place.

439   Cobet's deletion of χρήσθων leaves ἀτεχνῶς ὅ τι βούλονται almost without a syntactic construction; better, with Hermann and Guidorizzi, posit a lacuna after νῦν οὖν. Reisig's <οὗτοι> (= the members of the school) is plausible, but <μοῦτοι> would be even better.

509   For "hanging" read "peering".

554   For ἡμετέρας read ἡμετέρους. (Correction inserted in this edition.)

561   For εὐφραίνεσθ' read εὐφραίνησθ'. (Correction inserted in this edition.)

638   E. Degani, *GFF* 11 (1988) 55–56, strongly commends Hermann's conjecture ἢ ῥυθμῶν ἢ περὶ ἐπῶν, which is in keeping with the structure of the passage and the logical relations of the topics, "measures" and "rhythms" (which together form what we would call

metrics) being discussed first and in that order (639–645, 647–654) and followed by "words", i.e. grammar (658–693). The apparatus should read:

ῥυθμῶν ἢ περὶ ἐπῶν Hermann: περὶ ῥυθμῶν ἢ ἐπῶν NΘ: περὶ ἐπῶν ἢ ῥυθμῶν REK: περὶ ἐπῶν ἢ περὶ ῥυθμῶν Longinus *Prolegomena to Hephaestion* 83.19, Choeroboscus *in Heph.* 179.6: ἐπῶν ἢ περὶ ῥυθμῶν V ᵛˡChoeroboscus *loc.cit.*: ῥυθμῶν Choeroboscus *in Heph.* 203.2.

The translation should read: "About measures or rhythms, or about words?"

723–6   The rapid exit and re-entry I posit for Socrates is implausible; more likely he first appears at a window, coming out of the door only at 731 (so Guidorizzi).

740–1   For "slice your thought into minute parts" read "open out your thinking and refine it"; see D.M. MacDowell, *CR* 33 (1983) 175.

819   For τὸν (codd.) read τὸ (Valckenaer): Symmachus (in Σᴱ) seems not to have had an article at all in his text, for he says the second syllable of Δία should be scanned long!

849   The true reading ταὐτὸ is also in Θ (Dover, *The Greeks and their Legacy* 265).

894   For "I'll defeat you", since the Greek verb is present, read "I can beat you".

953   For the obelized words read ἀμείνων λέγων (Dover); cf. on 1028–9 below.

962   I should have mentioned (though no other editor does!) that the scholia here report that Aristophanes <of Byzantium> "strongly accepted these words (ταῦτα) as being well composed" – which implies that some mss. known to him had omitted them. The scholium does not specify precisely what words are referred to, but line 962 could well have been omitted in some copies by homoeoteleuton, and its absence would then not have been noticed except through collation with other copies. To show how easily this may happen, it may be noted that Π8 omits 969, apparently by homoearchon, even though this makes nonsense of the passage.

974   In ⊐ the last word of the line is επαχθει: grammar would require ἐπαχθές, but this is far more likely to have supplanted the rare ἀπηνές (as a gloss, a banalization – or the guess of an inattentive schoolboy taking dictation?) than vice versa.

975   The second and third apparatus citations should read:]νους Π8:]νοις Π8ˢ. The ostracon ⊐ reads ἀντεταμενους, thus confirming the plural offered by Π8 and *n*.

983 For "dainties" read "fancy fish".

995 Henderson (LCL) conjectures οὗ for ὅ τι, retaining μέλλεις and ἀναπλήσειν: the language is strained and probably refers euphemistically to sexual transgressions which this speaker finds too gross to mention.

1005–8 This passage has been discussed by J. Taillardat, *REG* 95.2 (1982) xvi–xviii; E.K. Borthwick, *Nikephoros* 2 (1989) 125–134; and (most convincingly) J. Jouanna, *BCH* 118 (1994) 35–49, who argues that (1) ἀποθρέξει means "you will go for a training run" (cf. Ar. fr. 645); (2) *pace* Taillardat and Borthwick, athletes are occasionally shown in vase-paintings wearing garlands or headbands; (3) for λευκῷ read λεπτῷ (van Leeuwen), not γλαυκῷ nor λιτῷ (Borthwick); (4) φυλλοβολούσης is correct and bears its ordinary meaning, since 1007 refers to autumn as is proved by the reference to green-brier (*mîlax*) which flowers in October/November. The only weakness in this analysis is that the text offers no particle or particles to mark the alleged contrast between autumn (1007) and spring (1008); this can be remedied by reading in 1008 e.g. ἦρός θ' ὥρᾳ χαίρων. The translation should read: "no, you will go down to the Academy and take a training run under the sacred olive-trees, wearing a light reed chaplet, together with a good decent companion of your own age, fragrant with green-brier and leaf-shedding poplar and freedom from cares, or delighting in the season of spring, when the plane tree whispers to the elm".

1028–9 Zimmermann ii 126–7 proposes the excellent emendation εὐδαίμονες ἄρ' ἦσαν (Ω = Laurentianus XXXI 35 (15th century)) οἱ ζῶντες ἐπὶ Κρόνου τότε "Happy, I see, were they who lived then, in the days of Cronus". Elsewhere in the play the name of Cronus labels people and practices as archaic or obsolete (398, 929, 1070); but it was also associated with the felicity of the Golden Age when Cronus had ruled the universe, before the harsh reign of Zeus (cf. Telecleides fr. 1; Cratinus fr. 176; Hes. *Works* 109–119; *Alcmeonis* fr. 7 Davies; Pl. *Polit.* 271c–272b; (Pl.) *Hipparchus* 229b; Arist. *Ath.Pol.* 16.7).

1113 Read δὲ σοὶ, since Strepsiades is being contrasted with Pheidippides and the Worse Argument (the subjects of the previous sentence).

1119 Coraes' emendation is far from satisfactory, but the transmitted text (accepted by Guidorizzi) lacks an essential definite article (as witness Del Corno's translation, "*le* vite gravide di grappoli"). Might one read τὰς καρπὸν τεκούσας ἀμπέλους ("your vines when they have borne their fruit")?

1137 The transmitted text is defensible; the lack of connection with the previous sentence (asyndeton) can be explained on the ground that

1137–41 is essentially a fuller statement of what is said in 1135–6. In translation, for "crush and destroy me; and when I make ..." read "crush and destroy me: when I make ...".

1142–77 In a forthcoming paper in *CQ*, David Konstan ingeniously suggests that when Socrates answers the door at 1145 he is accompanied by a silent disciple; that 1164 is addressed to this disciple, who, however, makes no move in response; and that either Socrates or the disciple himself then announces (1167) that he is none other than Pheidippides, whom, in his transformed state, his father (and many – I would suspect all – of the audience) had failed to recognize.

1155–6 For "moneylenders" read "loan-sharks"; an *obolostatēs* was one who made a living by lending small sums for short periods at very high rates of interest. See P.C. Millett, *Lending and Borrowing in Ancient Athens* (Cambridge, 1991) 179–188, 303 n.10. It does not follow from Strepsiades' use of this term that the creditors whom we see later are actually to be regarded as professional moneylenders; see comm. on 1216.

1171 An accent has been inadvertently omitted; read ἰοὺ ἰού.

1192 The last word of Strepsiades' question should read προσέθηχ'.

1287 An accent has been inadvertently omitted; read κατὰ μῆνα.

1308 Add to apparatus: λήψεταί τι Bergk: λήψεται RVE^{ac}K: τι λήψεται E^{pc}NΘ.

1473–4 It is attractively suggested by Revermann, *Comic Business* 234–5, that Strepsiades here smashes the *dinos* to the ground.

1494 For "*He sets fire to the rafters*" read "*He throws the torch down into the house*" (so Thiercy): a fire that starts at or near floor level, if it takes hold quickly, is more dangerous to life than one that starts at roof level, because the rising flame and smoke are more likely to trap and/or suffocate those in the building. Care would have been taken (if the revised script had ever been produced) to have some combustible material strategically placed so that the torch, falling on it, could kindle a realistic blaze (and also, one hopes, to place plenty of water within easy reach); cf. Addenda to comm. on 1484–5.

Notes[1]

18 The mechanics of Athenian interest-bearing loans were brilliantly expounded, almost entirely from this play, by D.M. MacDowell in a paper presented to the Leeds International Classical Seminar meeting of 16th May 2003. Loans were normally made for a month at a time (756); at the end of each month the loan could either be repaid (cf. 1267–78) or renewed; if it was renewed, a new tranche of interest became due and could either be paid (1287–9) or added to the loan (cf. 1156); but the creditor had the right to refuse a request for renewal of the loan or deferment of interest, and instead to insist on full payment and sue if payment was not made (cf. 1138–41). In Aristotle's time such a case ("if someone borrows at a drachma [per mina per month, i.e. 12%] and defaults") would have been dealt with by one of the five *eisagogeis* (Arist. *Ath.Pol.* 52.2), but this magistracy was of recent creation, and it is likely that in the fifth century the case would have gone to the relevant panel of the "deme-judges" (later called the Forty).

21 Twelve minas appears to have been a not untypical price for a top-class horse (cf. Lys. 8.10, Xen. *Anab.* 7.8.6 (50 darics = 10 minas)) and also, at least in the later fourth century, the maximum allowable compensation for a cavalry horse disabled or killed in service (see G.R. Bugh, *The Horsemen of Athens* (Princeton, 1988) 158, 169).

*23 **when I bought the horse:** both here and in 1224–5 the sale and the loan are so closely linked that we are probably expected to assume that this transaction was the Athenian equivalent of a sale on credit: the seller lent the purchase price to the buyer, thus enabling him to make the purchase as a cash transaction, and the buyer then became a debtor in a monthly loan arrangement as explained in the previous note. In view of this, it is reasonable to identify the First Creditor (1214–58) with the Pasias mentioned here, even though the Second Creditor is clearly *not* the same as the Amynias of 31. See D.M. MacDowell, *The Law in Classical Athens* (London, 1978) 138–9, and E.E. Cohen in M. Gagarin and D. Cohen ed. *The Cambridge Companion to Greek Law* (Cambridge, 2005) 293–6.

23 See also J.H. Kroll, *Hesperia* 46 (1977) 86–88.

34–35 MacDowell in his Leeds paper argues that the apparent contrast drawn here between lawsuits and distraint suggests that the first of my alternative interpretations should be preferred: some of Strepsiades' creditors had lent him money against specified securities,

---

[1] An asterisk prefixed to a note indicates that the note is a new one; all others are to be read as addenda to existing notes.

which they were entitled to seize forthwith, without the need to go to court, if he failed to pay interest when due.

37   Replace the reference to Harrison by one to D. Whitehead, *The Demes of Attica* (Princeton, 1986) 125–7, 131–2.

48   Coesyra appears, from the evidence of ostracism ballots cast against the elder Megacles, to have been his mother, not (as I implied) his wife; she may have been the daughter of the tyrant Peisistratus by an Eretrian wife (Peisistratus was in exile at Eretria for ten years: Hdt. 1.61.2–62.1). See B.M. Lavelle, *GRBS* 30 (1989) 503–513; F. Willemsen, *MDAI(A)* 106 (1991) 144–5; D.M. Lewis, *ZPE* 96 (1993) 51–52; G.R. Stanton, *ZPE* 111 (1996) 69–73.

64   **Callippides:** or, more simply, "the name of the much-mocked actor no doubt deflates aristocratic pretensions" (D.C. Braund, *ZPE* 156 (2006) 110 n.7).

67   The name Pheidippides is "internally contradictory" only from the peasant's point of view; to an aristocrat *pheidesthai tōn hippōn*, lit. "sparing one's horses", would merely suggest managing them well, feeding them properly and not over-straining them (cf. *Iliad* 5.201–3). See O. Panagl in P. Händel and W. Meid ed. *Festschrift für Robert Muth* (Innsbruck, 1983) 297–306.

*83   **by Poseidon here:** it may seem surprising that Strepsiades should have an image of Poseidon in his home, but this is doubtless to be viewed as further evidence of the extent to which his wife dominates the household.

91   Further evidence for the use of the *ekkyklēma* in this scene comes from other passages where there is ambivalence as to whether the characters are supposed to be inside or outside the house, notably 19 ("bring *out* my accounts"); see P. von Möllendorff, *Grundlagen einer Ästhetik der Alten Komödie* (Tübingen, 1995) 119–121.

103   Delete reference to Ar. fr. 377 Kock (= 393 K-A).

103   Not only Socrates' habit of going barefoot, but virtually all his outward and visible characteristics as described in *Clouds*, are referred to also by Plato: see comm. on 362, 415–6, 838. No doubt too his mask showed the ugly features remarked on by Alcibiades in Pl. *Symp.* 215a–b, Critobulus in Xen. *Symp.* 4.19, and Theodorus in *Theaet.* 143e (snub nose, protruding eyes). Nowhere outside *Clouds*, however, is it said or implied that Socrates was pale, and it is probably significant that he himself (as distinct from Chaerephon and the students) is never specifically described as pale in *Clouds* itself either. See D.F. Leão, *Humanitas* (Coimbra) 47 (1995) 327–339.

*126–132   It is acutely noted by Guidorizzi (on 1476–1511) that every major new turn taken by the plot of *Clouds* is preceded by a soliloquy from Strepsiades (cf. 791–2, 1131–44, 1201–5, 1476–85).

*137   **rendered abortive an idea that had been discovered:** many scholars have succumbed to the temptation to see here a parody of Socrates' well-known comparison of himself to a midwife in Pl. *Theaet.* 148e–151d, and hence evidence that the analogy was actually used by Socrates; but see M.F. Burnyeat, *BICS* 24 (1977) 7, who shows that Plato in the passage referred to does all he can to "make it abundantly clear that the comparison is *not*, in any sense, to be attributed to the historical Socrates".

178–9   G. Kloss, *Erscheinungsformen komischen Sprechens bei Aristophanes* (Berlin, 2001) 122–3 n.250 has a very attractive explanation of this passage. Socrates draws a circle in the ashes with a *diabetes*; then he deems the circle to be a wrestling-ring, the *diabetes* to be a wrestler (one who *diabainei* "plants his feet apart" in a firm fighting stance, cf. *Knights* 77) – and steals the imaginary cloak which this imaginary wrestler has laid aside for his bout in this imaginary ring.

229   On Diogenes of Apollonia, see now A. Laks, *Diogène d'Apollonie* (Lille, 1986). On the relationship between him and the Aristophanic Socrates, see P. Vander Waerdt, "Socrates in the *Clouds*", in Vander Waerdt ed. *The Socratic Movement* (Ithaca NY, 1994) 48–86 (esp. 61–64, 71–75), who however goes much too far in claiming that *all* the physical doctrines ascribed to Socrates in the play come from Diogenes.

*245   **the one that never pays its debts:** it is ironic that Strepsiades should immediately offer to swear that he will pay Socrates' fee for learning this Argument!

252   There is more to the Clouds than this; see especially D. Ambrosino, *QSt* 18 (1983) 3–60, who sees them above all as embodiments of the power of speech, which she finds to be the dominant idea of the play.

270–3   W.S. Teuffel in his edition (Leipzig, 1863) suggested, no doubt rightly, that while reciting these lines Socrates turns to face successively the four cardinal points.

275–290   P. von Möllendorff, *Aristophanes* (Hildesheim, 2002) 167–8, draws attention to the many echoes in this song of Socrates' prayer just before: from the very first, the Clouds are shown to be shaping themselves in the image of their worshippers' desires.

302–310   For this view of the role of the Clouds in the play, see also J. Hanuš, *Graecolatina Pragensia* 8 (1980) 19–22. M.C. Marianetti, *Religion and Politics in Aristophanes' Clouds* (Hildesheim, 1992) 79–81, 96–97 notes that already in the strophe (275–290) the Clouds' association of themselves with nature, brightness, agriculture, etc., tends to distance them from the urbanized, light-shunning Socratics, and that similarly in 1115–30 their blessings and curses are mostly of an agrarian nature.

303–4   A preferable interpretation, taking fuller account of the fact that the word translated "is opened" (*anadeiknutai*) means more precisely "is displayed by opening", is offered by C. Sourvinou-Inwood in M. Golden & P. Toohey ed. *Inventing Ancient Culture: Historicism, Periodization, and the Ancient World* (London, 1996) 140: the passage "indicates that the rite of the Eleusinian Mysteries included a ceremonial opening of the gates of the Telesterion to display its interior to the *mystai* who will be received in it, and probably also that this was a significant moment in the initiation ceremony".

323   Why did Ar. make Socrates point to Parnes when he knew Parnes could not be seen from the theatre? Because of all Attic mountains it is over Parnes that clouds most often gather; see G.V. Lalonde, *Hesperia* Suppl. 20 (1982) 80–81, citing Thphr. *On Weather Signs* 47.

332   (on medicine): Also relevant is the tendency for leading fifth-century medical men to be at least as concerned about the rhetorical success with which they promoted themselves and justified their theories as about the actual therapeutic success of their practice; relevant texts include Xen. *Mem.* 4.2.5, Pl. *Gorg.* 456b–c, 514d, and Hippocr. *On the Nature of Man* 1. On doctors and medicine in comedy see Imperio in Belardinelli et al. *Tessere* 63–75. It is striking that the three specific professions mentioned here (seers, doctors, poets) are precisely those named by Empedocles fr. 146 D-K as representing (together with rulers, reference to whom would not suit the context here) the highest form of earthly human existence; see A. Willi, *The Languages of Aristophanes* (Oxford, 2003) 109–110 (and cf. on 380 below).

333   See now B. Zimmermann, *Dithyrambos* (Göttingen, 1992) 117–136.

*334   **these ones have noses:** much nonsense has been written about this! The point is simply that while many natural objects (e.g. pebbles, eggs, many seeds, some fruits) have a general resemblance in shape to a human head, there is no kind of natural object, nor even any animal head known to ancient Greeks, which at all resembles a human head *with the nose.* The nose was thus the most prominently and distinctively human of all external anatomical features. Revermann, *Comic Business* 202–3, suggests in fact that the Clouds may be much less ugly than most comic personae: "this would facilitate and support the point made by the [play's] ending".

349   *PA* 7556 is not the Hieronymus mentioned here but his grandson.

353–4   Cleonymus also appears as the mover of decrees or amendments in *IG*

i^3 70.5 (not otherwise datable) and 1454 bis (426/5?). To the comic references to him, add *com. adesp.* 1151.5 K-A. His treatment by the comic poets is discussed by I.C. Storey, *RhM* 132 (1989) 247–261, who is, however, wrong to dismiss as a comic invention the allegation that he had thrown away his shield; if it is an invention, why is no similar accusation ever made in comedy against anyone *else*?

359   This indication of the Clouds' real opinion of Socrates (reinforced by 361–3 which implies that they do *not* regard Socrates as a man of "skill and intelligence") passes unnoticed by him and Strepsiades.

361   Prodicus' *Choice of Heracles* seems in several respects to have provided a model for the debate between the Better and Worse Arguments in *Clouds* itself: see A.M. Bowie, *Aristophanes: Myth, Ritual and Comedy* (Cambridge, 1993) 109–110.

380   The references to Democritus should be supplemented by Leucippus A1 D-K = D.L. 9.31–32; Epicurus ap. D.L. 10.90, ascribing a cosmogonic *dînos* to "one of the so-called physicists", may be referring to either of the two. Hence our passage cannot be regarded as evidence that Democritus had published anything before 423; Leucippus, on the other hand, had written early enough to influence Diogenes of Apollonia (Diogenes A5 D-K). In addition, Willi, *Languages* 104, points out that Empedocles (fr. 115 D-K) had spoken of *aitheros dînai*; this is one of a large number of Empedoclean echoes that Willi finds in *Clouds* (cf. pp.105–113). The term also appears – in the masculine form *dînos*, as here – in what appears to have been a cosmological section of Antiphon's *On Truth* (fr. 25 D-K).

398   Delete note and substitute: **the Cronia:** a festival in honour of Cronus, held on 12 Hecatombaeon (approximately July), and by the classical period considered of so little importance that legislative sessions could be held on that day (Dem. 24.26–31); see Parke 29–30. Similarly at 984 old-fashioned ways of thought are linked with another archaic ritual occasion, the Dipolieia.

*463–5   **with me ... you will lead the most envied life in the world:** cf. Pl. *Phd.* 81a "Such a soul ... , in the words used of those initiated in the mysteries, will truly dwell with the gods for the rest of time", also 69c. In Plato, however, and almost certainly in its original religious context too, this promise referred to the afterlife; the Clouds' promise refers to this world.

518–562   On eupolideans see also L.P.E. Parker, *PCPS* 34 (1988) 115–122. E.M. Hall in F.D. Harvey and J. Wilkins ed. *The Rivals of Aristophanes* (London/Swansea, 2000) 407–8 notes the extraordinary confusion of genders and identities in this parabasis: the speakers are directly or indirectly identified as (male) theatre performers, as (feminine) clouds, as Aristophanes, as an unmarried mother, as a (feminine) comedy (the shape of whose phallus, however, is a matter of concern), as Electra ... .

521–3   Old Comedy was almost certainly performed in southern Italy in the fourth century, and may have been introduced there as early as the foundation of Thurii in 444/3; see O.P. Taplin, *Comic Angels* (Oxford, 1993), esp. 14–17, 89–99. It is, nevertheless, unlikely that at this time any Athenian comic dramatist would choose to have his play performed for the *first* time anywhere but Athens – though at the very end of the fifth century at least two comedies may indeed have received their first performance in Italy, Metagenes' significantly named *Thurio-Persians* and Nicophon's *Sirens* (both of which, according to Athenaeus 6.269f–270a, were "unproduced", sc. at Athens).

*533   **since that time ... of your good opinion:** as is noted by D. Welsh, *Hermes* 118 (1990) 424, this line proves that "at least some of the spectators at the 'Banqueters' already knew that Aristophanes had written the play".

537   On Ar.'s practice of both disowning and employing "cheap and vulgar laughter-raising devices", see G.W. Dobrov in J. Redmond ed. *Themes in Drama 10: Farce* (Cambridge, 1988) 15–31.

545–556   Ar.'s claim of originality, and his attack on Eupolis, gain additional spice (not to say shamelessness) if, as is likely, *Clouds* (like one of its competitors, Ameipsias' *Connus*) was considerably indebted to Eupolis' *Goats*, which may well have won first prize at the Dionysia of 424 and whose main characters seem to have included a rustic (probably a goatherd) and a teacher who tried to instruct him in letters, music and dancing. See I.C. Storey, *Eupolis, Poet of Old Comedy* (Oxford, 2003) 67–74.

551   According to one source (Theophrastus, cited by Plutarch) it was Phaeax, not Nicias, who plotted with Alcibiades to secure Hyperbolus' ostracism; I have suggested in *CQ* 46 (1996) 332–3 that Hyperbolus' comic reputation may have made him an attractive target for such a plot.

553   The dating of *Demes* is disputed: 412 has long been the orthodox date, but I.C. Storey, *Eupolis, Poet of Old Comedy* (Oxford, 2003) 112–4 argues for 417 or 416; Giulia Torello, *Eupolis and Attic Comedy* (Diss. Nottingham 2006) favours Lenaea 414.

554   I certainly underestimated the extent to which *Maricas* can be shown to have imitated *Knights*: see I.C. Storey in Sommerstein et al. ed. *Tragedy, Comedy and the Polis* (Bari, 1993) 381–4, and my contribution to Harvey & Wilkins ed. *The Rivals of Aristophanes*, at

pp.440–2.

555   Eupolis seems to have portrayed Hyperbolus' mother as an itinerant bread-seller (cf. Eupolis fr. 209), as probably did Hermippus (see comm. on 557).

556   On Phrynichus see now F.D. Harvey in Harvey & Wilkins ed. *The Rivals of Aristophanes* 91–134.

562   This is the only place where Ar. alludes to the judgement of posterity *on his own work*, and is thus precious evidence that he expected his plays to survive, presumably *in the form of texts* which future generations would read (just as he himself read Homer or Aeschylus); see R.M. Rosen, *Yale Journal of Criticism* 10 (1997) 397–421, esp. 410–1.

563–574, 595–606   D. Blyth, *Scholia* 3 (1994) 36–41, points out that the four gods invoked in the strophe are all "sky and weather divinities" – i.e. are responsible for phenomena which according to Socrates were naturally, not divinely caused – while the four invoked in the antistrophe are all mentioned in connection with sites of the cultic worship which according to Socrates they ought not to receive. In this respect, it may be added, the parabasis corresponds neatly to the parodos: in 275–290 the chorus referred to the sky (Zeus), the sea (Poseidon), the aether, and the sun (as well as other divine aspects of nature such as the Ocean, the earth and the rivers), in 299–310 to the cults of Athens.

570   The reference to *trag. adesp.* 112 should be to Eur. fr. 908b Nauck-Snell.

621   After the death of Patroclus, Achilles insists on eating nothing until sunset the next day, even though he is going into battle (*Iliad* 19.209–214, 305–8); similarly Alexander ate nothing for two days after the death of Hephaestion (Arr. *Anab.* 7.14.8).

659   On Protagoras' remarks on grammatical gender, see now J. Lougovaya and R. Ast, *CQ* 54 (2004) 274–7, who show that his point was, not "that certain feminine nouns 'ought' to be masculine", but that some words were feminine when they were ordinary nouns and yet masculine when they were proper names. And for further evidence (derived from Xenophon's version in *Mem.* 2.1.21–33 of Prodicus' *Choice of Heracles*) that Prodicus too was interested in gender, and indeed favoured the use of distinctively feminine forms of nouns even where, like *alektruaina*, they had to be coined *ad hoc*, see D. Sansone, *JHS* 124 (2004) 133–4.

686   I.C. Storey, *JHS* 115 (1995) 182–4, adduces strong arguments to distinguish the Philoxenus of these passages both from the glutton referred to by later authors and from the father of the Eryxis of *Frogs*

934. Noting that almost all the other persons satirized in the opening scene of *Wasps* are politicians, he is inclined to identify our man with the mover of a decree on the cult of Apollo c.422–416 (*IG* i³ 137).

730 Note that Greek *epiballein* (which I have here rendered "throw over [me]") has as one of its meanings "bring (a woman) into sexual union with (a man)", cf. Diogenianus 2.72, and that the preposition *ex* "instead of" (lit. "out of") half suggests the idea that the blankets are to be *transformed* into a girl. See E. Degani, *Eikasmos* 1 (1990) 135.

749 On "drawing down the moon" cf. also Hippocr. *On the Sacred Disease* 4.

830 Diagoras is identified by R. Janko, *BICS* 46 (2002/3) 1–18 – more firmly than in his 1997 *ZPE* paper – as the author of the commentary on an Orphic poem preserved in the Derveni papyrus; Athenagoras, *In Defence of the Christians* 4, shows that he divulged Orphic as well as Eleusinian secrets (though he also says that Diagoras "declared outright that there was no god at all", which is certainly not the position of the Derveni commentator).

889 In the 1980s and 1990s there was a tendency to take the "fighting-cock scholium" seriously and to see the "Getty Birds vase" as illustrating this *agōn* (see especially E.G. Csapo, *Phoenix* 47 (1993) 1–28, 115–124); but there are serious difficulties with this view, to which attention was drawn by Taplin, *Comic Angels* 103–4. In Thiercy & Menu *Aristophane* 281–2 I suggested the scholium was due to confusion with 847ff. A better suggestion, however, has now been made by Revermann, *Comic Business* 213–7. Arguing (i) that the scholia on 889 cannot be supposed to be referring obscurely to *Clouds I* (when elsewhere they always refer to it clearly) and (ii) that the polemical tone in which scholia on 1032–3 assert that the Arguments appeared in human form suggests that someone had claimed they did not, he finds the likeliest explanation for the "fighting-cock scholium" to be that cock-fighting metaphors were used in a choral song written for *Clouds II* (whether or not it had also featured in *Clouds I*), and that this song was preserved in some branches of the tradition and lost in others (including those from which our text descends). One might speculate that it was written originally on a loose sheet which was mislaid during the period when the first generation of copies were being made.

957 The Clouds' "warm praise of the Better Argument", another clear pointer to their real opinion of the sophistic movement, is ignored by Strepsiades. I am indebted to my student Maria Middleton for pointing out the importance of this passage and 1024–35 (which in my 1997 paper on this *agōn* I entirely overlooked): these passages are so

inconsistent with the Clouds' earlier encouragement to Strepsiades to get himself or his son taught rhetoric by Socrates (412–475, 510–7, 700–716, 727–9, 794–6) that he really ought to have smelled a rat.

968   See now M.L. West, *Ancient Greek Music* (Oxford, 1992) 172–184, esp. 174–5 and 179–180.

969–971   Phrynis cannot have won a Panathenaic victory in 456, since that was not a Great Panathenaic year, and M. Hose, *Philologus* 137 (1993) 3–11, argues that the "archonship of Callias" referred to by the scholia here was that of 406/5; *pace* Hose, however, a victory in that year (seventeen years after *Clouds*) could hardly have been Phrynis' *first*, particularly as Arist. *Met.* 993b15 implies that Phrynis was famous well before Timotheus. Another possibility, first canvassed by M.H.E. Meier, is that "Callias" is an error for "Callimachus" (446/5), in which case the statement of the scholia that he was the first to win the competition in singing to the lyre at the Panathenaea will doubtless mean that he was the first winner after the reorganization of the festival, inspired by Pericles, at about this time; see J.A. Davison, *JHS* 78 (1958) 40–41.

972   Add: i.e. "obscuring the poetry and its intimate connection with the traditional music" by introducing melodic complexities (A. Andrisano, *MCr* 23/23 (1988/9) 194–7).

973–980   The implication of my note – that the Better Argument's evident sexual interest in young boys does not in itself undercut his high moral line – is made explicit by N. Papageorgiou, *Mnemosyne* 57 (2004) 284–294. It should, however, be noted that sexual exploitation of schoolboys *by paid teachers* was regarded as an evil, and laws enacted to reduce the opportunities for it (Aeschines 1.9–10).

983   Greek *opsa* denoted especially fish (modern Greek *psari* "fish" is descended from its diminutive, *opsarion*). On the association, in Athenian democratic thinking, between fish-eating, luxury, arrogance, subservience to bodily desires, and other deplorable qualities, see J.N. Davidson, *CQ* 43 (1993) 53–66, and his book *Courtesans and Fishcakes* (London, 1997).

984   On the cicada brooch see especially A. Rumpf in *Symbola Coloniensia Iosepho Kroll ... oblata* (Cologne, 1949) 85–99.

985   On the Dipolieia see also W. Burkert, *Homo Necans* (Eng. tr. Berkeley, 1983) 136–143.

988   On the pyrrhic dance see now P. Ceccarelli in P.A. Murray and P.J. Wilson ed. *Music and the Muses* (Oxford, 2004) 91–117.

989   In fact *kōlê* "penis" does appear to be attested on two magical amulets (C. Bonner, *Studies in Magical Amulets chiefly Greco-Egyptian* (Ann

Arbor, 1950) 215; id., *Hesperia* 20 (1951) 335–6 #51); see D.M. Bain, *Eikasmos* 3 (1992) 149–152.

997   On the erotic symbolism of apples cf. also Sappho fr. 105a, Stesichorus *PMG* 187, and Berlin Papyrus 21243 (published by W. Brashear, *ZPE* 33 (1979) 261–278), and see A.P. Burnett, *Three Archaic Poets* (London, 1983) 267–8. The symbolism survives in Greece to the present day, but the apple is virtually always thrown at the woman (as in the myth of Melanion and Atalanta), not by her.

1001   The "tasteless vegetable" is now officially named *Amaranthus lividus*. On the use of its name as a term of abuse in Greek, Latin and Italian, see M.G. Carilli, *Studi e Ricerche dell'Istituto di Latino* (Genoa) 4 (1981) 23–30.

1075   On *phusis* = "genitals" cf. also Hippocr. *Mul.* 2.143, *PGM* xxxvi 284, and see K.McLeish, *CQ* 27 (1977) 76–79, and J.J. Winkler, *The Constraints of Desire* (New York, 1990) 217–220.

1083   On how the use of wood-ash would facilitate depilation (and render it extremely painful), see my note on *Thesm.* 537. These punishments for adulterers (or, more accurately, forms of private revenge licensed by custom) are, not surprisingly, never mentioned outside comedy, but Xen. *Mem.* 2.1.5 alludes to them as plainly as is consistent with the dignity of serious literature. They constituted in theory the serious crime of *hybris* (cf. Xen. *loc.cit.*), but a prosecution would have no chance of success unless the victim/accuser could convince the jury that he was not in fact guilty of adultery. See C. Carey, *LCM* 18 (1993) 53–55.

1102   I have discussed this passage in *Museum Criticum* 25–28 (1990–3) 175–9. My original interpretation was not fully satisfactory, as had been pointed out by R.K. Fisher, *Aristophanes' Clouds: Purpose and Technique* (Amsterdam, 1984) 205 n.8, since after 1096–1100 one would have expected "you buggers" to be an address to (the majority of) the audience. I therefore suggested that the Better Argument flung his cloak towards the audience (or perhaps rather towards one of the individuals in it who had been singled out in 1099–1101) and thereby revealed that he was wearing beneath it an inner garment (*khitōn*) of an effeminate style and colour, probably a saffron-dyed *krokōtos* (cf. *Thesm.* 138, 253, 941, 945, 1044, 1220; see Stone 174–5). I would now be inclined, additionally, to adopt, or adapt, a proposal made by von Möllendorff in Pöhlmann et al. *Studien zur Bühnendichtung* ... 147 and suggest that after throwing the cloak (as a right-handed man naturally would) towards the spectators on his *right* side, the actor ran up one of the gangways in the *left* (western) part of the auditorium (perhaps pausing to dally flirtatiously with a spectator or two?), eventually disappearing from view to return to the performing area around the outside of the theatre complex (cf. Addenda to text/translation of 275–328).

1115–30   P. Totaro, *Le seconde parabasi di Aristofane* (Stuttgart, 1999) 66–67 n.8 points out that in this second parabasis, just as in the first, the chorus speak in the name of justice and religion. One may also note that the threats in the latter part of the speech foreshadow the end of the play (stoning, 1508; breaking down roofs, 1488ff); this *may* indicate that the speech is a new one written for the revised version of the play.

1136   Delete "and probably also the defendant"; as MacDowell pointed out in his Leeds paper (see on 18 above), if Strepsiades had himself been required to pay *prytaneia* he would surely at some point in the play have complained about it. Pollux (8.38) is the only source who states that the defendant as well as the plaintiff had to pay *prytaneia*.

1154–70   It is striking that in all the known tragic songs which provide partial parallels to this one, the character who sings is a *woman*. J. Angel y Espinós, in A. López Eire ed. *Sociedad, política y literatura: comedia griega antigua* (Salamanca, 1997) 243–8, argues that the play parodied in 1154–5 is likely to be Euripides' *Peleus* rather than Sophocles', since the continuation of the tragic passage as cited in the scholia ("Oho, who is at the door or in the house?") shows typically Euripidean features (cf. *Phoen.* 1067, *Ba.* 170, and numerous passages in which *pulē* "door, gate" and *domos* "house" appear in close proximity); if he is right, it is reasonable to suppose that much in 1156–64 is modelled on Euripides too.

*1162   **who will dispel the grief:** Greek *lūsaniās*, which is also a fairly common personal name, and which I.C. Storey, *CQ* 39 (1989) 549–550 suggests may allude to one of two actual contemporaries of that name. The more promising of the two, in my view, is Lysanias of Thoricus (*PA* 9312, *LGPN* 54), father of the cavalryman Dexileos (*IG* ii² 6217) born in 414/3, killed at Corinth in 394/3, and commemorated by a famous surviving monument; this Lysanias would probably be in his early or middle twenties in 423 and thus of similar age, status and original tastes to Pheidippides. "The reader for *CQ*" (viz. myself) speculated that Lysanias might recently have won renown by saving his father's life in battle (at Delium?) and that this was why it was appropriate for Strepsiades to compare *his* son and potential saviour to Lysanias. Storey's own preference was for Lysanias of Sphettus (*PA* 9324, *LGPN* 53), whose son Aeschines became a well-known associate of Socrates and later a writer of Socratic dialogues, and who was himself present to support Socrates at his trial in 399 (Pl. *Apol.* 33e).

*1178 Revermann, *Comic Business* 223, points out that Pheidippides will now have shed the speech impediment referred to at 872–3. He will also be so different in complexion and probably in costume that, were it not for the clear verbal identification, the audience might have found it hard to recognize him.

*1214 **so ought a man ... his own money away?:** the witness has apparently been trying to persuade the creditor not to press for payment.

*1234 **Zeus, Hermes and Poseidon:** Zeus as the supreme god, Hermes as the god of trading (*Empolaios,* cf. *Ach.* 816, *Wealth* 1155), Poseidon because the loan was for buying a horse (so Hermann).

*1269 **particularly when I'm in distress:** we may be meant to assume that the man urgently needs his money back to pay for medical treatment.

1299 For "his forthcoming book *Hybris*" read "his book *Hybris* (Warminster, 1992)".

1300 Alternatively the point of *seirāphoros* may be that the offside race-horse, because of its role in the race, was the one most likely to need goading; see F. García Romero, *CFC* 6 (1996) 94–95.

1356 On the Crius-ode see now further J.H. Molyneux, *Simonides: A Historical Study* (Wauconda IL, 1992) 47–54.

1358 In his objection to singing at table, Pheidippides significantly has the support both of his admired Euripides (cf. *Medea* 190–203) and of the Platonic Socrates (cf. *Prot.* 347c–348a, *Symp.* 176e). See G. Crane, *Mnemosyne* 43 (1990) 435–8.

1380 D.E. O'Regan, *Rhetoric, Comedy and the Violence of Language in Aristophanes' Clouds* (New York, 1992) 120 notes the irony of Strepsiades' appeal to the "debt of nurture" due to him as parent (cf. also 861–4, 999) when he has been trying to evade paying *his* debts to others. Presently Pheidippides will claim the right (duty?) to repay a somewhat different kind of "debt" to his father by giving him beatings in return for the beatings he received as a child.

1382–1384 All these nursery words are still in use in Greece in almost the same form; see Th. Stephanopoulos, *Glotta* 61 (1983) 12–15 (who notes that in modern usage *mamma* often refers specifically to bread). For a comprehensive overview of what is known about "baby talk and child language" in ancient Greece, see M. Golden in F. De Martino and A.H. Sommerstein ed. *Lo spettacolo delle voci* (Bari, 1995) ii 11–34.

*1423–6 E.M. Harris, *ZPE* 140 (2002) 3–5, points out that the phrase *to loipon* "in the future" (barring retroactive application) and forms of *hosoi* "as many as, all that" (defining an exempted class) are common in Athenian legislative enactments: Pheidippides has been taught the forensic trade all right!

1484–5   The burning of Troy had been the final catastrophe of at least one earlier tragedy, the *Sack of Troy* by Iophon (son of Sophocles); cf. Ar. fr. 234 K-A "Hecuba wailing and the heap of straw burning" (sc. backstage to simulate the conflagration).

Select Bibliography

Aristophanes

Editions of the complete plays. The standard critical edition of Aristophanes will henceforth be the new Oxford Classical Text by N.G. Wilson (Oxford, 2007), which will be accompanied by a volume of textual discussions (*Aristophanea: Studies on the Text of Aristophanes*); other complete modern editions are that of V. Coulon (Collection Budé: Paris, 1923–30), with French translation, introductions, and brief notes by H. van Daele, and the Loeb Classical Library edition by J.J. Henderson (Cambridge MA, 1998–2002). Of importance for their commentaries are the editions of J. van Leeuwen (Leiden, 1896–1909) and B.B. Rogers (London, 1902–15). Two series of editions with commentary, by various editors, are currently in progress (Oxford, 1964– , 9 vols. so far published, with two more expected soon; Milan, 1985– , with Italian translation by D. Del Corno, 5 vols. so far published). The edition of the first five plays with Italian translation and substantial annotation (but not a full commentary) by G. Mastromarco (Turin, 1983) has now (2006) been continued as far as *Frogs* in collaboration with P. Totaro.

Fragments of lost plays. R. Kassel and C. Austin, *Poetae Comici Graeci* (Berlin, 1983–), is superseding, as its publication progresses, all previous collections of comic fragments; the fragments of Aristophanes are in volume III.2 (1984).

Scholia (ancient and medieval commentaries). The edition of all the *Scholia in Aristophanem* under the direction of W.J.W. Koster and D. Holwerda (Groningen, 1960–) is now complete for nine of the eleven plays. The scholia to *Lysistrata* are contained in Pars II, Fasc. 4 (ed. J. Hangard, 1996).

There is an *index verborum* to Aristophanes by O.J. Todd (Cambridge MA, 1932).

Bibliographies. Reports on research on, and literature about, Aristophanes appeared in *(Bursians) Jahresbericht über die Fortschritte der klassischen Altertumswissenschaft* every few years from 1877 to 1939. Subsequent surveys (those asterisked also cover other writers of Old Comedy) include those by K.J. Dover, *Lustrum* 2 (1957) 52–112 (for 1938–55); W. Kraus, *Anzeiger für die Altertumswissenschaft* 24 (1971) 161–180 (for 1949–70); *H.J. Newiger, *Aristophanes und die alte Komödie* (Darmstadt, 1975) 487–510 (for 1955–73); *I.C. Storey, *EMC* 6 (1987) 1–46 (for 1975–84) and *Antichthon* 26 (1992) 1–29 (for 1982–91); and B. Zimmermann, *Anzeiger für die Altertumswissenschaft* 45 (1992) 161–184 and 47 (1994) 1–18 (for 1971–92).

General studies

W. Schmid, *Geschichte der griechischen Literatur* I.iv (Munich, 1946) 174–440.

A. Lesky, *A History of Greek Literature* (tr. J. Willis and C. de Heer) (London,1966) 417–452.

T. Gelzer, "Aristophanes (12)", in *RE* Supplementband XII cols. 1391–1570; also published separately as *Aristophanes der Komiker* (Stuttgart, 1971).

E.W. Handley, "Comedy", in P.E. Easterling and B.M.W. Knox ed. *The Cambridge History of Classical Literature* i (Cambridge, 1985) 355–425 = *Greek Drama* (Cambridge, 1989) 103–173 (for bibliography, by M. Drury, see pp.773–9 = 189–195).

H.J. Newiger ed. *Aristophanes und die alte Komödie* (Darmstadt, 1975). An anthology of twentieth-century articles.

E. Segal ed. *Oxford Readings in Aristophanes* (Oxford, 1996). Another anthology.

K.J. Dover, *Aristophanic Comedy* (London, 1972).

A. Solomos, *The Living Aristophanes* (tr. A. Solomos and M. Felheim) (Ann Arbor, 1974).

K.J. Reckford, *Aristophanes' Old-and-New Comedy I: Six Essays in Perspective* (Chapel Hill NC, 1987).

J.M. Bremer and E.W. Handley ed. *Aristophane (Entretiens sur l'antiquité classique* 38) (Geneva, 1993).

A.M. Bowie, *Aristophanes: Myth, Ritual and Comedy* (Cambridge, 1993).

L.K. Taaffe, *Aristophanes and Women* (London, 1993).

G. Mastromarco, *Introduzione a Aristofane* (Bari, 1994).

D.M. MacDowell, *Aristophanes and Athens: An Introduction to the Plays* (Oxford, 1995).

G.W. Dobrov ed. *Beyond Aristophanes: Transition and Diversity in Greek Comedy* (Atlanta, 1995).

P. Thiercy and M. Menu ed. *Aristophane: la langue, la scène, la cité* (Bari, 1996).

S. Halliwell, *Aristophanes: Birds, Lysistrata, Assembly-Women, Wealth* (Oxford, 1997) ix–lxxix.

G.W. Dobrov ed. *The City as Comedy: Society and Representation in Athenian Drama* (Chapel Hill, 1997).

B. Zimmermann, *Die griechische Komödie* (Düsseldorf/Zürich, 1998) 9–188.

P. Thiercy, *Aristophane et l'Ancienne Comédie* (Paris, 1999).

M.S. Silk, *Aristophanes and the Definition of Comedy* (Oxford, 2000).

P. von Möllendorff, *Aristophanes* (Hildesheim, 2002).

B. Zimmermann, *Die griechische Komödie*² (Frankfurt, 2006) 9–154.

Dramatic technique

T. Zieliński, *Die Gliederung der altattischen Komödie* (Leipzig, 1885).

P. Mazon, *Essai sur la composition des comédies d'Aristophane* (Paris, 1904).

H.J. Newiger, *Metapher und Allegorie: Studien zu Aristophanes* (Munich, 1957).

T. Gelzer, *Der epirrhematische Agon bei Aristophanes* (Munich, 1960).

C.H. Whitman, *Aristophanes and the Comic Hero* (Cambridge MA, 1964).

K.D. Koch, *Kritische Idee und komisches Thema* (Bremen, 1965).

P. Rau, *Paratragodia: Untersuchungen einer komischen Form des Aristophanes* (Munich, 1967).

G.M. Sifakis, *Parabasis and Animal Choruses* (London, 1971).

M. Landfester, *Handlungsverlauf und Komik in den frühen Komödien des Aristophanes* (Berlin, 1977).

K. McLeish, *The Theatre of Aristophanes* (London, 1980).

B. Zimmermann, "The parodoi of the Aristophanic comedies", *SIFC* (3rd ser.) 2 (1984) 13–24; reprinted with revisions in Segal ed. *Oxford Readings in Aristophanes* 182–193.

P. Thiercy, *Aristophane: fiction et dramaturgie* (Paris, 1986).

N.J. Lowe, "Greek stagecraft and Aristophanes", in J. Redmond ed. *Themes in Drama 10: Farce* (Cambridge, 1988) 33–52.

T.K. Hubbard, *The Mask of Comedy: Aristophanes and the Intertextual Parabasis* (Ithaca NY, 1991).

G.M. Sifakis, "The structure of Aristophanic comedy", *JHS* 112 (1992) 123–142.

W.G. Arnott, "Comic openings", *Drama* 2 (1993) 14–32, with response by N. Felson-Rubin (33–38).

P. von Möllendorff, *Grundlagen einer Ästhetik der Alten Komödie* (Tübingen, 1995).

G. Mastromarco, "La commedia antica fra tradizione e innovazione", in J.A. López Férez ed. *La comedia griega y su influencia en la literatura española* (Madrid, 1998) 23–42.

B. Zimmermann, "Innovation und Tradition in den Komödien des Aristophanes", *SRCG* 1 (1998) 275–287.

J.P. Poe, "Entrances, exits, and the structure of Aristophanic comedy", *Hermes* 127 (1999) 189–207.

N.W. Slater, "Making the Aristophanic audience", *AJP* 120 (1999) 351–368.

P. Totaro, *Le seconde parabasi di Aristofane* (Stuttgart, 1999).

M. Treu, *Undici cori comici: aggressività, derisione e tecniche drammatiche in Aristofane* (Genoa, 1999).

J. Hesk, "Intratext and irony in Aristophanes", in A.R. Sharrock and H. Morales ed. *Intratextuality* (Oxford, 2000) 227–261.

A.F.H. Bierl, *Der Chor in der Alten Komödie* (Munich, 2001).

G.W. Dobrov, *Figures of Play: Greek Drama and Metafictional Poetics* (Oxford, 2001).

A. Ercolani ed. *Spoudaiogeloion: Form und Funktion der Verspottung in der aristophanischen Komödie* (= Drama 11) (Stuttgart, 2002).

N.W. Slater, *Spectator Politics: Metatheater and Performance in Aristophanes* (Philadelphia, 2002).

G. Compton-Engle, "Control of costume in three plays of Aristophanes", *AJP* 124 (2003) 507–535.

C. Calame, "Choral forms in Aristophanic comedy: musical mimesis and dramatic performance in classical Athens", in P.A. Murray and P.J. Wilson ed. *Music and the Muses* (Oxford, 2004) 157–184.

S. Beta, *Il linguaggio nelle commedie di Aristofane: parola positiva e parola negativa nella commedia antica* (Rome, 2004).

O. Imperio, *Parabasi di Aristofane: Acarnesi, Cavalieri, Vespe, Uccelli* (Bari, 2004).

C. Calame ed. *Poétique d'Aristophane et langue d'Euripide en dialogue* = *Études de lettres* 2004/4 (Lausanne, 2004).

R.M. Rosen, "Aristophanes, Old Comedy, and Greek tragedy", in R. Bushnell ed. *A Companion to Tragedy* (Oxford, 2005) 251–268.

R. Saetta Cottone, *Aristofane e la poetica dell'ingiuria: per una introduzione alla loidori/a comica* (Rome, 2005).

M. Revermann, *Comic Business: Theatricality, Dramatic Technique, and Performance Contexts of Aristophanic Comedy* (Oxford, 2006).

L.A. Kozak and J.W. Rich ed. *Playing around Aristophanes: Essays in celebration of the completion of the edition of the comedies of Aristophanes by Alan Sommerstein* (Oxford, 2006).

C. Platter, *Aristophanes and the Carnival of Genres* (Baltimore, forthcoming).

Language and style

J. Taillardat, *Les images d'Aristophane*[2] (Paris, 1965).

E.S. Spyropoulos, *L'accumulation verbale chez Aristophane* (Thessaloniki, 1974).

K.J. Dover, "The style of Aristophanes", in *Greek and the Greeks* (Oxford, 1987) 224–236.

K.J. Dover, "Language and character in Aristophanes", *ibid.* 237–248[1].

J.J. Henderson, *The Maculate Muse: Obscene Language in Attic Comedy*[2] (Oxford, 1991).

S.D. Olson, "Names and naming in Aristophanic comedy", *CQ* 42 (1992) 304–319.

A. López Eire, *La lengua coloquial de la comedia aristofánica* (Murcia, 1996).

A. López Eire, "Lengua y política en la comedia aristofánica", in A. López Eire ed. *Sociedad, política y literatura: comedia griega antigua* (Salamanca, 1997) 45–80.

A.H. Sommerstein, "The anatomy of euphemism in Aristophanic comedy", in F. De Martino and A.H. Sommerstein ed. *Studi sull'eufemismo* (Bari, 1999) 181–217.

---

[1]These two articles are revised versions of papers originally published in Italian in 1970 and 1976 respectively.

S. Colvin, *Dialect in Aristophanes* (Oxford, 1999).

L. McClure, *Spoken like a Woman: Speech and Gender in Athenian Drama* (Princeton, 1999), esp. ch. 2 and 6.

J.M. Labiano Ilundain, *Estudio de las interjecciones en las Comedias de Aristófanes* (Amsterdam, 2000).

G. Kloss, *Erscheinungsformen komischen Sprechens bei Aristophanes* (Berlin, 2001).

A. Willi ed. *The Language of Greek Comedy* (Oxford, 2002).

A. Willi, *The Languages of Aristophanes* (Oxford, 2003).

J.E. Thorburn, "Winter in the comedies of Aristophanes", *Mouseion* 3 (2003) 325–338.

J. Robson, *Humour, Obscenity and Aristophanes* (Tübingen, 2006).

Metre

J.W. White, *The Verse of Greek Comedy* (London, 1912). Still valuable on the spoken and chanted (as distinct from lyric) metres.

A.M. Dale, *The Lyric Metres of Greek Drama*[2] (Cambridge, 1968).

B. Zimmermann, *Untersuchungen zur Form und dramatischen Technik der aristophanischen Komödien* (3 vols., Königstein/Frankfurt, 1984–7).

L.P.E. Parker, *The Songs of Aristophanes* (Oxford, 1996).

Production

T.B.L. Webster, *Monuments Illustrating Old and Middle Comedy*[3] (rev. J.R. Green) (*BICS* Suppl. 39, 1978).

C.W. Dearden, *The Stage of Aristophanes* (London, 1976).

H.J. Newiger, "Drama und Theater", in G.A. Seeck ed. *Das griechische Drama* (Darmstadt, 1979) 434–503.

L.M. Stone, *Costume in Aristophanic Comedy* (New York, 1981).

A.W. Pickard-Cambridge, *The Dramatic Festivals of Athens*[3] (rev. J. Gould and D.M. Lewis) (Oxford, 1988).

J.R. Green, "On seeing and depicting the theatre in classical Athens", *GRBS* 32 (1991) 15–50.

O.P. Taplin, *Comic Angels and Other Approaches to Greek Drama through Vase-Paintings* (Oxford, 1993).

C.F. Russo, *Aristophanes: An Author for the Stage* (London, 1994).

J.P. Poe, "Multiplicity, discontinuity, and visual meaning in Aristophanic comedy", *RhM* 143 (2000) 256–295.

J. Whitehorne, "Aristophanes' representation of 'intellectuals'", *Hermes* 130 (2002) 28–35.

N.J. Lowe, "Aristophanic spacecraft", in L.A. Kozak and J.W. Rich ed. *Playing around Aristophanes* (Oxford, 2006) 48–64.

Comedy and society

G.E.M. de Ste Croix, *The Origins of the Peloponnesian War* (London, 1972), Appendix XXIX.

J.J. Winkler and F.I. Zeitlin ed. *Nothing to Do with Dionysos?* (Princeton, 1990), esp. chapters by Goldhill, Ober & Strauss, and Henderson.

S. Halliwell, "Comic satire and freedom of speech in classical Athens", *JHS* 111 (1991) 48–70.

A.H. Sommerstein, "Old Comedians on Old Comedy", *Drama* 1 (1992) 14–33.

A.H. Sommerstein et al. ed. *Tragedy, Comedy and the Polis* (Bari, 1993), esp. chapters by Henderson, Halliwell, Mastromarco and Handley.

A.T. Edwards, "Historicizing the popular grotesque: Bakhtin's *Rabelais* and Attic Old Comedy", in R.S. Scodel ed. *Theater and Society in the Classical World* (Ann Arbor, 1993).

C. Carey, "Comic ridicule and democracy", in R.G. Osborne and S. Hornblower ed. *Ritual, Finance, Politics: Athenian Democratic Accounts Presented to David Lewis* (Oxford, 1994) 69–83.

E.G. Csapo and W.J. Slater, *The Context of Ancient Drama* (Ann Arbor, 1994); a sourcebook of texts and images on all aspects of the theatrical and social environment of drama.

P.A. Cartledge, *Aristophanes and his Theatre of the Absurd* (3rd ed., Bristol, 1995).

J.R. Green, *Theatre in Ancient Greek Society* (London, 1995).

A.H. Sommerstein, "How to avoid being a *komodoumenos*", *CQ* 46 (1996) 327–356.

M. Heath, "Aristophanes and the discourse of politics", in Dobrov ed. *The City as Comedy* (Chapel Hill, 1997; see above) 230–249.

A.H. Sommerstein, "The theatre audience and the Demos", in J.A. López Férez ed. *La comedia griega y su influencia en la literatura española* (Madrid, 1998) 43–62.

I.C. Storey, "Poets, politicians and perverts: personal humour in Aristophanes", *Classics Ireland* 5 (1998) 85–134.

J.J. Henderson, "Attic Old Comedy, frank speech, and democracy", in D. Boedeker and K.A. Raaflaub ed. *Democracy, Empire and the Arts in Fifth-century Athens* (Cambridge MA, 1998) 255–273.

M.M. Mactoux, "Esclaves-femmes dans le Corpus d'Aristophane", in F. Reduzzi Merola and A. Storchi Marino ed. *Femmes-esclaves: modèles d'interprétation anthropologique, économique, juridique* (Naples, 1999) 21–46.

C.B.R. Pelling, *Literary Texts and the Greek Historian* (London, 2000) 123–163.

L. Bertelli, "La memoria storica di Aristofane", in C. Bearzot et al. ed. *Storiografia locale e storiografia universale* (Como, 2001) 41–99.

P. Reinders, *Demos Pyknites: Untersuchungen zur Darstellung des Demos in der Alten Komödie* (Stuttgart, 2001).

SELECT BIBLIOGRAPHY

J. Spielvogel, *Wirtschaft und Geld bei Aristophanes* (Frankfurt, 2001).

M. Farioli, *Mundus alter: Utopie e distopie nella commedia greca antica* (Milan, 2001).

C. Mann, "Aristophanes, Kleon und eine angebliche Zäsur in der Geschichte Athens", in A. Ercolani ed. *Spoudaiogeloion* (see above) 105–124.

A.H. Sommerstein, "Die Komödie und das 'Unsagbare'", *ibid.* 125–145; also to appear (as "Comedy and the unspeakable") in D.L. Cairns ed. *Law, Rhetoric and Comedy in Classical Athens* (London/Swansea, forthcoming).

D. Rosenbloom, "From *ponêros* to *pharmakos*: theater, social drama, and revolution in Athens, 428–404 BCE", *CA* 21 (2002) 283–346.

C. Brockmann, *Aristophanes und die Freiheit der Komödie* (Munich, 2003).

B. Pütz, *The Symposium and Komos in Aristophanes* (Stuttgart, 2003).

J. Spielvogel, "Die politische Position des athenischen Komödiendichters Aristophanes", *Historia* 52 (2003) 3–22.

D.M. O'Higgins, *Women and Humor in Classical Greece* (Cambridge, 2003).

J.J. Henderson, "Demos, demagogue, tyrant in Old Comedy", in K.A. Morgan ed. *Popular Tyranny* (Austin, 2003) 155–179.

A.H. Sommerstein, "Harassing the satirist: the alleged attempts to prosecute Aristophanes", in I. Sluiter and R.M. Rosen ed. *Free Speech in Classical Antiquity* (Leiden, 2004) 145–174.

S. Halliwell, "Aischrology, shame, and comedy", *ibid.* 115–144.

A.H. Sommerstein, "Comedy and the unspeakable", in D.L. Cairns and R.A. Knox ed. *Law, Rhetoric and Comedy in Classical Athens* (Swansea, 2004) 205–222.

P.J. Rhodes, "Aristophanes and the Athenian assembly", *ib.* 223–237.

I. Stark, *Die hämische Muse: Spott als soziale und mentale Kontrolle in der griechischen Komödie* (Munich, 2004).

A.H. Sommerstein, "*Nephelokokkygia* and *Gynaikopolis*: Aristophanes' dream cities", in M.H. Hansen ed. *The Imaginary Polis* (Copenhagen, 2005) 73–99.

A.H. Sommerstein, "An alternative democracy and an alternative to democracy in Aristophanic comedy", in U. Bultrighini ed. *Democrazia e antidemocrazia nel mondo greco* (Alessandria, 2005 (2006)) 195–207 (discussion, 229–233).

B. Zimmermann, "Poetics and politics in the comedies of Aristophanes", in L.A. Kozak and J.W. Rich ed. *Playing around Aristophanes* (Oxford, 2006) 1–16.

Miscellaneous

E. Fraenkel, *Beobachtungen zu Aristophanes* (Rome, 1962).

V. Ehrenberg, *The People of Aristophanes: A Sociology of Old Attic Comedy*[3] (New York, 1962).

W. Süss, *Aristophanes und die Nachwelt* (Leipzig, 1911).

G.A.H. van Steen, *Venom in Verse: Aristophanes in Modern Greece* (Princeton, 2000).

SELECT BIBLIOGRAPHY

M. Holtermann, *Der deutsche Aristophanes* (Göttingen, 2004).

J.M. Walton, *Found in Translation: Greek Drama in English* (Cambridge, 2006)

E.M. Hall and A. Wrigley ed. *Aristophanes in Performance, 421 BC – AD 2007: Peace, Birds and Frogs* (Oxford, 2007).

Bibliography to *Clouds*

Editions of the play
W.J.M. Starkie (London, 1911); K.J. Dover (Oxford, 1968); G. Guidorizzi and D. Del Corno (Milan, 1996).

Books and articles
C.P. Segal, "Aristophanes' cloud-chorus", *Arethusa* 2 (1969) 143–161. Reprinted in H.J. Newiger ed. *Aristophanes und die alte Komödie* (Darmstadt, 1975) 174–197, and in E. Segal ed. *Oxford Readings in Aristophanes* (Oxford, 1996) 162–181.

A.W.H. Adkins, "Clouds, mysteries, Socrates and Plato", *Antichthon* 4 (1970) 13–24.

E.A. Havelock, "The Socratic self as it is parodied in Aristophanes' *Clouds*", *YCS* 22 (1972) 1–18.

K.J. Reckford, "Father-beating in Aristophanes' *Clouds*", in S. Bertman ed. *The Conflict of Generations in Ancient Greece and Rome* (Amsterdam, 1976) 89–118.

P. Green, "Strepsiades, Socrates and the abuses of intellectualism", *GRBS* 20 (1979) 15–25.

M.C. Nussbaum, "Aristophanes and Socrates on learning practical wisdom", *YCS* 26 (1980) 43–97.

J. Hanuš, "The gods in the *Clouds*", *Graecolatina Pragensia* 8 (1980) 11–23.

L. Woodbury, "Strepsiades' understanding: five notes on the *Clouds*", *Phoenix* 34 (1980) 108–127.

A. Köhnken, "Der Wolken-Chor des Aristophanes", *Hermes* 108 (1980) 154–169.

D. Ambrosino, "Nuages et sens: autour des *Nuées* d'Aristophane", *Quaderni di Storia* 18 (1983) 3–60.

R.K. Fisher, *Aristophanes' Clouds: Purpose and Technique* (Amsterdam, 1984).

R.K. Fisher, "The relevance of Aristophanes: a new look at *Clouds*", *G&R* 35 (1988) 23–28.

T.K. Hubbard, *The Mask of Comedy* (Ithaca NY, 1991) ch.5.

A. Grilli, *Inganni d'autore: due studi sulla funzione del protagonista nel teatro di Aristofane* (Pisa, 1992).

M.C. Marianetti, *Religion and Politics in Aristophanes' Clouds* (Hildesheim, 1992).

D.E. O'Regan, *Rhetoric, Comedy and the Violence of Language in Aristophanes' Clouds* (New York, 1992).

E.G. Csapo, "Deep ambivalence: notes on a Greek cockfight", *Phoenix* 47 (1993) 1–28, 115–124.

I.C. Storey, "The date of Aristophanes' *Clouds II* and Eupolis' *Baptai*: a reply to E.C. Kopff", *AJP* 114 (1993) 71–84.

J.J. Henderson, "Problems in Greek literary history: the case of Aristophanes' *Clouds*", in R.M. Rosen and J. Farrell ed. *Nomodeiktes: Greek Studies in Honor of Martin Ostwald* (Ann Arbor, 1993) 591–601.

S.D. Olson, "*Clouds* 537–44 and the original version of the play", *Philologus* 138 (1994) 32–37.

P. Vander Waerdt, "Socrates in the *Clouds*", in Vander Waerdt ed. *The Socratic Movement* (Ithaca NY, 1994) 48–86.

D. Blyth, "Cloudy morality and the meteorology of some choral odes", *Scholia* 3 (1994) 24–45.

M. Hose, "Der aristophanische Held", *Drama* 3 (1995) 27–50.

R. Janko, "The physicist as hierophant: Aristophanes, Socrates and the authorship of the Derveni papyrus", *ZPE* 118 (1997) 61–94.

R.M. Rosen, "Performance and textuality in Aristophanes' *Clouds*", *Yale Journal of Criticism* 10 (1997) 397–421.

A.H. Sommerstein, "The silence of Strepsiades and the *agon* of the first *Clouds*", in P. Thiercy and M. Menu ed. *Aristophane: la langue, la scène, la cité* (Bari, 1997) 269–282.

O. Imperio, "La figura dell'intellettuale nella commedia greca", in A.M. Belardinelli et al. *Tessere. Frammenti della commedia greca: studi e commenti* (Bari, 1998) 43–130, esp. 99–120.

A. Casanova, "La revisione delle *Nuvole* di Aristofane", *Prometheus* 26 (2000) 19–34.

C. Carey, "Old Comedy and the sophists", in F.D. Harvey and J. Wilkins ed. *The Rivals of Aristophanes* (London/Swansea, 2000) 419–436.

R. Janko, "God, science and Socrates", *BICS* 46 (2002/3) 1–18.

A. Willi, *The Languages of Aristophanes* (Oxford, 2003) 96–156.

N. Papageorgiou, "Ambiguities in *kreitton logos*", *Mnemosyne* 57 (2004) 284–294.

A.F.H. Bierl, "Alt und Neu bei Aristophanes (unter besonderer Berücksichtigung der Wolken)", in A. von Müller and J. von Ungern-Sternberg ed. *Die Wahrnehmung des Neuen in Antike und Renaissance* (Munich, 2004) 1–24.

M. Revermann, *Comic Business* (Oxford, 2006) 179–235, 326–332.

A.H. Sommerstein, "Cloudy swearing: when (if ever) is an oath not an oath?", in A.H. Sommerstein and J. Fletcher ed. *Horkos: The Oath in Greek Society* (Exeter, 2007).

B. Zimmermann, "*Pathei mathos*: strutture tragiche nelle *Nuvole* di Aristofane", in E. Medda et al. ed. *Komoidotragoidia: intersezioni del tragico e del comico nel teatro del V secolo a.C.* (Pisa, 2006) 327–335.

REFERENCES AND ABBREVIATIONS

REFERENCES

Fragments of iambic and elegiac poetry are cited from M.L. West, *Iambi et Elegi Graeci* (Oxford, 1971-2) and also where appropriate from B. Gentili and C. Prato, *Poetae Elegiaci: Testimonia et Fragmenta* (Leipzig, 1979-). Fragments of Sappho and Alcaeus have been cited from E. Lobel and D.L. Page, *Poetarum Lesbiorum Fragmenta* (Oxford, 1955); of Pindar, from B. Snell and H. Maehler, *Pindari Carmina cum Fragmentis: Pars II* (Leipzig, 1975); of other lyric poets, from D.L. Page, *Poetae Melici Graeci* (Oxford, 1962); of Aeschylus, from A. Nauck, *Tragicorum Graecorum Fragmenta*[2] (Leipzig, 1889) and H.J. Mette, *Die Fragmente der Tragödien des Aischylos* (Berlin, 1959); of Sophocles, from S.L. Radt's fourth volume of the new *Tragicorum Graecorum Fragmenta* (Göttingen, 1977)*; of Euripides, from Nauck; of the minor tragedians, from B. Snell's first volume of *TrGF* (Göttingen, 1971); of Attic comedy, from T. Kock, *Comicorum Atticorum Fragmenta* (Leipzig, 1880-8)** or C. Austin, *Comicorum Graecorum Fragmenta in Papyris Reperta* (Berlin, 1973), the latter indicated by *CGF*.

Fragments of, and testimonies concerning, the Presocratics and Sophists, are cited from H. Diels, *Die Fragmente der Vorsokratiker*[6] ed. W. Kranz (Berlin, 1951-2). Fragments of Aristotle are cited from the edition of V. Rose (Leipzig, 1886).

References to Menander by play and line are to the edition of F.H. Sandbach (Oxford, 1972).

For the law-code of Gortyn, cited on 1425-6, see R.F. Willetts, *The Law Code of Gortyn* (Berlin, 1967).

*Except where "Radt" is specified, the references also apply to A.C. Pearson, *The Fragments of Sophocles* (Cambridge, 1917).

**Unless otherwise stated, the references also apply to J.M. Edmonds, *The Fragments of Attic Comedy* (Leiden, 1957-61).

SELECT LIST OF ABBREVIATIONS

Ach.	*Acharnians.*
Aesch.	Aeschylus.
AJPh	*American Journal of Philology.*
Andoc.	Andocides.
Ap. Rh.	Apollonius Rhodius.
Ar.	Aristophanes.
Arist.	Aristotle.
BCH	*Bulletin de Correspondance Hellénique.*
CGF	Austin, *Comicorum Graecorum Fragmenta in Papyris Reperta* (see References).
Char.	*Characters* (Theophrastus).
CP	*Classical Philology.*
CQ	*Classical Quarterly.*
CR	*Classical Review.*
Dein.	Deinarchus.
Dem.	Demosthenes.
Demetr. *Eloc.*	Demetrius of Phalerum, *On Style.*
D-K	Diels-Kranz, *Die Fragmente der Vorsokratiker* (see References).
D.L.	Diogenes Laertius.
D.S.	Diodorus Siculus.
Eccl.	*Ecclesiazusae.*
epigr.	epigram (cited from Page, *Epigrammata Graeca*, q.v.)
Et. Mag.	*Etymologicum Magnum.*
Eur.	Euripides.
Euthd.	*Euthydemus* (Plato).
FGrH	F. Jacoby, *Fragmente der griechischen Historiker* (Berlin and Leiden, 1923-58).
fr.	fragment.
G-P	Gentili and Prato (see References).
gr.	graecus.
GRBS	*Greek, Roman and Byzantine Studies.*
HA	*Historia Animalium* (Aristotle).
Hdt.	Herodotus.
Hes.	Hesiod.
HF	*Hercules Furens* (*The Madness of Heracles*) (Euripides).
h.Hom.Dem.	Homeric Hymn to Demeter.
h.Hom.Pan.	Homeric Hymn to Pan.

Hippocr.	Hippocratic treatise.
HP	*Historia Plantarum* (Theophrastus).
HSCP	*Harvard Studies in Classical Philology.*
Hyp.	Hypereides.
ICS	*Illinois Classical Studies.*
IG	*Inscriptiones Graecae.*
Isocr.	Isocrates.
JHS	*Journal of Hellenic Studies.*
Kinkel	G. Kinkel, *Epicorum Graecorum Fragmenta* vol. i (Leipzig, 1877).
Lex. Vind.	*Lexicon Vindobonense.*
Lys.	Lysias.
Lys.	*Lysistrata.*
MDAI(A)	*Mitteilungen des Deutschen Archäologischen Instituts (Athenische Abteilung).*
Men.	Menander.
N.H.	*Naturalis Historia* (Pliny the Elder).
PA	J. Kirchner, *Prosopographia Attica* (Berlin, 1901-3).
Page	(i) *Poetae Melici Graeci* (see References). Citations with "Page" are to fragment numbers for individual poets, not to the continuous numbering.
	(ii) D.L. Page, *Epigrammata Graeca* (Oxford, 1975).
Paus.	Pausanias.
Peregr.	*On the Death of Peregrinus* (Lucian).
Phd.	*Phaedo* (Plato).
Phdr.	*Phaedrus* (Plato).
Pind.	Pindar.
Pl.	Plato.
Plut.	Plutarch.
PMG	*Poetae Melici Graeci* (see References). Citations with "*PMG*" (used only for anonymous poems) are to the continuous numbering running through the book.
Proleg.	W.J.W. Koster, *Scholia in Aristophanem: Pars I: Fasc. Ia: Prolegomena de Comoedia* (Groningen, 1975)
PSI	*Pubblicazioni della Società Italiana per la Ricerca dei Papiri Greci e Latini in Egitto: Papiri Greci e Latini.*
QUCC	*Quaderni Urbinati di Cultura Classica.*
schol.	scholium or scholia.
SEG	*Supplementum Epigraphicum Graecum.*
Snell	*TrGF* vol. i (see References).

Soph.	Sophocles.
Thesm.	*Thesmophoriazusae.*
Thg.	*Theogony* (Hesiod).
Thphr.	Theophrastus.
Threatte	L. Threatte, *The Grammar of Attic Inscriptions* (Berlin, 1980-).
Tht.	*Theaetetus* (Plato).
Thuc.	Thucydides.
TrGF	*Tragicorum Graecorum Fragmenta* (Göttingen, 1971-); "*TrGF* 20" means that the person in question is author no. 20 in *TrGF* vol. i.
YCS	*Yale Classical Studies.*
ZPE	*Zeitschrift für Papyrologie und Epigraphik.*

CLOUDS

INTRODUCTORY NOTE

Clouds was originally produced at the City Dionysia of 423 B.C., when
it was placed third and last, Cratinus being victorious with *The Wine-flask*
(*Pūtínē*), a brilliant satire on his own bibulousness, and Ameipsias second with
Connus. This reverse seems to have hurt Aristophanes deeply, for he regarded
Clouds as his best play (*Wasps* 1047), and after an interval[1] he began to revise
the play, apparently intending to produce it again. The task of revision was
abandoned incomplete[2]; nevertheless, soon afterwards[3], copies of the revised
version were circulating among the literary public alongside copies of the version produced in 423, and it is the revised version that has survived. The extent
of the revision will be considered below.

The main subject of the play is the growth, in the Athens of the late fifth
century, of new and untraditional forms of education, above all education in
rhetoric, which Aristophanes here professes to regard as the art of winning
arguments (in assembly, courts and elsewhere) which on the merits of the case
one deserves to lose, or, in a phrase which must already have been current (see
on 112-5). "making the worse argument into the better". With rhetoric are
associated other things studied and taught by the thinkers and educators
whom, following Plato, we are accustomed to label "the sophists", such as cosmology and meteorology (e.g. 95-97, 368-407), biology (144-168) and grammar
(658-691)[4]. All these pursuits are depicted as useless and absurd. The gravest
accusation made against the sophists, however, is that of atheism: they are

1. An indication of date is provided by lines 551-9, which can hardly have been
written before 419 —since they imply that at least three comedies attacking Hyperbolus
had been produced since Eupolis' *Maricas* (Lenaea 421), and we know that no such play
appeared at the 421 City Dionysia — but must have been written before Hyperbolus was
ostracized, which probably occurred early in 416.

2. This is shown (i) by the absence of a formally and theatrically indispensable
choral ode after 888, (ii) by the retention of passages (notably 575-594) closely tied to
the ephemeral circumstances of the year 423.

3. A *terminus ante quem* is given by the production of Eupolis' *Baptai*, which contained a rejoinder (Eupolis fr. 78) to the charge of plagiarism made against Eupolis in
Clouds 553-4. *Baptai* satirized Alcibiades among others (schol. Aristides 3.444 Dindorf)
and is unlikely to be later than 415.

4. For an account of the sophists and their contribution to Greek thought see
W.K.C. Guthrie, *A History of Greek Philosophy* iii (Cambridge, 1969) 3-319.

2

presented as denying the existence of Zeus and the other traditional gods and as believing in new deities of their own (cf. *Frogs* 888-894; Pl. *Apol.* 26b), and it is primarily for this that the Clouds, who from the first (302ff, 563ff, 595ff) indicate to the audience that they *do* honour the traditional gods, engineer the punishment of the sophists and of their dupe Strepsiades (1461; cf. 1508-9).   *

It was necessary to the plot that some one person should be singled out as the typical sophist, and Aristophanes' choice fell upon Socrates: partly because this relentless questioner and arguer, who frequented the Agora and the wrestling-schools and hardly ever left the city, must have been a more familiar figure to a greater number of people than teachers such as Prodicus and Hippias, who taught mostly in private for high fees and were often away from Athens; partly no doubt because certain aspects of Socrates the man lent themselves particularly easily to caricature, for example his notoriously ugly appearance (Pl. *Symp.* 215a-b) That Socrates was far from a typical sophist, Aristophanes either did not know or did not care: he may not have taught dishonest rhetoric, but he certainly (like the Worse Argument in the play) questioned and confuted those whose zeal for traditional beliefs was stronger than their understanding of the grounds on which these beliefs might be based, and his young admirers will have been encouraged by his example to do likewise; he may not have disbelieved in the gods, but he certainly (if the early Platonic dialogue *Euthyphro* is anything to go by) queried the foundations of the conventional concept of piety. It may well be that in this play there is not one serious accusation made by Aristophanes against Socrates which he did not sincerely believe to be justified[5]. It must of course be noted that the unfair image of Soc-   * rates created by comedy and public opinion will have played its part, many years later, in bringing about his condemnation (the Platonic Socrates [*Apol.* 18b-c] asserts that this prejudice is more dangerous to him than the charges   * made by his actual accusers); but it should also be noted that by devoting time to refuting the false allegations of teaching science and dishonest rhetoric, Socrates in his defence speech was trying to divert attention from other matters on which the prosecution's case was far stronger[6].

The fragments of the original version of *Clouds* (Ar. fr. 376-386) are too slight to give much idea of how it differed from the version we possess. Our main information comes from one of the ancient synopses (Hypotheses) to our play (Hypothesis VI Hall-Geldart = VII Coulon = I Dover):

⸱ 5. M. Nussbaum, *YCS* 26 (1980) 43-97, goes so far as to argue that in *Clouds* Socrates' theory and method of education are presented with essential faithfulness and subjected to valid and telling criticisms that anticipate those made by Plato in the *Republic*.

6. Such as the fact that some of those who had been most in his company had done great harm to Athens (cf. Aeschines 1.173).

3

* This play is the same as the first[7], but has been revised in details, as though the poet intended to produce it again but, for whatever reason, did not do so. To speak generally, there has been revision in almost every part of the play; some parts have been removed, new sections have been woven in, and changes have been made in arrangement and in the exchanges between characters. Certain parts in their present form belong entirely to the revised version: thus the parabasis of the chorus[8] has been replaced, and where the just argument talks to the unjust[9], and lastly where the school of Socrates is burned.

Of the three major changes here mentioned, only the last will have seriously affected the structure of the play, and altogether the revision does not seem to have been as far-reaching as has sometimes been supposed[10].

There is an excellent edition of *Clouds* by Sir Kenneth Dover (Oxford, 1968); the very full commentary of W.J.M. Starkie (London, 1911) remains valuable. W.J.W. Koster's edition of the Aristophanic scholia is now complete for *Clouds*: D. Holwerda has edited the ancient scholia (Groningen, 1977) and those of Tzetzes (Groningen, 1960), while the scholia of Eustathius, Thomas Magister, Triclinius and later commentators have been edited by Koster himself (Groningen, 1974).

7. That is, it is not an entirely new play like the second *Thesmophoriazusae*.

8. This refers only to the speech 518-562 (the "parabasis" in the narrower sense of the term), which discusses, among other things, the failure of the original play. A scholion on 520 states that the corresponding speech in the original play was in a different metre (no doubt anapaestic tetrameters).

9. Referring perhaps to the altercation 889-948. Others take it as referring to the speech of the Better Argument in 961-1023, or to the entire *agōn* 889-1104; but it is only in the initial altercation that the Better Argument can properly be said to be talking to the Worse.

* 10. In addition to the passages in our play whose content shows that they were composed for production in 423 and not later, several others (1113-30, 1196-1200, 1417) are positively attested by various sources as having been included in the original play. See further Dover's introduction to his edition (pp. lxxx-xcviii) and my notes on 888-9 and 1437-9.

NOTE ON THE TEXT

Both in antiquity and in the Middle Ages *Clouds* was one of the most popular of Aristophanes' comedies. Six papyri[1] preserve at least part of some 180 lines of the play, and there are over a hundred and thirty medieval manuscripts, divided basically into two families, with RV on the one side and the later mss. (*n*) on the other. Where there is a clear-cut division between the two families, RV are more often wrong than right. There is, however, a good deal of contamination, as well as some evidence that variants were inherited from antiquity, and no reading found in R or in V or in the bulk of the relatively uninterpolated *n* mss. can be excluded from consideration merely on stemmatic grounds [2].

Within the *n* family two main groups of mss. are discernible. Of the four mss. which represent the family in the apparatus of this edition, K belongs to one group and NΘ to the other, while E is a ms. of the first group with corrections derived from a ms. of the second group. Continually, however, readings straddle the divide between the two groups.

All the *n* mss. contain some conjectures by scholars of the thirteenth and fourteenth centuries. Two of the later of these, Thomas Magister and Demetrius Triclinius, can be said to have produced recensions of the text, the latter, at any rate, more than once.

In the apparatus RVEKNΘ[3] and (where available) the papyri are cited regularly, other mss. only for true or plausible readings. A reading is ascribed to Thomas or Triclinius when it is sufficiently widespread in mss. reflecting

---

*   1. Two of these happen not to be cited in the apparatus: Π5 (Oxyrhynchus Papyrus 1371), of the fifth century, which contains parts of lines 1-11 and 38-48, and Π62 (Laurentian Papyrus III 318), of the fourth century, which contains parts of lines 1-7.

    2. I do not think that the passages (predominantly in the first 630 lines of the play) where V preserves the truth alone or almost alone can all be explained away as Dover, p. cx, attempts to do. Actually, over the play as a whole, V is right alone more often than R is.

    3. The four *n* mss. selected are the same four chosen by Dover. Between them they contain almost all the medieval readings absent from RV that have some chance of being inherited from antiquity. The main exception is the remarkable reading of Vb3 at 1373, which conceivably may derive from the commentary of Tzetzes (cf. schol. U ad loc.)

the recension of the scholar in question to make it probable that it originates with him. The good conjectures at 151, 533, 538 and 680 are probably post-Triclinian.

The manuscripts of *Clouds* are not well reported. Dover's edition gives a full report of the readings of RVEKNΘ and selected readings of other mss.; in his introduction, pp. xcix-cxxv, he lists, with references, the mss. collated by him and those on which published information exists, and discusses the history of the text. For further information and corrections see Koster's and Holwerda's introductions to their editions of the scholia (though their conclusions about ms. relationships with respect to the scholia are not necessarily, and do not profess to be, valid with respect to the text of the play).

* SIGLA

Manuscripts		Century
Π6	Berlin Papyrus 13225+13226 (contains fragments of 177-270, 936-973)	5th
Π7	PSI 1171 (contains 577-635)	3rd
Π8	Berlin Papyrus 13219 (contains fragments of 946-1015)	5th/6th
Π9	Strasbourg Papyrus inv. 621 (contains 1372-85, 1407-28)	5th/7th
R	Ravennas 429	10th
V	Venetus Marcianus 474	11th/12th
E	Estensis gr. 127 (=*a.*U.5.10)	14th
K	Ambrosianus C222 inf.	13th/14th
N	Neapolitanus 184 (=II F 27)	15th
Θ	Laurentianus *conv. soppr.* 140	14th
A	Parisinus Regius 2712	14th
M	Ambrosianus L39 sup.	early 14th
Md1	Matritensis 4683	late 13th
Np1	Neapolitanus 179 (= II F 22)	late 14th
Np5	Neapolitanus 182 (= II F 25)	15th
P14	Parisinus Regius 2827	15th
U	Vaticanus Urbinas 141	14th

Vb3	Vaticanus Barberinianus I 126	14th
Vs1	Vaticanus Reginae Suecorum 147	early 14th
X	Laurentianus XXXI 13	15th

al.   one or more mss. among those with a basically pre-Thoman text in addition to the ms. or mss. specifically cited

Thom.	the recension of Thomas Magister (c. 1300)	
Tricl.	one or another of the successive recensions of Demetrius Triclinius (c. 1315-30)	

Vv2	Vaticanus gr. 57 (text Thoman)	14th
Vv4	Vaticanus gr. 918 (text Thoman)	(1362)

Ct1	Cantabrigiensis 2626, first part (representing an early state of the Triclinian text)	(c.1320)
L	(Oxoniensis Bodleianus) Holkhamensis 88 (representing the final state of the Triclinian text)	early 15th

Ct3	Cantabrigiensis 2614	15th
Ln5	(Londiniensis) Harleianus 5725	15th or 16th
V3	Venetus Marcianus 473	14th

Ald.   the Aldine *editio princeps* (Venice, 1498)

n	the agreement of EKNΘ
n'	*n* with the exception of that ms. (or correction, variant, etc.) which is cited for a different reading

codd.   = RV*n*

Other Sigla

Σ	scholion
λ	lemma (of scholion)
γρ	reading noted in ms. or scholia as a variant
i	implied by or inferable from
ac	before correction
pc	after correction

s	above or below the line
E^1 (et sim.)	the hand of the original copyist
E^2 (et sim.)	a later hand
Suda^F, Suda^{rell} etc.	variant readings in the Suda are thus referred to ("rell." = the remaining mss)
$[E^1]$ (et sim.)	the reading of the hand in question is no longer legible.

ΝΕΦΕΛΑΙ

CLOUDS

TA TOY ΔΡΑΜΑΤΟΣ ΠΡΟΣΩΠΑ

ΣΤΡΕΨΙΑΔΗΣ Φείδωνος Κικυννεύς, πατήρ.
ΦΕΙΔΙΠΠΙΔΗΣ, υἱός.
ΟΙΚΕΤΗΣ Στρεψιάδου.
ΜΑΘΗΤΗΣ Σωκράτους.
ΣΩΚΡΑΤΗΣ.
ΧΟΡΟΣ Νεφελῶν.
ΚΡΕΙΤΤΩΝ ΛΟΓΟΣ.
ΗΤΤΩΝ ΛΟΓΟΣ.
ΧΡΗΣΤΗΣ Α, δημότης Στρεψιάδου.
ΧΡΗΣΤΗΣ Β.
ΧΑΙΡΕΦΩΝ.

ΚΩΦΑ ΠΡΟΣΩΠΑ
    ΜΑΘΗΤΑΙ Σωκράτους.
    ΚΛΗΤΗΡ τοῦ προτέρου χρήστου.
    ΞΑΝΘΙΑΣ καὶ ἄλλοι οἰκέται Στρεψιάδου.

CHARACTERS OF THE PLAY

STREPSIADES, *son of Pheidon, of Cicynna.*
PHEIDIPPIDES, *his son.*
SLAVE *of Strepsiades.*
STUDENT *of Socrates.*
SOCRATES.
CHORUS *of Clouds.*
THE BETTER ARGUMENT.
THE WORSE ARGUMENT.
FIRST CREDITOR, *a fellow-demesman of Strepsiades.*
SECOND CREDITOR.
CHAEREPHON.

SILENT CHARACTERS

STUDENTS *of Socrates.*
WITNESS *accompanying First Creditor.*
XANTHIAS *and other slaves of Strepsiades.*

ΣΤΡΕΨΙΑΔΗΣ
 Ἰοὺ ἰού.

 ὦ Ζεῦ βασιλεῦ, τὸ χρῆμα τῶν νυκτῶν ὅσον.

 ἀπέραντον. οὐδέποθ' ἡμέρα γενήσεται;

 καὶ μὴν πάλαι γ' ἀλεκτρυόνος ἤκουσ' ἐγώ·

 οἱ δ' οἰκέται ῥέγκουσιν. ἀλλ' οὐκ ἂν πρὸ τοῦ. 5

 ἀπόλοιο δῆτ', ὦ πόλεμε, πολλῶν οὕνεκα,

 ὅτ' οὐδὲ κολάσ' ἔξεστί μοι τοὺς οἰκέτας.

 ἀλλ' οὐδ' ὁ χρηστὸς οὑτοσὶ νεανίας

 ἐγείρεται τῆς νυκτός, ἀλλὰ πέρδεται

 ἐν πέντε σισύραις ἐγκεκορδυλημένος. 10

 ἀλλ', εἰ δοκεῖ, ῥέγκωμεν ἐγκεκαλυμμένοι.—

 ἀλλ' οὐ δύναμαι δείλαιος εὕδειν δακνόμενος

 ὑπὸ τῆς δαπάνης καὶ τῆς φάτνης καὶ τῶν χρεῶν

 διὰ τουτονὶ τὸν υἱόν. ὁ δὲ κόμην ἔχων

 ἱππάζεταί τε καὶ ξυνωρικεύεται, 15

 ὀνειροπολεῖ θ' ἵππους· ἐγὼ δ' ἀπόλλυμαι

 ὁρῶν ἄγουσαν τὴν σελήνην εἰκάδας·

 οἱ γὰρ τόκοι χωροῦσιν. ἅπτε, παῖ, λύχνον,

 κἄκφερε τὸ γραμματεῖον, ἵν' ἀναγνῶ λαβὼν

 ὁπόσοις ὀφείλω καὶ λογίσωμαι τοὺς τόκους. 20

 φέρ' ἴδω, τί ὀφείλω; δώδεκα μνᾶς Πασίᾳ.

 τοῦ δώδεκα μνᾶς Πασίᾳ; τί ἐχρησάμην;

 ὅτ' ἐπριάμην τὸν κοππατίαν. οἴμοι τάλας,

 εἴθ' ἐξεκόπην πρότερον τὸν ὀφθαλμὸν λίθῳ.

ΦΕΙΔΙΠΠΙΔΗΣ
 Φίλων, ἀδικεῖς· ἔλαυνε τὸν σαυτοῦ δρόμον. 25

Στ. τοῦτ' ἐστὶ τουτὶ τὸ κακὸν ὅ μ' ἀπολώλεκεν·

[*Strepsiades and Pheidippides are lying asleep. Strepsiades is rest-less, and presently he wakes and sits up.*]

STREPSIADES: Ough! Lord Zeus, what a length of night-time! It's unending! Is it never going to be day? Though I heard a cock crow quite a time ago – but the slaves are snoring. They wouldn't have been in the old days. Damn you, War, damn you on a hundred counts, when it's not even possible for me to punish my slaves! And this fine young man here, he doesn't wake up before daylight either; he's farting away swathed in five fleeced cloaks. All right, if you want to, let's cover our heads and snore. [*He lies down and tries to sleep, but soon abandons the attempt.*] No, I just can't sleep, heaven help me, with being bitten and nagged by expenses and mangers and debts, on account of this son of mine. He wears his hair long, and he rides and he chariot-and-pairs, and he lives and dreams horses. As for me, I'm fit to perish when I see the moon in its twenties, for the interest is mounting up. [*Calling within*] Boy! light a lamp and bring out my accounts, so I can see how many creditors I have and calculate the interest. [*A slave brings the waxed tablets on which the accounts are written, and stays holding the lamp for Strepsiades to read by.*] Now let me see, what do I owe? "Twelve minas to Pasias." Twelve minas to Pasias? What for? Why did I borrow it? Oh yes, when I bought the horse with the *koppa* brand. My god! I wish I'd had my eye knocked out first with a stone.

PHEIDIPPIDES [*in his sleep*]: Philon, you're cheating; drive in your own lane.

STREPSIADES: That's it, that's the trouble, that's what's

ὀνειροπολεῖ γὰρ καὶ καθεύδων ἱππικήν.

Φε. πόσους δρόμους ἐλᾷ τὰ πολεμιστήρια;

Στ. ἐμὲ μὲν σὺ πολλοὺς τὸν πατέρ' ἐλαύνεις δρόμους.
 ἀτὰρ τί χρέος ἔβα με μετὰ τὸν Πασίαν;   30
 τρεῖς μναῖ διφρίσκου καὶ τροχοῖν 'Αμυνίᾳ.

Φε. ἄπαγε τὸν ἵππον ἐξαλύσας οἴκαδε.

Στ. ἀλλ', ὦ μέλ', ἐξήλικας ἐμέ γ' ἐκ τῶν ἐμῶν,
 ὅτε καὶ δίκας ὦφληκα χἄτεροι τόκου
 ἐνεχυράσεσθαί φασιν.

* Φε.   ἐτεόν, ὦ πάτερ,   35
 τί δυσκολαίνεις καὶ στρέφει τὴν νύχθ' ὅλην;

Στ. δάκνει μέ τις δήμαρχος ἐκ τῶν στρωμάτων.

Φε. ἔασον, ὦ δαιμόνιε, καταδαρθεῖν τί με.

Στ. σὺ δ' οὖν κάθευδε· τὰ δὲ χρέα ταῦτ' ἴσθ' ὅτι
 εἰς τὴν κεφαλὴν ἅπαντα τὴν σὴν τρέψεται.   40
 φεῦ·
 εἴθ' ὤφελ' ἡ προμνήστρι' ἀπολέσθαι κακῶς,
 ἥτις με γῆμ' ἐπῆρε τὴν σὴν μητέρα.
 ἐμοὶ γὰρ ἦν ἄγροικος ἥδιστος βίος,
 εὐρωτιῶν, ἀκόρητος, εἰκῇ κείμενος,
 βρύων μελίτταις καὶ προβάτοις καὶ στεμφύλοις·   45
 ἔπειτ' ἔγημα Μεγακλέους τοῦ Μεγακλέους
 ἀδελφιδῆν ἄγροικος ὢν **ἐξ** ἄστεως,

---

31 'Αμυνίᾳ R̲n̲: 'Αμεινίᾳ V.
35 ἐνεχυράσεσθαί $^{i}_{\Sigma}$VAM $^{i}_{\Sigma(i)}$ΕΘΝp1: ἐνεχυράσασθαί (-ρίσ- N)
  codd. Σ(ii)ΕΘΝp1.
47 ἄστεως Dindorf: ἄστεος codd. ^{λ}Suda, Lex. Vind.

ruined me; even in his sleep, it's racing he dreams of.

PHEIDIPPIDES [*as before*]: How many laps are the war-chariots going to drive?

STREPSIADES: You're driving me, your father, round enough bends! — But after Pasias what sad debt befell? "Three minas to Amynias for a small chariot-board and a pair of wheels."   30

PHEIDIPPIDES [*as before*]: Let the horse have a roll, and then take him off home.

STREPSIADES: You've been rolling all right, my lad — rolling in *my* money. Now I've got judgements against me, and other creditors are saying they will distrain for their interest.   35

PHEIDIPPIDES [*waking and raising his head*]: Tell me, father, why have you been fretting and twisting and turning all night long?

STREPSIADES: I'm getting bitten by a . . . deme official in the bedding.

PHEIDIPPIDES: If you please, father dear, let me get a bit of sleep. [*He lies down again and covers his head.*]

STREPSIADES: All right, you sleep; but I tell you, one day all these debts will be *your* headache! Ah, would that she most   40
miserably had perished, the matchmaker who incited me to marry your mother! I had a rustic life, a delightful life, nice and mouldy and unswept, spreading one's limbs as one pleased, a life teeming   45
with honey-bees and sheep and pressed olive; and then I married the niece of Megacles son of Megacles, I a rustic, she from town, a

15

σεμνήν, τρυφῶσαν, ἐγκεκοισυρωμένην.
ταύτην ὅτ' ἐγάμουν, συγκατεκλινόμην ἐγὼ
ὄζων τρυγός, τρασιᾶς, ἐρίων, περιουσίας,   50
ἡ δ' αὖ μύρου, κρόκου, καταγλωττισμάτων,
δαπάνης, λαφυγμοῦ, Κωλιάδος, Γενετυλλίδος.
οὐ μὴν ἐρῶ γ' ὡς ἀργὸς ἦν, ἀλλ' ἐσπάθα·
ἐγὼ δ' ἂν αὐτῇ θοἰμάτιον δεικνὺς τοδὶ
πρόφασιν ἔφασκον· "ὦ γύναι, λίαν σπαθᾷς."   55

ΟΙΚΕΤΗΣ
    ἔλαιον ἡμῖν οὐκ ἔνεστ' ἐν τῷ λύχνῳ.

Στ. οἴμοι· τί γάρ μοι τὸν πότην ἧπτες λύχνον;
    δεῦρ' ἔλθ', ἵνα κλάῃς.

Οι.   διὰ τί δῆτα κλαύσομαι;

Στ. ὅτι τῶν παχειῶν ἐνετίθεις θρυαλλίδων.
    μετὰ ταῦθ', ὅπως νῷν ἐγένεθ' υἱὸς οὑτοσί,   60
    ἐμοί τε δὴ καὶ τῇ γυναικὶ τἀγαθῇ,
    περὶ τοὐνόματος δὴ 'νταῦθ' ἐλοιδορούμεθα.
    ἡ μὲν γὰρ ἵππον προσετίθει πρὸς τοὔνομα,
    Ξάνθιππον ἢ Χαίριππον ἢ Καλλιππίδην,
    ἐγὼ δὲ τοῦ πάππου 'τιθέμην Φειδωνίδην.   65
    τέως μὲν οὖν ἐκρινόμεθ'· εἶτα τῷ χρόνῳ
    κοινῇ ξυνέβημεν κἀθέμεθα Φειδιππίδην.
    τοῦτον τὸν υἱὸν λαμβάνους' ἐκορίζετο,
    "ὅταν σὺ μέγας ὢν ἅρμ' ἐλαύνῃς πρὸς πόλιν,
    ὥσπερ Μεγακλέης, ξυστίδ' ἔχων—'· ἐγὼ δ' ἔφην·   70
    "ὅταν μὲν οὖν τὰς αἶγας ἐκ τοῦ φελλέως,

---

62 δὴ 'νταῦθ' Reisig: δὴ 'ντεῦθεν vel sim. RK: δὴν ἐντεῦθεν V:
    δὴ ταῦτ' n'.

64 Χαίριππον V: Χάριππον n: Κάλλιππον R.

16

spoilt, stuck-up snob, all Coesyrated. When I married her
I went to bed smelling of new wine, drying figs, fleeces, and afflu-   50
ence; and she of perfume, saffron, deep kisses, extravagance, over-
eating, Colias and Genetyllis. Still, I won't say she was idle; she did
use to weave, packing the threads close; and I used to say to her,   *
showing her this cloak by way of evidence, "Missus, you weave *too*   55
close."

    [*The lamp held by the slave goes out.*]

    SLAVE: We've no oil in the lamp.

    STREPSIADES: Dammit, why did you light me the lamp with
the big thirst? You'll have a hiding for that; come here!

    SLAVE: Why should I have a hiding?

    STREPSIADES: Because you put in one of the fat wicks. [*The
slave evades him and goes inside.*] — After that, when this son was   60
born to us, to me, that is, and my good wife, then we were quarrel-
ling over his name. She wanted to add -*hippus* to the name, thus
"Xanthippus" or "Chaerippus" or "Callippides", while I wanted to   65
name him Pheidonides after his grandfather. For a time we argued;
then eventually we came to a mutual agreement and named him
Pheidippides. She used to take this boy and say to him lovingly,
"When you're big and drive a chariot to the Acropolis, like Megacles,   70
wearing a rich smooth robe—"; but I'd say, "No, when you drive
the goats home from the Rocklands, like your father, dressed in a

ὥσπερ ὁ πατήρ σου, διφθέραν ἐνημμένος."
ἀλλ' οὐκ ἐπείθετο τοῖς ἐμοῖς οὐδὲν λόγοις,
ἀλλ' ἵππερόν μου κατέχεεν τῶν χρημάτων.
νῦν οὖν ὅλην τὴν νύκτα φροντίζων ὁδοῦ .   75
μίαν ηὗρον ἀτραπὸν δαιμονίως ὑπερφυᾶ,
ἣν ἢν ἀναπείσω τουτονί, σωθήσομαι.
ἀλλ' ἐξεγεῖραι πρῶτον αὐτὸν βούλομαι.
πῶς δῆτ' ἂν ἥδιστ' αὐτὸν ἐπεγείραιμι;   πῶς;
Φειδιππίδη, Φειδιππίδιον.

Φε.   τί, ὦ πάτερ;   80

Στ. κύσον με καὶ τὴν χεῖρα δὸς τὴν δεξιάν.

Φε. ἰδού. τί ἐστιν;

Στ.   εἰπέ μοι, φιλεῖς ἐμέ;

Φε. νὴ τὸν Ποσειδῶ τουτονὶ τὸν ἵππιον.

Στ. μὴ 'μοιγε τοῦτον μηδαμῶς τὸν ἵππιον·
οὗτος γὰρ ὁ θεὸς αἴτιός μοι τῶν κακῶν.   85
ἀλλ' εἴπερ ἐκ τῆς καρδίας μ' ὄντως φιλεῖς,
ὦ παῖ, πιθοῦ.

Φε.   τί οὖν πίθωμαι δῆτά σοι;

Στ. ἔκστρεφον ὡς τάχιστα τοὺς σαυτοῦ τρόπους,
καὶ μάνθαν' ἐλθὼν ἂν ἐγὼ παραινέσω.

Φε. λέγε δή, τί κελεύεις;

Στ.   καί τι πείσει;

Φε.   πείσομαι,   90

87 πίθωμαι Vv2: πείθομαι RV: πιθοῦμαι vel sim. E^{pc}<u>n'</u>: $[E^{ac}]$.

18

leather smock." But he took no notice at all of what I said; instead he's now made the family exchequer sick with *galloping consumption*. So now all night I've been trying to think of a way out, and I've found one path, a heaven-sent miracle of a path, which if I can persuade this boy to follow, I'll be saved. But first I want to wake him up. Now what would be the nicest way for me to wake him up? what now? — Pheidippides! my sweet little Pheidippides!

PHEIDIPPIDES: What is it, father?

STREPSIADES: Kiss me and give me your right hand.

PHEIDIPPIDES [*getting up and doing so*]: There. What's the matter?

STREPSIADES: Tell me, do you love me?

PHEIDIPPIDES: Yes, by Poseidon here [*gesturing towards a statue on stage*], the Lord of horses.

STREPSIADES: None of that Lord of horses for me on any account! That's the god that's been the cause of my troubles. But, my son, if you truly love me from your heart, obey me now.

PHEIDIPPIDES: Obey you in what way?

STREPSIADES: Turn your way of life inside out at once, and go and learn what I'm going to ask you to.

PHEIDIPPIDES: Tell me, then, what do you ask me to learn?

STREPSIADES: And you will obey?

PHEIDIPPIDES: I will, I swear it by Dionysus.

νὴ τὸν Διόνυσον.

Στ.   δεῦρό νυν ἀπόβλεπε.
  ὁρᾷς τὸ θύριον τοῦτο καὶ τοὐκίδιον;

Φε.   ὁρῶ. τί οὖν τοῦτ' ἐστὶν ἐτεόν, ὦ πάτερ;

Στ.   ψυχῶν σοφῶν τοῦτ' ἐστὶ φροντιστήριον.
  ἐνταῦθ' ἐνοικοῦσ' ἄνδρες, οἳ τὸν οὐρανὸν   95
  λέγοντες ἀναπείθουσιν ὡς ἔστιν πνιγεύς,
  κἄστιν περὶ ἡμᾶς οὗτος, ἡμεῖς δ' ἄνθρακες.
  οὗτοι διδάσκουσ', ἀργύριον ἤν τις διδῷ,
  λέγοντα νικᾶν καὶ δίκαια κἄδικα.

Φε.   εἰσὶν δὲ τίνες;

Στ.   οὐκ οἶδ' ἀκριβῶς τοὔνομα.   100
  μεριμνοφροντισταὶ καλοί τε κἀγαθοί.

Φε.   αἰβοῖ, πονηροί γ'. οἶδα· τοὺς ἀλαζόνας,
  τοὺς ὠχριῶντας, τοὺς ἀνυποδήτους λέγεις,
  ὧν ὁ κακοδαίμων Σωκράτης καὶ Χαιρεφῶν.

Στ.   ἢ ἤ, σιώπα· μηδὲν εἴπῃς νήπιον.   105
  ἀλλ' εἴ τι κήδει τῶν πατρῴων ἀλφίτων,
  τούτων γενοῦ μοι, σχασάμενος τὴν ἱππικήν.

Φε.   οὐκ ἂν μὰ τὸν Διόνυσον εἰ δοίης γέ μοι
  τοὺς φασιανοὺς οὓς τρέφει Λεωγόρας.

Στ.   ἴθ', ἀντιβολῶ σ', ὦ φίλτατ' ἀνθρώπων ἐμοί,   110
  ἐλθὼν διδάσκου.

Φε.   καὶ τί σοι μαθήσομαι;

Στ.   εἶναι παρ' αὐτοῖς φασιν ἄμφω τὼ λόγω,
  τὸν κρείττον', ὅστις ἐστί, καὶ τὸν ἥττονα.
  τούτοιν τὸν ἕτερον τοῖν λόγοιν, τὸν ἥττονα,

20

STREPSIADES: Very well, now look over here. You see that nice little door and that nice little house?

PHEIDIPPIDES: I do. What is it actually, father?

STREPSIADES: That is a Reflectory for clever spirits. Men 95
live there who try to argue us into believing that the sky is a baking-cover, and we're the charcoal, and it's all around us. These people teach you, if you pay them, how to carry the day in argument, whether your cause is just or unjust.

PHEIDIPPIDES: And who are they? 100

STREPSIADES: I don't know the name exactly. Reflective thinkers, fine upstanding people.

PHEIDIPPIDES: Ugh, the rotten lot! I know them; you're talking about the charlatans, the palefaces, the men with no shoes, such as that god-forsaken Socrates and Chaerephon.

STREPSIADES: Hey! Be quiet, don't say anything so child- 105
ish! Now, if you care at all for your father's groats, drop your racing, I beg you, and become one of that company.

PHEIDIPPIDES: By Dionysus, no, not if you gave me the pheasants that Leogoras rears.

STREPSIADES: Come on, I beseech you, my best beloved 110
in the world, go there and learn.

PHEIDIPPIDES: And what do you want me to learn?

STREPSIADES: It's said that they have in their house both the Arguments, the Better, whatever that may be, and the Worse; and that one of this pair of Arguments, the Worse, can plead an un- 115

21

νικᾶν λέγοντά φασι τἀδικώτερα.   115
ἢν οὖν μάθῃς μοι τὸν ἄδικον τοῦτον λόγον,
ἃ νῦν ὀφείλω διὰ σέ, τούτων τῶν χρεῶν
οὐκ ἂν ἀποδοίην οὐδ' ἂν ὀβολὸν οὐδενί.

Φε. οὐκ ἂν πιθοίμην· οὐ γὰρ ἂν τλαίην ἰδεῖν
τοὺς ἱππέας τὸ χρῶμα διακεκναισμένος.   120

Στ. οὐκ ἄρα μὰ τὴν Δήμητρα τῶν γ' ἐμῶν ἔδει,
οὔτ' αὐτὸς οὔθ' ὁ ζύγιος οὔθ' ὁ σαμφόρας·
ἀλλ' ἐξελῶ σ' ἐς κόρακας ἐκ τῆς οἰκίας.

Φε. ἀλλ' οὐ περιόψεταί μ' ὁ θεῖος Μεγακλέης
ἄνιππον. ἀλλ' εἴσειμι, σοῦ δ' οὐ φροντιῶ.   125

Στ. ἀλλ' οὐδ' ἐγὼ μέντοι πεσών γε κείσομαι,
ἀλλ' εὐξάμενος τοῖσιν θεοῖς διδάξομαι
αὐτὸς βαδίζων εἰς τὸ φροντιστήριον.
πῶς οὖν γέρων ὢν κἀπιλήσμων καὶ βραδὺς
λόγων ἀκριβῶν σχινδαλάμους μαθήσομαι;   130
ἰτητέον. τί ταῦτ' ἔχων στραγγεύομαι,
ἀλλ' οὐχὶ κόπτω τὴν θύραν; παῖ, παιδίον.

ΜΑΘΗΤΗΣ
βάλλ' ἐς κόρακας. τίς ἐσθ' ὁ κόψας τὴν θύραν;

Στ. Φείδωνος υἱὸς Στρεψιάδης Κικυννόθεν.

Μα. ἀμαθής γε νὴ Δί', ὅστις οὑτωσὶ σφόδρα   135
ἀπεριμερίμνως τὴν θύραν λελάκτικας,
καὶ φροντίδ' ἐξήμβλωκας ἐξηυρημένην.

Στ. σύγγνωθί μοι· τηλοῦ γὰρ οἰκῶ τῶν ἀγρῶν.
ἀλλ' εἰπέ μοι τὸ πρᾶγμα τοὐξημβλωμένον.

Μα. ἀλλ' οὐ θέμις πλὴν τοῖς μαθηταῖσιν λέγειν.   140

Στ. λέγε νυν ἐμοὶ θαρρῶν· ἐγὼ γὰρ οὑτοσὶ

                                        22

just cause and prevail. Well, if you learn this Wrongful Argument
for me, then of these debts that I owe now because of you, I
wouldn't have to pay an obol to anyone.

PHEIDIPPIDES: I can't obey you: I couldn't bear to set eyes
on the Knights with all the colour withered from **my** face.   120

STREPSIADES: Then, by Demeter, you shan't eat anything
of mine, not you nor your yoke-horse nor your *san*-branded thoroughbred; I'll throw you out of the house, and you can go to
blazes.

PHEIDIPPIDES: Ah, but uncle Megacles won't let me remain
horseless. I'm going inside, and not giving a thought to you. [*He*   125
goes into his father's house.]

STREPSIADES: And *I'm* not going to take this blow lying
down; with a prayer to the gods, I shall go to the Reflectory and
get *myself* taught. But then how am I to learn splinter-like exac-   130
titudes of argument, when old, forgetful and slow? — No, I have got
to go. Why do I keep dallying like this, instead of knocking on the
door? [*Knocking*] Boy! Little boy!

STUDENT [*within*]: Oh, get stuffed! [*Opening the door*]
Who's been knocking at this door?

STREPSIADES: Strepsiades, son of Pheidon, of Cicynna.

STUDENT: An ignoramus, for sure, the way you've kicked   135
so hard at the door without circumspect cogitation, and rendered
abortive an idea that had been discovered. [*He comes out and closes*
the door behind him.]

STREPSIADES: Forgive me; I live a long way off in the country. But do tell me about the thing that miscarried.

STUDENT: It may not lawfully be divulged except to the   140
students.

STREPSIADES: Then tell me, you've nothing to worry about;

*　　　ἥκω μαθητὴς εἰς τὸ φροντιστήριον.

Μα.　λέξω· νομίσαι δὲ ταῦτα χρὴ μυστήρια.
　　　ἀνήρετ' ἄρτι Χαιρεφῶντα Σωκράτης
　　　ψύλλαν ὁπόσους ἅλλοιτο τοὺς αὑτῆς πόδας·　　　　145
　　　δακοῦσα γὰρ τοῦ Χαιρεφῶντος τὴν ὀφρῦν
　　　ἐπὶ τὴν κεφαλὴν τὴν Σωκράτους ἀφήλατο.

Στ.　πῶς δῆτα διεμέτρησε;

Μα.　　　　　　　　δεξιώτατα.
　　　κηρὸν διατήξας, εἶτα τὴν ψύλλαν λαβὼν
　　　ἐνέβαψεν εἰς τὸν κηρὸν αὑτῆς τὼ πόδε,　　　　150
　　　κᾆτα ψυχείσῃ περιέφυσαν Περσικαί.
　　　ταύτας ὑπολύσας ἀνεμέτρει τὸ χωρίον.

Στ.　ὦ Ζεῦ βασιλεῦ, τῆς λεπτότητος τῶν φρενῶν.

Μα.　τί δῆτ' ἄν, ἕτερον εἰ πύθοιο Σωκράτους
　　　φρόντισμα;

Στ.　　　　　ποῖον; ἀντιβολῶ, κάτειπέ μοι.　　　　155

Μα.　ἀνήρετ' αὐτὸν Χαιρεφῶν ὁ Σφήττιος
　　　ὁπότερα τὴν γνώμην ἔχοι, τὰς ἐμπίδας
　　　κατὰ τὸ στόμ' ᾄδειν ἢ κατὰ τοὐρροπύγιον.

Στ.　τί δῆτ' ἐκεῖνος εἶπε περὶ τῆς ἐμπίδος;

145　ἅλλοιτο vel sim. K^{sac} θ^{2}AVb3 al. Suda^F λ$_Σ$Np1 Σ Soph. Aj. 103,
　　　El. 1101: ἅλοιτο vel sim. RVn Suda$^{rell.}$ λ$_Σ$RE i$_Σ$RVEMNp1,
　　　Σ^{RV} 831.

148　διεμέτρησε n, Lucian, Theophylactus Bulgarus: τοῦτο διεμέτρησε
　　　R: τοῦτ' ἐμέτρησε V.

151　ψυχείσῃ Ct3: ψυγείσῃ codd. Suda.

156　Χαιρεφῶν codd.: perh. e.g. Χαιρεκράτης or Κλειτοφῶν.

it's as a student that I have come here to the Reflectory.

STUDENT: I'll tell you, but you must regard these things as holy secrets. A little while ago Socrates asked Chaerephon how 145 many of its own feet a flea could jump; because one had bitten Chaerephon's eyebrow and jumped off onto Socrates' head.

STREPSIADES: And how did he measure it out?

STUDENT: Very cleverly. He melted wax, then took the flea and dipped both its feet in the wax, and then when it cooled it had 150 Persian boots clinging to it. He had taken these off, and was measuring the distance.

STREPSIADES: Lord Zeus, what mental subtlety!

STUDENT: What would you say if you heard another idea 155 Socrates had?

STREPSIADES: What idea? Tell me, I implore you.

STUDENT: Chaerephon of Sphettus asked him whether he was of the opinion that gnats hum through their mouth or through their rump.

STREPSIADES: Well, what did he say about the gnat?

Μα. ἔφασκεν εἶναι τοὔντερον τῆς ἐμπίδος   160
     στενόν, διὰ λεπτοῦ δ' ὄντος αὐτοῦ τὴν πνοὴν
     βίᾳ βαδίζειν εὐθὺ τοὐρροπυγίου·
     ἔπειτα κοῖλον πρὸς στενῷ προσκείμενον
     τὸν πρωκτὸν ἠχεῖν ὑπὸ βίας τοῦ πνεύματος.

Στ. σάλπιγξ ὁ πρωκτός ἐστιν ἄρα τῶν ἐμπίδων.   165
     ὢ τρισμακάριος τοῦ διεντερεύματος.
     ἦ ῥᾳδίως φεύγων ἂν ἀποφύγοι δίκην,
     ὅστις δίοιδε τοὔντερον τῆς ἐμπίδος.

Μα. πρώην δέ γε γνώμην μεγάλην ἀφῃρέθη
     ὑπ' ἀσκαλαβώτου.

Στ.   τίνα τρόπον; κάτειπέ μοι.   170

Μα. ζητοῦντος αὐτοῦ τῆς σελήνης τὰς ὁδοὺς
     καὶ τὰς περιφοράς, εἶτ' ἄνω κεχηνότος
     ἀπὸ τῆς ὀροφῆς νύκτωρ γαλεώτης κατέχεσεν.

Στ. ἥσθην γαλεώτῃ καταχέσαντι Σωκράτους.

Μα. ἐχθὲς δέ γ' ἡμῖν δεῖπνον οὐκ ἦν ἑσπέρας.   175

Στ. εἶέν· τί οὖν πρὸς τἄλφιτ' ἐπαλαμήσατο;

Μα. κατὰ τῆς τραπέζης καταπάσας λεπτὴν τέφραν,
*   κάμψας ὀβελίσκον, εἶτα διαβήτην λαβὼν
     ἐκ τῆς παλαίστρας θοἰμάτιον ὑφείλετο.

Στ. τί δῆτ' ἐκεῖνον τὸν Θαλῆν θαυμάζομεν;   180
     ἄνοιγ' ἄνοιγ' ἀνύσας τὸ φροντιστήριον,
     καὶ δεῖξον ὡς τάχιστά μοι τὸν Σωκράτη·
     μαθητιῶ γάρ. ἀλλ' ἄνοιγε τὴν θύραν.

182 Σωκράτη Ald.: Σωκράτην codd.: so also 1465, 1477.

26

STUDENT: He said that the gnat's intestine is narrow, and   160
that the air is forced through this small tube right the way to
the rump; and then the arsehole, being a cavity adjacent to a narrow passage, emits sound as a result of the force of the wind.

STREPSIADES: So the arsehole of gnats is a trumpet. Happy,   165
happy man, what a feat of evisceration! He'd surely find it easy to
defend a lawsuit successfully, when he has such a deep knowledge
of the intestine of the gnat.

STUDENT: Then the other day he was robbed of a great idea
by a spotted lizard.   170

STREPSIADES: In what way? Tell me.

STUDENT: He was investigating the paths and revolutions of   *
the moon, and then when he was gazing open-mouthed at the sky a
gecko shat on him from the eaves in the dark.

STREPSIADES [*laughing*]: I like that gecko shitting on
Socrates!

STUDENT: Then last night there was no dinner for us to eat.   175

STREPSIADES: I see, so what did he contrive to get you your
groats?

STUDENT: He covered the table with a thin sprinkling of ash,
bent a spit, then picked up a faggot . . . from the wrestling-school and
stole his cloak.

STREPSIADES: After that, why do we still admire old Thales?   180
Open up, quick, open up the Reflectory, and show me Socrates as
quickly as you can — I'm bursting to learn! Open the door! [*A platform is rolled out of the door, on which are a number of thin, pale*

ὦ Ἡράκλεις, ταυτὶ ποδαπὰ τὰ θηρία;

Μα. τί ἐθαύμασας; τῷ σοι δοκοῦσιν εἰκέναι;   185

Στ. τοῖς ἐκ Πύλου ληφθεῖσι, τοῖς Λακωνικοῖς.
    ἀτὰρ τί ποτ' εἰς τὴν γῆν βλέπουσιν οὑτοιί;

Μα. ζητοῦσιν οὗτοι τὰ κατὰ γῆς.

Στ.   βολβοὺς ἄρα
    ζητοῦσι. μή νυν τοῦτό γ' ἔτι φροντίζετε·
    ἐγὼ γὰρ οἶδ' ἵν' εἰσὶ μεγάλοι καὶ καλοί.   190
    τί γὰρ οἵδε δρῶσιν οἱ σφόδρ' ἐγκεκυφότες;

Μα. οὗτοι δ' ἐρεβοδιφῶσιν ὑπὸ τὸν Τάρταρον.

Στ. τί δῆθ' ὁ πρωκτὸς εἰς τὸν οὐρανὸν βλέπει;

Μα. αὐτὸς καθ' αὑτὸν ἀστρονομεῖν διδάσκεται.
    ἀλλ' εἴσιθ', ἵνα μὴ 'κεῖνος ὑμῖν ἐπιτύχῃ.   195

Στ. μήπω γε, μήπω γ', ἀλλ' ἐπιμεινάντων, ἵνα
    αὐτοῖσι κοινώσω τι πραγμάτιον ἐμόν.

Μα. ἀλλ' οὐχ οἷόν τ' αὐτοῖσι πρὸς τὸν ἀέρα
    ἔξω διατρίβειν πολὺν ἄγαν ἐστὶν χρόνον.

Στ. πρὸς τῶν θεῶν, τί γὰρ τάδ' ἐστίν; εἰπέ μοι.   200

Μα. ἀστρονομία μὲν αὑτηί.

Στ.   τουτὶ δὲ τί;

Μα. γεωμετρία.

Στ.   τοῦτ' οὖν τί ἐστι χρήσιμον;

189 γ' ἔτι Reisig: γε RKΘ: ἔτι VE^{pc}N: [E^{ac}].
195 ὑμῖν ^{i}Σ^{R}: ἡμῖν codd. Suda ^{i}Σ^{Vb3}.

28

students in attitudes presently to be described.] Heracles! where
do these creatures come from?

STUDENT: Why are you surprised? What do you think they   185
look like?

STREPSIADES: Like the men captured at Pylos, the Lacon-
ians. But tell me [*pointing to one group of students*] why on earth
are these ones looking at the ground?

STUDENT: They are trying to discover what is under the
earth.

STREPSIADES: Oh, I see, they're looking for bulbs to eat!
Well, you don't need to give that another thought, because I know   190
where there are lovely big ones. And what are these people doing,
the ones who are bent right over?

STUDENT: They are searching into the nether darkness below
Tartarus.

STREPSIADES: Then why is their arse looking at the sky?

STUDENT: It's learning astronomy on its own account. [*To
the students forming the tableau*] Go inside, we don't want *him* to   195
find you here.

STREPSIADES: Not yet, not yet! Let them stay, so that I can
inform them about a little problem that I have.

STUDENT: No, they aren't allowed to spend too much time
outside in the air. [*The other students go inside.*]

STREPSIADES [*pointing to instruments hanging up at the
back of the vacated platform*]: Tell me, what in heaven's name are   200
these?

STUDENT: This here is astronomy.

STREPSIADES: And what's this?

STUDENT: Geometry.

STREPSIADES: So what's that useful for?

Μα. γῆν ἀναμετρεῖσθαι.

Στ.   πότερα τὴν κληρουχικήν;

Μα. οὔκ, ἀλλα τὴν σύμπασαν.

Στ.   ἀστεῖον λέγεις·
τὸ γὰρ σόφισμα δημοτικὸν καὶ χρήσιμον.   205

Μα. αὕτη δέ σοι γῆς περίοδος πάσης. ὁρᾷς;
αἵδε μὲν 'Αθῆναι.

Στ.   τί σὺ λέγεις; οὐ πείθομαι,
ἐπεὶ δικαστὰς οὐχ ὁρῶ καθημένους.

Μα. ὡς τοῦτ' ἀληθῶς 'Αττικὴ τὸ χωρίον.

Στ. καὶ ποῦ Κικυννῆς εἰσιν, οὑμοὶ δημόται;   210

Μα. ἐνταῦθ' ἔνεισιν. ἡ δέ γ' Εὔβοι', ὡς ὁρᾷς,
ἡδὶ παρατέταται μακρὰ πόρρω πάνυ.

Στ. οἶδ'· ὑπὸ γὰρ ἡμῶν παρετάθη καὶ Περικλέους.
ἀλλ' ἡ Λακεδαίμων ποῦ 'σθ';

Μα.   ὅπου 'στίν; αὑτηί.

Στ. ὡς ἐγγὺς ἡμῶν. τοῦτο μεταφροντίζετε,   215
ταύτην ἀφ' ἡμῶν ἀπαγαγεῖν πόρρω πάνυ.

Μα. ἀλλ' οὐχ οἷόν τε.

Στ.   νὴ Δί' οἰμώξεσθ' ἄρα.
φέρε, τίς γὰρ οὗτος οὑπὶ τῆς κρεμάθρας ἀνήρ;

209   'Αττικὴ Dobree: 'Αττικὸν codd., Et. Mag.:]ν Π6.
215   μεταφροντίζετε Bentley, cf. Σ^R: μέγα φροντίζετε Suda ^iΣ^M:
        πάνυ φροντίζετε codd.

30

STUDENT: For measuring land.

STREPSIADES: You mean land for cleruchs?

STUDENT: No, land generally.

STREPSIADES: A charming notion! It's a useful and demo-   205
cratic device.

STUDENT: And this is a map of the whole world. Do you
see? here's Athens.

STREPSIADES: What do you mean? I don't believe you; I
don't see any jurors on their benches.

STUDENT: I assure you this area is Attica.

STREPSIADES: Then where are the men of Cicynna, my   210
fellow-demesmen?

STUDENT [*indicating the area south-east of Athens*]: They're
in this part. And here, as you see, is Euboea, lying stretched out
beside the mainland for a very long distance.

STREPSIADES: I know; we laid it out, we and Pericles. But
where's Sparta?

STUDENT: Where is it? Here.

STREPSIADES: How close to us! Rethink that one, please,   215
so as to take it a good long way away from us.

STUDENT: It can't be done.

STREPSIADES [*raising his stick*]: In that case, by Zeus,
you're going to howl! [*Looking up, where the crane has swung
Socrates into view*] Here. tell me, who's that man dangling from the
hook?

Μα.   αὐτός.

Στ.   τίς αὐτός;

Μα.   Σωκράτης.

Στ.   ὦ Σώκρατες.
ἴθ' οὗτος, ἀναβόησον αὐτόν μοι μέγα.   220

Μα. αὐτὸς μὲν οὖν σὺ κάλεσον· οὐ γάρ μοι σχολή.

Στ. ὦ Σώκρατες,
ὦ Σωκρατίδιον.

ΣΩΚΡΑΤΗΣ
             τί με καλεῖς, ὦφήμερε;

Στ. πρῶτον μὲν ὅ τι δρᾷς, ἀντιβολῶ, κάτειπέ μοι.

Σω. ἀεροβατῶ καὶ περιφρονῶ τὸν ἥλιον.   225

Στ. ἔπειτ' ἀπὸ ταρροῦ τοὺς θεοὺς ὑπερφρονεῖς,
ἀλλ' οὐκ ἀπὸ τῆς γῆς, εἴπερ;

Σω.   οὐ γὰρ ἄν ποτε
ἐξηῦρον ὀρθῶς τὰ μετέωρα πράγματα,
εἰ μὴ κρεμάσας τὸ νόημα καὶ τὴν φροντίδα
λεπτὴν καταμείξας εἰς τὸν ὅμοιον ἀέρα.   230
εἰ δ' ὢν χαμαὶ τἄνω κάτωθεν ἐσκόπουν,
οὐκ ἄν ποθ' ηὗρον· οὐ γὰρ ἀλλ' ἡ γῆ βίᾳ
ἕλκει πρὸς αὑτὴν τὴν ἰκμάδα τῆς φροντίδος.
πάσχει δὲ ταὐτὸ τοῦτο καὶ τὰ κάρδαμα.

Στ. πῶς φής;   235
ἡ φροντὶς ἕλκει τὴν ἰκμάδ' εἰς τὰ κάρδαμα;
ἴθι νυν κατάβηθ', ὦ Σωκρατίδιον, ὡς ἐμέ,

235 πῶς Π6: τί codd.

32

STUDENT: It's the master.

STREPSIADES: Who's the master?

STUDENT: Socrates.

STREPSIADES: Socrates! — Here, you, call out to him for   220
me, good and loud.

STUDENT: No, you call him yourself; I'm busy. [*He goes
inside.*]

STREPSIADES: Socrates! my sweet little Socrates!

SOCRATES [*aloft*]: Why dost thou call me, thou creature
of a day?

STREPSIADES: First of all, I beg you, tell me what you're
doing.

SOCRATES: I walk the air and descry the sun.   225

STREPSIADES: You mean you decry the gods from a wicker   *
cage? Why not do it on the ground, if at all?

SOCRATES: I could never have made correct discoveries
about celestial phenomena, except by hanging up my mind and mix-   229-
ing the minute particles of my thought into the air which it resembles.   230
If I had been on the ground and investigated the upper regions from
below, I would never have made my discoveries; for it is certain that
the earth forcibly draws the moisture of thought to itself. Just the
same thing happens to cress.

STREPSIADES [*baffled*]: How do you mean? Thought draws   235
moisture to cress? — Here, my sweet Socrates, come down now to
me, so that you can teach me the things I've come to be taught.

ἵνα μ' ἐκδιδάξῃς ὧνπερ ἕνεκ' ἐλήλυθα.

Σω. ἦλθες δὲ κατὰ τί;

Στ.   βουλόμενος μαθεῖν λέγειν·
ὑπὸ γὰρ τόκων χρήστων τε δυσκολωτάτων   240
ἄγομαι, φέρομαι, τὰ χρήματ' ἐνεχυράζομαι.

Σω. πόθεν δ' ὑπόχρεως σαυτὸν ἔλαθες γενόμενος;

Στ. νόσος μ' ἐπέτριψεν ἱππική, δεινὴ φαγεῖν.
ἀλλά με δίδαξον τὸν ἕτερον τοῖν σοῖν λόγοιν,
τὸν μηδὲν ἀποδιδόντα. μισθὸν δ' ὅντιν' ἂν   245
πράττῃ μ', ὀμοῦμαί σοι καταθήσειν τοὺς θεούς.

Σω. ποίους θεοὺς ὀμεῖ σύ; πρῶτον γὰρ θεοὶ
ἡμῖν νόμισμ' οὐκ ἔστι.

Στ.   τῷ γὰρ ὄμνυτ'; ἢ
σιδαρέοισιν, ὥσπερ ἐν Βυζαντίῳ;

Σω. βούλει τὰ θεῖα πράγματ' εἰδέναι σαφῶς   250
ἅττ' ἐστὶν ὀρθῶς;

Στ.   νὴ Δί', εἴπερ ἐστί γε.

Σω. καὶ συγγενέσθαι ταῖς Νεφέλαισιν εἰς λόγους,
ταῖς ἡμετέραισι δαίμοσιν;

Στ.   μάλιστά γε.

Σω. κάθιζε τοίνυν ἐπὶ τὸν ἱερὸν σκίμποδα.

Στ. ἰδού, κάθημαι.

Σω.   τουτονὶ τοίνυν λαβὲ   255

---

238 ἕνεκ' Vv4: οὕνεκ' codd.

SOCRATES [*descending to the ground*]: And why have you come?

STREPSIADES: Because I want to learn oratory. I'm being 240-1
ravaged and plundered, and having my goods distrained on, at the
hands of usury and of creditors whom nothing can satisfy.

SOCRATES: And how did you come to get into debt without
realizing it?

STREPSIADES: I've been ruined by an equine affliction,
which has been eating me up fearfully. Anyway, please teach me
one of your two Arguments, the one that never pays its debts. What- 245
ever fee you require from me, I'll swear to you by the gods to pay
cash down.

SOCRATES: What do you mean, swear by the gods? Apart
from anything else, we don't credit gods here.

STREPSIADES: Then what currency *do* you use for oaths? Is
it iron coins, like at Byzantium?

SOCRATES: Do you desire certain knowledge of the true 250
nature of things divine?

STREPSIADES: I do indeed, if it's really possible.

SOCRATES: And to commune and converse with the Clouds,
who are our deities?

STREPSIADES: Very much so.

SOCRATES: Then please sit on the sacred bed.

STREPSIADES: There, I'm sitting. 255

SOCRATES: Now take this wreath.

τὸν στέφανον.

Στ.　　　　　ἐπὶ τί στέφανον; οἴμοι, Σώκρατες,
ὥσπερ με τὸν 'Αθάμανθ' ὅπως μὴ θύσετε.

Σω.　οὔκ, ἀλλὰ πάντας ταῦτα τοὺς τελουμένους
ἡμεῖς ποιοῦμεν.

Στ.　　　　　εἶτα δὴ τί κερδανῶ;

Σω.　λέγειν γενήσει τρῖμμα, κρόταλον, παιπάλη.　　　　　260
ἀλλ' ἔχ' ἀτρεμεί.

Στ.　　　　　μὰ τὸν Δί' οὐ ψεύσει γέ με·
καταπαττόμενος γὰρ παιπάλη γενήσομαι.

Σω.　εὐφημεῖν χρὴ τὸν πρεσβύτην καὶ τῆς εὐχῆς ἐπακούειν.
ὦ δέσποτ' ἄναξ ἀμέτρητ' 'Αήρ, ὃς ἔχεις τὴν γῆν μετέωρον,
λαμπρός τ' Αἰθήρ, σεμναί τε θεαὶ Νεφέλαι βροντησικέραυνοι,　265
ἄρθητε, φάνητ', ὦ δέσποιναι, τῷ φροντιστῇ μετέωροι.

Στ.　μήπω, μήπω γε, πρὶν ἂν τουτὶ πτύξωμαι, μὴ καταβρεχθῶ.
τὸ δὲ μηδὲ κυνῆν οἴκοθεν ἐλθεῖν ἐμὲ τὸν κακοδαίμον' ἔχοντα.

Σω.　ἔλθετε δῆτ', ὦ πολυτίμητοι Νεφέλαι, τῷδ' εἰς ἐπίδειξιν·
εἴτ' ἐπ' 'Ολύμπου κορυφαῖς ἱεραῖς χιονοβλήτοισι κάθησθε,　　270
εἴτ' 'Ωκεανοῦ πατρὸς ἐν κήποις ἱερὸν χορὸν ἵστατε Νύμφαις,
εἴτ' ἄρα Νείλου προχοαῖς ὑδάτων χρυσέαις ἀρύτεσθε πρόχοισιν,
ἢ Μαιῶτιν λίμνην ἔχετ', ἢ σκόπελον νιφέντα Μίμαντος·
ὑπακούσατε δεξάμεναι θυσίαν καὶ τοῖς ἱεροῖσι χαρεῖσαι.　　274

ΧΟΡΟΣ
　ἀέναοι Νεφέλαι,　　　　　　　　　　　　　　　　　　(στρ.

258　πάντας ταῦτα Reiske: πάντα ταῦτα ΕΚ: ταῦτα πάντα RVNθ.
268　μηδὲ E: μὴ RVn', Eustathius, Σ^{RVΓ} Wasps 445.
272　ἀρῦτ- Suda: ἀρύ- codd.

36

STREPSIADES: Why a wreath? Heavens, Socrates, don't on any account make a sacrifice of me, like Athamas.

SOCRATES: No, no; we do this to everyone when they're being initiated.

STREPSIADES: And so what shall I gain by it?

SOCRATES: You'll become a smooth talker, a tinkling cym- 260
bal, the sieved meal of subtlety. Now keep still. [*He sprinkles fine meal over Strepsiades.*]

STREPSIADES: By Zeus, you can't fool me. I *shall* become sieved meal — by being sprinkled with it!

SOCRATES: Let the old man speak fair and listen to the prayer. O Sovereign Lord, immeasurable Air, who upholdest the floating earth, and thou, bright Sky, and ye august thunder-fulmi- 265
nating Cloud-goddesses, arise, appear, blessed Ladies, appear on high to him who thinks on you.

STREPSIADES [*trying to cover himself with his cloak*]: Not yet, not yet, not till I've wrapped myself in this so as not to get drenched. What can have possessed me to leave home without even a cap?

SOCRATES: Yea, most glorious Clouds, come to display your-
selves to this man: whether ye now sit on the holy snow-clad peaks 270
of Olympus, or call the Nymphs to a holy dance in the gardens of
father Ocean; or whether again at the mouths of the Nile ye draw of
its waters with golden ewers, or haunt Lake Maeotis or the snowy
crag of Mimas: hearken to me, accepting my sacrifice and rejoicing
in these holy rites.

CHORUS [*in the distance*]:
Everlasting Clouds, 275 *

37

ἀρθῶμεν φανεραὶ δροσερὰν φύσιν εὐάγητον
πατρὸς ἀπ' Ὠκεανοῦ βαρυαχέος
   ὑψηλῶν ὀρέων κορυφὰς ἔπι
   δενδροκόμους, ἵνα   28
   τηλεφανεῖς σκοπιὰς ἀφορώμεθα
   καρπούς τ' ἀρδομέναν ἱερὰν χθόνα
   καὶ ποταμῶν ζαθέων κελαδήματα
   καὶ πόντον κελάδοντα βαρύβρομον·
   ὄμμα γὰρ αἰθέρος ἀκάματον σελαγεῖται   28
μαρμαρέαισιν αὐγαῖς.
ἀλλ' ἀποσεισάμεναι νέφος ὄμβριον
   ἀθανάτας ἰδέας ἐπιδώμεθα
   τηλεσκόπῳ ὄμματι γαῖαν.   29

Σω. ὦ μέγα σεμναὶ Νεφέλαι, φανερῶς ἠκούσατέ μου καλέσαντος.
     ᾔσθου φωνῆς ἅμα καὶ βροντῆς μυκησαμένης θεοσέπτου;

Στ. καὶ σέβομαί γ', ὦ πολυτίμητοι, καὶ βούλομαι ἀνταποπαρδεῖν
     πρὸς τὰς βροντάς· οὕτως αὐτὰς τετραμαίνω καὶ πεφόβημαι·
     κεἴ θέμις ἐστίν, νυνί γ' ἤδη—κεἴ μὴ θέμις ἐστί—χεσείω.   29

Σω. οὐ μὴ σκώψει, μηδὲ ποιήσεις ἅπερ οἱ τρυγοδαίμονες οὗτοι;
     ἀλλ' εὐφήμει· μέγα γάρ τι θεῶν κινεῖται σμῆνος ἀοιδαῖς.

Χο. παρθένοι ὀμβροφόροι,   (ἀντ
     ἔλθωμεν λιπαρὰν χθόνα Παλλάδος, εὔανδρον γᾶν   30
     Κέκροπος ὀψόμεναι πολυήρατον·
        οὗ σέβας ἀρρήτων ἱερῶν, ἵνα
        μυστοδόκος δόμος

282 ἱερὰν VK^{pc}: θ' ἱερὰν R̲n̲'.
296 σκώψει Elmsley: σκώψῃς codd.
299 χθόνα K: ἐς χθόνα RV̲n̲'.

38

let us rise and make visible our radiant dewy form,
leaving deep-roaring father Ocean
for the peaks of lofty mountains
crowned with trees, that we   280
may gaze on the hill-tops conspicuous from afar
and the holy earth whose crops we water
and sacred rivers' rushing flow
and the deep thunder of the sounding sea;
for the unwearying eye of heaven is blazing   285
with sparkling rays.
Then let us shake off the rainy mist
from our immortal form, and look
upon the earth with far-seeing eye.   290

SOCRATES: O most revered Clouds, manifest it is that you heard my call. [*To Strepsiades*] Did you hear their voice, and together with it the bellow of awe-inspiring divine thunder?

STREPSIADES: Yes, and I revere you, most glorious ones, and in response to that thunder I want to fart back, so much do they put me in fear and trembling; and right now, if it is lawful —   295
and even if it isn't — I need to crap.

SOCRATES: Will you stop playing the fool and acting like those goddamned comedians? Now speak fair; for a great swarm of deities is on the move, singing.

CHORUS [*nearer*]:
Rain-bearing maidens,
let us go to the gleaming land of Pallas, to see   300
the lovely land of Cecrops, home of fine men;
where are the august rites none may speak of, where
to receive the initiates the temple

ἐν τελεταῖς ἁγίαις ἀναδείκνυται·
οὐρανίοις τε θεοῖς δωρήματα,   305
ναού θ' ὑψερεφεῖς καὶ ἀγάλματα,
καὶ πρόσοδοι μακάρων ἱερώταται
εὐστέφανοί τε θεῶν θυσίαι θαλίαι τε
παντοδαπαῖσιν ὥραις,   310
ᾗρί τ' ἐπερχομένῳ Βρομία χάρις
εὐκελάδων τε χορῶν ἐρεθίσματα
καὶ μοῦσα βαρύβρομος αὐλῶν.

Στ. πρὸς τοῦ Διός, ἀντιβολῶ σε, φράσον, τίνες εἶσ', ὦ Σώκρατες,
                                                               αὗται
    αἱ φθεγξάμεναι τοῦτο τὸ σεμνόν; μῶν ἡρῷναί τινές εἰσιν;   315

Σω. ἥκιστ', ἀλλ' οὐράνιαι Νεφέλαι, μεγάλαι θεαὶ ἀνδράσιν ἀργοῖς,
    αἵπερ γνώμην καὶ διάλεξιν καὶ νοῦν ἡμῖν παρέχουσιν
    καὶ τερατείαν καὶ περίλεξιν καὶ κροῦσιν καὶ κατάληψιν.

Στ. ταῦτ' ἄρ' ἀκούσασ' αὐτῶν τὸ φθέγμ' ἡ ψυχή μου πεπότηται,
    καὶ λεπτολογεῖν ἤδη ζητεῖ καὶ περὶ καπνοῦ στενολεσχεῖν   320
    καὶ γνωμιδίῳ γνώμην νύξασ' ἑτέρῳ λόγῳ ἀντιλογῆσαι·
    ὥστ', εἴ πώς ἐστιν, ἰδεῖν αὐτὰς ἤδη φανερῶς ἐπιθυμῶ.

Σω. βλέπε νυν δευρὶ πρὸς τὴν Πάρνηθ'· ἤδη γὰρ ὁρῶ κατιούσας
    ἡσυχῇ αὐτάς.

Στ.   φέρε, ποῦ; δεῖξον.

Σω.   χωροῦσ' αὗται πάνυ πολλαὶ
    διὰ τῶν κοίλων καὶ τῶν δασέων, αὗται πλάγιαι.

Στ.   τί τὸ χρῆμα;   325

310 παντοδαπαῖσιν Blaydes: παντοδαπαῖσιν ἐν E^{pc}: παντοδαπαῖς ἐν
    RVn'.
324 ἡσυχῇ (-ῆ) Elmsley: ἡσύχως codd.

is opened at the holy Mystic festival;
giving of gifts to the gods of heaven, 305
high-roofed temples, sacred statues,
holy processions in honour of the Blest Ones,
garlanded sacrifices to the gods and festivities
at each and every season, 310
and at the onset of spring Dionysian delight,
the excitement of melodious choruses
and the deep-sounding music of the pipes.

STREPSIADES: In the name of Zeus, Socrates, tell me, I beg
you, who are these ladies who voiced that majestic song? They're 315
not some kind of female heroes, are they?

SOCRATES: Not at all; they are the heavenly Clouds, great
goddesses for men of idleness, who bestow on us intelligence and
discourse and understanding, fantasy and circumlocution and incisive and repressive power.

STREPSIADES: So that is why my soul, on hearing their
voice, has taken wing, and now longs to chop logic and to chatter 320
minutely about smoke, to puncture a maxim with a little maxim of
my own and meet argument with counter-argument; and therefore,
if it's at all possible, I'm eager now to see them face to face.

SOCRATES: Then look this way, towards Mount Parnes; for
now I see them coming gently down.

STREPSIADES: Let's see — where? Show me.

SOCRATES: [*pointing off to the side*]: There they come, a
great many of them, through the woods and the hollows — there, 325
to your side.

STREPSIADES [*peering at the sky in that direction*]: What's
all this about? I can't see them.

41

ὡς οὐ καθορῶ.

Σω.   παρὰ τὴν εἴσοδον.

Στ.   ἤδη νυνὶ μόλις οὕτως.

Σω. νῦν γέ τοι ἤδη καθορᾷς αὐτάς, εἰ μὴ λημᾷς κολοκύνταις.

Στ. νὴ Δί' ἔγωγ'. ὦ πολυτίμητοι· πάντα γὰρ ἤδη κατέχουσιν.

Σω. ταύτας μέντοι σὺ θεὰς οὔσας οὐκ ᾔδησθ' οὐδ' ἐνόμιζες;

Στ. μὰ Δί', ἀλλ' ὁμίχλην καὶ δρόσον αὐτὰς ἡγούμην καὶ καπνὸν εἴ·

Σω. οὐ γὰρ μὰ Δί' οἶσθ' ὅτι ἢ πλείστους αὗται βόσκουσι σοφιστάς,
θουριομάντεις, ἰατροτέχνας, σφραγιδονυχαργοκομήτας·
κυκλίων τε χορῶν ᾀσματοκάμπτας, ἄνδρας μετεωροφένακας,
οὐδὲν δρῶντας βόσκουσ' ἀργούς, ὅτι ταύτας μουσοποιοῦσιν.

Στ. ταῦτ' ἄρ' ἐποίουν "ὑγρᾶν νεφελᾶν στρεπταιγλᾶν δάϊον ὁρμάν",
"πλοκάμους θ' ἑκατογκεφάλα Τυφῶ", "πρημαινούσας τε θυέλλας"
*   εἶτ' "ἀερίας διεράς, γαμψοὺς οἰωνοὺς ἀερονηχεῖς"
"ὄμβρους θ' ὑδάτων δροσερᾶν νεφελᾶν"· εἶτ' ἀντ' αὐτῶν κατέπι
κεστρᾶν τεμάχη μεγαλᾶν ἀγαθᾶν κρέα τ' ὀρνίθεια κιχηλᾶν.

Σω. διὰ μέντοι τάσδ'. οὐχὶ δικαίως;

* Στ.   λέξον δή μοι, τί παθοῦσαι,
εὔπερ νεφέλαι γ' εἰσὶν ἀληθῶς, θνηταῖς εἴξασι γυναιξίν;
οὐ γὰρ ἐκεῖναί γ' εἰσὶ τοιαῦται.

Σω.   φέρε, ποῖαι γάρ τινές εἰσιν

326 παρὰ PE^{ac}KΘ: πρὸς VE^{pc}N.
329 ᾔδησθ' Hirschig: ᾔδεις codd.
340 δή K (K^s adds νύν): δὴ νῦν RVEΘ: δὲ νῦν N.

SOCRATES: Just at the wing-entrance!

STREPSIADES: Ah, *now*, looking this way, I just about can.

[*The Clouds, in the guise of women, enter the orchestra.*]

SOCRATES: Now surely you see them, unless you've got styes the size of pumpkins.

STREPSIADES: Yes, I do. Glory be! they're filling the whole place.

SOCRATES: And you didn't know they were goddesses, and didn't believe in them?

STREPSIADES: No, indeed; I thought they were mist and dew and vapour.   330

SOCRATES: Because you aren't aware that these goddesses sustain and nourish a whole host of "experts", diviners from Thurii, professors of the medical art, long-haired do-nothings with onyx signet-rings; and composers of convoluted songs for dithyrambic choruses, men of airy quackery, they maintain in idleness doing nothing, because they poeticize about the Clouds.

STREPSIADES: Ah, that's why they write about the "fear-   335 ful onset of rain-filled clouds edged with twists of radiance" and the "locks of hundred-headed Typhos" and "flatulent squalls", and then "aerial aquifers, crook-taloned birds floating in air" and "waters raining from the dewy clouds", and as a reward for that, guzzle slices of lovely big barracuda fish and the avian flesh of thrushes!

SOCRATES: All thanks to these Clouds; and rightly too, don't   340 you think?

STREPSIADES: Well, tell me, if they really are clouds, what's happened to them, that they look like mortal women? I mean, the clouds up there aren't like that.

SOCRATES: Well, what are they like?

Στ. οὐκ οἶδα σαφῶς· εἴξασιν δ' οὖν ἐρίοισιν πεπταμένοισιν,
     κοὐχὶ γυναιξίν, μὰ Δί', οὐδ' ὁτιοῦν· αὗται δὲ ῥῖνας ἔχουσιν.

Σω. ἀπόκριναί νυν ἅττ' ἂν ἔρωμαι.

Στ.   λέγε νυν ταχέως ὅ τι βούλει.   345

Σω. ἤδη ποτ' ἀναβλέψας εἶδες νεφέλην κενταύρῳ ὁμοίαν
     ἢ παρδάλει ἢ λύκῳ ἢ ταύρῳ;

Στ.   νὴ Δί' ἔγωγ'. εἶτα τί τοῦτο;

Σω. γίγνονται πάνθ' ὅ τι βούλονται· κᾆτ' ἢν μὲν ἴδωσι κομήτην
     ἄγριόν τινα τῶν λασίων τούτων, οἷόνπερ τὸν Ξενοφάντου,
     σκώπτουσαι τὴν μανίαν αὐτοῦ κενταύροις ἤκασαν αὐτάς.   350

Στ. τί γὰρ ἢν ἅρπαγα τῶν δημοσίων κατίδωσι Σίμωνα, τί δρῶσιν;

Σω. ἀποφαίνουσαι τὴν φύσιν αὐτοῦ λύκοι ἐξαίφνης ἐγένοντο.

Στ. ταῦτ' ἄρα, ταῦτα Κλεώνυμον αὗται τὸν ῥίψασπιν χθὲς ἰδοῦσαι,
     ὅτι δειλότατον τοῦτον ἑώρων, ἔλαφοι διὰ τοῦτ' ἐγένοντο.

Σω. καὶ νῦν γ', ὅτι Κλεισθένη εἶδον, ὁρᾷς; διὰ τοῦτ' ἐγένοντο
                                                    γυναῖκες.

Στ. χαίρετε τοίνυν, ὦ δέσποιναι· καὶ νῦν, εἴπερ τινὶ κἄλλῳ,   356
     οὐρανομήκη ῥήξατε κἀμοὶ φωνήν, ὦ παμβασίλειαι.

Χο. χαῖρ', ὦ πρεσβῦτα παλαιογενές, θηρατὰ λόγων φιλομούσων·
     σύ τε, λεπτοτάτων λήρων ἱερεῦ, φράζε πρὸς ἡμᾶς ὅ τι χρῄζεις·
     οὐ γὰρ ἂν ἄλλῳ γ' ὑπακούσαιμεν τῶν νῦν μετεωροσοφιστῶν   360
     πλὴν ἢ Προδίκῳ, τῷ μὲν σοφίας καὶ γνώμης οὕνεκα, σοὶ δὲ

343 δ' οὖν Rn Suda, Lex. Vind.: γοῦν V Choeroboscus, Et. Mag.:
     οὖν Zonaras.
344 δὲ E $^{\lambda}\Sigma^{M}$: δέ γε RVE^{s}n': $^{\lambda}\Sigma^{E}$.
345 ἂν E^{pc}: ἂν σ' RVE^{ac}n'.
355 Κλεισθένη Σ^{E}: Κλεισθένην codd. Σ^{RVM} $^{\lambda}\Sigma^{M}$.

44

STREPSIADES: I don't know exactly; but what they *look* like is flocks of wool spread out, not like women in the least, for certain; while these ones have noses.

SOCRATES: Now answer the questions I ask you. 345

STREPSIADES: Ask whatever you like, straight away.

SOCRATES: Have you ever looked up and seen a cloud resembling a centaur, or a leopard, or a wolf, or a bull?

STREPSIADES: I have indeed; so what of that?

SOCRATES: They take any form they like; so if they see a long-haired savage, one of those shaggy characters, like the son of Xenophantus, they make fun of his passions by making themselves 350 look like centaurs.

STREPSIADES: And what if they see a plunderer of the public purse like Simon, what do they do?

SOCRATES: They expose him for what he is by at once turning into wolves.

STREPSIADES: So that's why they turned into deer yesterday — that's why, because they saw Cleonymus the shield-dropper and recognized him for a great coward.

SOCRATES: And this time, because they've seen Cleisthenes, 355 do you see, that's made them turn into women.

STREPSIADES [*to the chorus*]: Then hail, sovereign Ladies: and now, if you have ever done so for another, then for me too, almighty Queens, utter forth a sound to scale the heavens.

CHORUS: All hail, old man of ripe years, hunter after artistic arguments; [*to Socrates*] and you, priest of the subtlest balderdash, tell us what you desire; for we would not give ear to any other 360 present-day celestial expert except for Prodicus, in his case because of his skill and intelligence, in yours because you swagger in the

45

ὅτι βρενθύει τ' ἐν ταῖσιν ὁδοῖς καὶ τὠφθαλμὼ παραβάλλεις
κἀνυπόδητος κακὰ πόλλ' ἀνέχει κἀφ' ἡμῖν σεμνοπροσωπεῖς.

Στ. ὦ Γῆ, τοῦ φθέγματος· ὡς ἱερὸν καὶ σεμνὸν καὶ τερατῶδες.   3

Σω. αὗται γάρ τοι μόναι εἰσὶ θεαί· τἄλλα δὲ πάντ' ἐστὶ φλύαρος.

Στ. ὁ Ζεὺς δ' ὑμῖν, φέρε, πρὸς τῆς Γῆς, οὑλύμπιος οὐ θεός ἐστιν;

Σω. ποῖος Ζεύς; οὐ μὴ ληρήσεις; οὐδ' ἐστὶ Ζεύς.

Στ.   τί λέγεις σύ;
ἀλλὰ τίς ὕει; τουτὶ γὰρ ἔμοιγ' ἀπόφηναι πρῶτον ἁπάντων.

Σω. αὗται δήπου· μεγάλοις δέ σ' ἐγὼ σημείοις αὐτὸ διδάξω.
φέρε, ποῦ γὰρ πώποτ' ἄνευ νεφελῶν ὕοντ' ἤδη τεθέασαι;   3
καίτοι χρῆν αἰθρίας ὕειν αὐτόν, ταύτας δ' ἀποδημεῖν.

Στ. νὴ τὸν Ἀπόλλω, τοῦτό γέ τοι τῷ νυνὶ λόγῳ εὖ προσέφυσας.
καίτοι πρότερον τὸν Δί' ἀληθῶς ᾤμην διὰ κοσκίνου οὐρεῖν.
ἀλλ' ὅστις ὁ βροντῶν ἐστι φράσον, τοῦθ' ὅ με ποιεῖ τετραμαί|

Σω. αὗται βροντῶσι κυλινδόμεναι.

Στ.   τῷ τρόπῳ, ὦ πάντα σὺ τολμῶν;   3

Σω. ὅταν ἐμπλησθῶσ' ὕδατος πολλοῦ κἀναγκασθῶσι φέρεσθαι
κατακριμνάμεναι πλήρεις ὄμβρου δι' ἀνάγκην, εἶτα βαρεῖαι
εἰς ἀλλήλας ἐμπίπτουσαι ῥήγνυνται καὶ παταγοῦσιν.

Στ. ὁ δ' ἀναγκάζων ἐστὶ τίς αὐτάς—οὐχ ὁ Ζεύς;—ὥστε φέρεσθαι;

Σω. ἥκιστ', ἀλλ' αἰθέριος δῖνος.

Στ.   Δῖνος; τουτί μ' ἐλελήθει,   3
ὁ Ζεὺς οὐκ ὤν, ἀλλ' ἀντ' αὐτοῦ Δῖνος νυνὶ βασιλεύων.

366 ὑμῖν E^{ac}: ἡμῖν RVE^{pc} n'.
374 τοῦθ' ὅ VKθ: τοῦτο vel sim. REN.

46

streets and cast your eyes sideways, go barefoot and endure much suffering, and give yourself airs on our account.

STREPSIADES: Holy Earth, what a sound they make! how divine and majestic and wondrous!

SOCRATES: Yes, you know, these are the only gods; all the rest is codswallop.

STREPSIADES: But look, in the name of Earth, don't you consider Olympian Zeus a god?

SOCRATES: What do you mean, Zeus? Will you stop talking nonsense? Zeus doesn't even exist.

STREPSIADES: What's that you say? Then who makes the rain? Give me your answer to that, to begin with.

SOCRATES: These Clouds do, of course; and I'll prove it to you by strong evidence. Tell me, where have you ever yet seen it raining without clouds? And yet one might have expected Zeus to make rain by himself from a clear sky while the Clouds were away from home.

STREPSIADES: By Apollo, you've made that point marry well with what you were just saying. And I really used to think that it was Zeus pissing through a sieve! But tell me who causes the thunder that makes me tremble.

SOCRATES: These Clouds thunder when they roll about.

STREPSIADES: You'll stop at nothing. How?

SOCRATES: When they are filled with a great deal of water and are compelled by necessity to move, hanging full of rain, then when they collide with each other, being heavy they burst with a crash.

STREPSIADES: But who is it that compels them to move? Isn't that Zeus?

SOCRATES: Not in the least; it's a celestial vortex.

STREPSIADES: Vortex? That I hadn't realised, that Zeus is no more, and Vortex is now king in his place. But you haven't yet

365

370

375

380

47

ἀτὰρ οὐδέν πω περὶ τοῦ πατάγου καὶ τῆς βροντῆς μ' ἐδίδαξας.

Σω.   οὐκ ἤκουσάς μου, τὰς νεφέλας ὕδατος μεστὰς ὅτι φημὶ
ἐμπιπτούσας εἰς ἀλλήλας παταγεῖν διὰ τὴν πυκνότητα;

Στ.   φέρε, τουτὶ τῷ χρὴ πιστεύειν;

Σω.   ἀπὸ σαυτοῦ 'γώ σε διδάξω.   385
ἤδη ζωμοῦ Παναθηναίοις ἐμπλησθεὶς εἶτ' ἐταράχθης
τὴν γαστέρα, καὶ κλόνος ἐξαίφνης αὐτὴν διεκορκορύγησεν;

Στ.   νὴ τὸν Ἀπόλλω, καὶ δεινὰ ποιεῖ γ' εὐθύς μοι καὶ τετάρακται,
χὥσπερ βροντὴ τὸ ζωμίδιον παταγεῖ καὶ δεινὰ κέκραγεν,
ἀτρέμας πρῶτον "παππὰξ παππάξ", κἄπειτ' ἐπάγει, "παπαπαππάξ",
χὥταν χέζω, κομιδῇ βροντᾷ "παπαπαππάξ", ὥσπερ ἐκεῖναι.   391

Σω.   σκέψαι τοίνυν ἀπὸ γαστριδίου τυννουτουὶ οἷα πέπορδας·
τὸν δ' ἀέρα τόνδ' ὄντ' ἀπέραντον πῶς οὐκ εἰκὸς μέγα βροντᾶν;

Στ.   ταῦτ' ἄρα καὶ τὠνόματ' ἀλλήλοιν, "βροντὴ" καὶ "πορδή", ὁμοίω.
ἀλλ' ὁ κεραυνὸς πόθεν αὖ φέρεται λάμπων πυρί, τοῦτο δίδαξον,
καὶ καταφρύγει βάλλων ἡμᾶς, τοὺς δὲ ζῶντας περιφλεύει;   396
τοῦτον γὰρ δὴ φανερῶς ὁ Ζεὺς ἵησ' ἐπὶ τοὺς ἐπιόρκους.

Σω.   καὶ πῶς, ὦ μῶρε σὺ καὶ Κρονίων ὄζων καὶ βεκκεσέληνε,
εἴπερ βάλλει τοὺς ἐπιόρκους, δῆτ' οὐχὶ Σίμων' ἐνέπρησεν   399
οὐδὲ Κλεώνυμον οὐδὲ Θέωρον; καίτοι σφόδρα γ' εἶσ' ἐπίορκοι.
ἀλλὰ τὸν αὑτοῦ γε νεὼν βάλλει καὶ Σούνιον, ἄκρον Ἀθηνέων,
καὶ τὰς δρῦς τὰς μεγάλας· τί μαθών; οὐ γὰρ δὴ δρῦς γ' ἐπιορκεῖ

396   -φλεύει Blaydes: -φλύει REKNθ^s: -φλέγει VE^sθ Σ^{RE}.
399   δῆτ' VE^{pc}: πῶς δῆτ' RE^{ac}Kθ² Suda σ477, Σ^{ΕΓ2} Ach. 134: πῶς
      Nθ¹ Suda κ1379.
401   Ἀθηνέων Porson: Ἀθηναίων RVEθ^s, Σ Dionysius Periegeta 506:
      Ἀθηνῶν ΚΝθ Demetr. Eloc. 150.

48

given me any explanation about the crash of the thunder.

SOCRATES: Didn't you hear me? I say that the clouds, when they are full of water and collide with one another, make a noise owing to their density.

STREPSIADES: Come on, who do you expect to believe that?   385 *

SOCRATES: I'll demonstrate it to you from your own body. Have you ever filled yourself full of soup at the Panathenaea and then had an upset stomach, which a sudden agitation has set all rumbling?

STREPSIADES: By Apollo, yes; and I find it makes a great fuss and turmoil right away, and that little bit of soup crashes about and makes a fearful noise just like thunder: gently first of all, "pap-   390 pax pappax", then it steps things up, "*papapappax*", and when I crap, it absolutely does thunder, "***papapappax***", just as those clouds do.

SOCRATES: Well now, consider what a fart you can produce from a little stomach like that; is it not to be expected that the air around us, which is boundless, should produce mighty thunder?

STREPSIADES: Ah, that's why the two words sound alike, *brontē* "thunder" and *pordē* "fart"! But tell me this: where does   395 the lightning-bolt come from, blazing with fire as it flies, to strike us and burn us to a cinder, or sometimes singe us and spare our lives? Plainly that is the weapon of Zeus let loose against perjurers.

SOCRATES: You babbling prelunar idiot, smelling of the age   * of Cronus! If he really strikes perjurers, how come, pray, that he hasn't set fire to Simon or Cleonymus or Theorus? After all, they're   400 as perjured as can be! On the contrary, he strikes his own temple and Sunium, "headland of Athens", and the mighty oak trees. What's his idea? An oak tree certainly doesn't commit perjury!

Στ. οὐκ οἶδ'· ἀτὰρ εὖ σὺ λέγειν φαίνει. τί γάρ ἐστιν δῆθ' ὁ
                                                                κεραυνός;

Σω. ὅταν εἰς ταύτας ἄνεμος ξηρὸς μετεωρισθεὶς κατακλῃσθῇ,
     ἔνδοθεν αὐτὰς ὥσπερ κύστιν φυσᾷ, κἄπειθ' ὑπ' ἀνάγκης   405
     ῥήξας αὐτὰς ἔξω φέρεται σοβαρὸς διὰ τὴν πυκνότητα,
     ὑπὸ τοῦ ῥοίβδου καὶ τῆς ῥύμης αὐτὸς ἑαυτὸν κατακάων.

Στ. νὴ Δί' ἐγὼ γοῦν ἀτεχνῶς ἔπαθον τουτί ποτε Διασίοισιν.
     ὀπτῶν γαστέρα τοῖς συγγένεσιν κᾆτ' οὐκ ἔσχων ἀμελήσας·
     ἡ δ' ἄρ' ἐφυσᾶτ', εἶτ' ἐξαίφνης διαλακήσασα πρὸς αὐτὼ   410
*   τὠφθαλμώ μου προσετίλησεν καὶ κατέκαυσεν τὸ πρόσωπον.

Χο. ὦ τῆς μεγάλης ἐπιθυμήσας σοφίας ἄνθρωπε παρ' ἡμῶν,
     ὡς εὐδαίμων ἐν 'Αθηναίοις καὶ τοῖς Ἕλλησι γενήσει,
     εἰ μνήμων εἶ καὶ φροντιστής, καὶ τὸ ταλαίπωρον ἔνεστιν
     ἐν τῇ ψυχῇ, καὶ μὴ κάμνεις μήθ' ἑστὼς μήτε βαδίζων,   415
     μήτε ῥιγῶν ἄχθει λίαν μήτ' ἀριστᾶν ἐπιθυμεῖς,
     οἴνου τ' ἀπέχει καὶ γυμνασίων καὶ τῶν ἄλλων ἀνοήτων,
     καὶ βέλτιστον τοῦτο νομίζεις, ὅπερ εἰκὸς δεξιὸν ἄνδρα,
     νικᾶν πράττων καὶ βουλεύων καὶ τῇ γλώττῃ πολεμίζων.

Στ. ἀλλ' ἕνεκέν γε ψυχῆς στερρᾶς δυσκολοκοίτου τε μερίμνης   420
     καὶ φειδωλοῦ καὶ τρυσιβίου γαστρὸς καὶ θυμβρεπιδείπνου,
     ἀμέλει, θαρρῶν οὕνεκα τούτων ἐπιχαλκεύειν παρέχοιμ' ἄν.

Σω. ἄλλο τι δῆτ' οὐ νομιεῖς ἤδη θεὸν οὐδένα πλὴν ἅπερ ἡμεῖς,
     τὸ Χάος τουτὶ καὶ τὰς Νεφέλας καὶ τὴν Γλῶτταν, τρία ταυτί; 424

Στ. οὐδ' ἂν διαλεχθείην γ' ἀτεχνῶς τοῖς ἄλλοις οὐδ' ἂν ἀπαντῶν,

409 ἔσχων θ $^i\Sigma^{RVM}$: ἔσχον RVn' Suda, $^\lambda\Sigma^{RVM}$, Eustathius.
412-7 are cited, with many corruptions (some inadvertent, some
      deliberate), by Diogenes Laertius 2.27.
417 οἴνου codd. Suda, $^i\Sigma^V$, Diogenes: ὕπνου Et. Mag.

STREPSIADES: I don't know; but you seem to have a good point. Well, what *is* the thunderbolt?

SOCRATES: When a dry wind rises aloft and gets shut up inside these Clouds, it blows them up from within like a bladder, and then by necessity it bursts them and flies out with a violent rush due to its compressed density, and with the friction and the impetus it burns itself up.   405

STREPSIADES: I certainly had just the same thing happen to me once at the Diasia. I was roasting a haggis for my relations, and forgot to slit it; and it began to puff out, and then all of a sudden it   410
exploded, spitting blood right in my eyes and burning my face.   *

CHORUS-LEADER: You who desire the higher wisdom from us, how happy you will become in the eyes of the Athenians and of all Greeks — if you have a good memory and the capacity for thought, if there is endurance in your soul, if neither standing nor   415
walking tires you, if you are not too put out by being cold or yearn for your breakfast, if you abstain from wine and physical exercise and all other follies, and if your notion of the ultimate good is what one might expect a clever man to hold, that it is success in action and deliberation, and in the warfare of the tongue.

STREPSIADES: Well, as far as a tough soul is concerned, and   420
the capacity to cogitate on a restless bed, and a niggardly, thread-bare-living stomach that can dine off savory — never fear, so far as these are concerned I'd hand myself over with confidence to be forged on your anvil.

SOCRATES: Is it correct, then, that you will now recognize no god but those we recognize, the Void around us, the Clouds, and the Tongue, these three?

STREPSIADES: I'd absolutely refuse even to speak to the   425
other gods if I met them; and I won't sacrifice to them, or pour

οὐδ' ἂν θύσαιμ', οὐδ' ἂν σπεύσαιμ', οὐδ' ἐπιθείην λιβανωτόν.

Χο. λέγε νυν ἡμῖν ὅ τι σοι δρῶμεν θαρρῶν· ὡς οὐκ ἀτυχήσεις,
     ἡμᾶς τιμῶν καὶ θαυμάζων καὶ ζητῶν δεξιὸς εἶναι.

Στ. ὦ δέσποιναι, δέομαι τοίνυν ὑμῶν τουτὶ πάνυ μικρόν,
     τῶν Ἑλλήνων εἶναί με λέγειν ἑκατὸν σταδίοισιν ἄριστον.   430

Χο. ἀλλ' ἔσται σοι τοῦτο παρ' ἡμῶν, ὥστε τὸ λοιπόν γ' ἀπὸ τουδὶ
     ἐν τῷ δήμῳ γνώμας οὐδεὶς νικήσει πλείονας ἢ σύ.

Στ. μὴ 'μοιγε λέγειν γνώμας μεγάλας· οὐ γὰρ τούτων ἐπιθυμῶ,
     ἀλλ' ὅσ' ἐμαυτῷ στρεφοδικῆσαι καὶ τοὺς χρήστας διολισθεῖν.

Χο. τεύξει τοίνυν ὧν ἱμείρεις· οὐ γὰρ μεγάλων ἐπιθυμεῖς.   435
     ἀλλὰ σεαυτὸν θαρρῶν παράδος τοῖς ἡμετέροις προπόλοισιν.

Στ. δράσω ταῦθ' ὑμῖν πιστεύσας· ἡ γὰρ ἀνάγκη με πιέζει
     διὰ τοὺς ἵππους τοὺς κοππατίας καὶ τὸν γάμον ὅς μ' ἐπέτριψεν.
*   νῦν οὖν ἀτεχνῶς ὅ τι βούλονται
        τουτὶ τό γ' ἐμὸν σῶμ' αὐτοῖσιν   440
        παρέχω τύπτειν, πεινῆν, διψῆν,
        αὐχμεῖν, ῥιγῶν, ἀσκὸν δείρειν,
        εἴπερ τὰ χρέα διαφευξοῦμαι
        τοῖς τ' ἀνθρώποις εἶναι δόξω
        θρασύς, εὔγλωττος, τολμηρός, ἴτης,   445
        βδελυρός, ψευδῶν συγκολλητής,
        εὑρησιεπής, περίτριμμα δικῶν,
        κύρβις, κρόταλον, κίναδος, τρύμη,
        μάσθλης, εἴρων, γλοιός, ἀλαζών,

439 ἀτεχνῶς Cobet: χρήσθων ἀτεχνῶς codd.
442 ῥιγῶν Dobree: ῥιγοῦν codd.
442 δείρειν Scaliger: δέρειν RVn': δαύρειν Kˢ.

libations to them, or put incense on their altars.

CHORUS-LEADER: Then tell us what we are to do for you, and do so with confidence; for you will not come to grief, if you honour and respect us and seek to be an educated man.

STREPSIADES: Well then, sovereign Ladies, I beg of you this very small boon, that I may be by miles and miles the best speaker in the Greek world. 430

CHORUS-LEADER: That you shall have from us: so much so that in future, from now on, no one will carry more motions in the Assembly than you.

STREPSIADES: No proposing important motions for me, please! That's not what I desire: only to be able to twist justice for my own benefit and give my creditors the slip.

CHORUS-LEADER: Then you will gain the object of your 435 longing, for it is no great thing that you desire. Now hand yourself over with confidence to our ministers.

STREPSIADES: I shall do so, trusting in you; for necessity presses hard on me, owing to those *koppa*-branded horses and the marriage that has been my ruin. So now I unconditionally deliver 439-to them this body of mine to be beaten, to hunger, to thirst, to be 441 dirty, to freeze, to be flayed into a wineskin, if only I can escape my debts and make men think me audacious, glib, daring, forward, loath- 445 some, a sticker-together of lies, ready with words, a lawcourt veteran, a walking statute-book, a tinkling cymbal, a fox, a needle's eye, a supple rogue, a dissembler, a sticky customer, a fraud, a whipping- 450

κέντρων, μιαρός, στρόφις, ἀργαλέος,   450
ματιολοιχός.
ταῦτ' εὖ με καλοῦσ' ἀπαντῶντες,
δρώντων ἀτεχνῶς ὅ τι χρῄζουσιν·
κεἰ βούλονται,
νὴ τὴν Δήμητρ' ἔκ μου χορδὴν   455
τοῖς φροντισταῖς παραθέντων.

Χο. λῆμα μὲν πάρεστι τῷδέ γ'
     οὐκ ἄτολμον, ἀλλ' ἕτοιμον.
     ἴσθι δ' ὡς
     ταῦτα μαθὼν παρ' ἐμοῦ κλέος οὐρανόμηκες   460
     ἐν βροτοῖσιν ἕξεις.

Στ. τί πεύσομαι;

Χο.   τὸν πάντα χρόνον μετ' ἐμοῦ
     ζηλωτότατον βίον ἀνθρώπων διάξεις.   465

Στ. ἆρά γε τοῦτ' ἄρ' ἐγώ ποτ' ὄψομαι;

Χο.   ὥστε γέ σου
     πολλοὺς ἐπὶ ταῖσι θύραις ἀεὶ καθῆσθαι,
     βουλομένους ἀνακοινοῦσθαί τε καὶ εἰς λόγον ἐλθεῖν   470
     πράγματα κἀντιγραφὰς πολλῶν ταλάντων,
     ἄξια σῇ φρενί, συμβουλευσομένους μετὰ σοῦ.   475

     ἀλλ' ἐγχείρει τὸν πρεσβύτην ὅ τι περ μέλλεις προδιδάσκειν,
     καὶ διακίνει τὸν νοῦν αὐτοῦ, καὶ τῆς γνώμης ἀποπειρῶ.

Σω. ἄγε δή, κάτειπέ μοι σὺ τὸν σαυτοῦ τρόπον,
     ἵν' αὐτὸν εἰδὼς ὅστις ἐστὶ μηχανὰς
     ἤδη 'πὶ τούτοις πρός σε καινὰς προσφέρω.   480

471 λόγον Tricl., Heliodorus (in Σ^{VVs1} 467): λόγους codd.

post, a villain, a twister, a pest, a greedy feeder on quibbles. If they can make people who meet me give me these names, they may do absolutely anything they like with me; and if they wish, by Demeter, 455 they can make sausages of me and serve them up to the thinking-students.

CHORUS: This man has a spirit
that is resolute and does not flinch.
I tell you,
when you have learned these things from 460
me you will have among men
a renown that reaches to heaven.

STREPSIADES: What will happen to me?

CHORUS: With me, for all time to come,
you will lead the most envied life in the world. 465

STREPSIADES: You mean that is really what I'll one day see?

CHORUS: Yes, so that crowds
will always be sitting at your door,
wanting to consult you and speak with you, 470
to take your advice on actions and pleadings 472-5
involving many talents, worthwhile business
for your mind.

CHORUS-LEADER [to Socrates]: Now try to give the old man whatever preliminary teaching you mean to give him, stir up his mind and make trial of his intelligence.

SOCRATES [to Strepsiades]: Now then, tell me about your disposition, so that, knowing what it is, I can forthwith bring the 480 latest artillery to bear on you.

Στ. τί δέ; τειχομαχεῖν μοι διανοεῖ, πρὸς τῶν θεῶν;

Σω. οὔκ, ἀλλὰ βραχέα σου πυθέσθαι βούλομαι,
εἰ μνημονικὸς εἶ.

Στ.   δύο τρόπω, νὴ τὸν Δία·
ἢν μέν γ' ὀφείληταί τί μοι, μνήμων πάνυ·
ἐὰν δ' ὀφείλω σχέτλιος, ἐπιλήσμων πάνυ.   485

Σω. ἔνεστι δῆτά σοι λέγειν ἐν τῇ φύσει;

Στ. λέγειν μὲν οὐκ ἔνεστ', ἀποστερεῖν δ' ἔνι.

Σω. πῶς οὖν δυνήσει μανθάνειν;

Στ.   ἀμέλει, καλῶς.

Σω. ἄγε νυν ὅπως, ὅταν τι προβάλωμαι σοφὸν
περὶ τῶν μετεώρων, εὐθέως ὑφαρπάσει.   490

Στ. τί δαί; κυνηδὸν τὴν σοφίαν σιτήσομαι;

Σω. ἄνθρωπος ἀμαθὴς οὑτοσὶ καὶ βάρβαρος.
δέδοικά σ', ὦ πρεσβῦτα, μὴ πληγῶν δέει.
φέρ' ἴδω, τί δρᾷς, ἢν τίς σε τύπτῃ;

Στ.   τύπτομαι,
κᾆπειτ' ἐπισχὼν ὀλίγον ἐπιμαρτύρομαι·   495
εἶτ' αὖθις ἀκαρῆ διαλιπὼν δικάζομαι.

Σω. ἴθι νυν, κατάθου θοἰμάτιον.

Στ.   ἠδίκηκά τι;

Σω. οὔκ, ἀλλὰ γυμνοὺς εἰσιέναι νομίζεται.

Στ. ἀλλ' οὐχὶ φωράσων ἔγωγ' εἰσέρχομαι.

489 προβάλωμαι n: προβάλλωμαί σοι RV: προβάλω σοι Hirschig.

STREPSIADES: Eh? Are you intending, in heaven's name, to lay siege to me?

SOCRATES: No; I want to find out a few things from you — such as whether you have a good memory.

STREPSIADES: It works two ways, I tell you: if something is owed to me, it's very retentive; but if it's poor old me that's in 485 debt, I'm very forgetful.

SOCRATES: Then you have a natural gift for speaking?

STREPSIADES: For speaking, no; for evading my debts, yes.

SOCRATES: Then how will you be able to learn?

STREPSIADES: I will all right, don't worry.

SOCRATES: Well then, make sure that whenever I throw out a piece of learning on celestial matters, you snap it up at once. 490

STREPSIADES: Eh? Am I going to have to eat my learning like a dog?

SOCRATES: This man's an ignorant barbarian. Old man, I fear you may need the rod. Let me see: what do you do if someone strikes you?

STREPSIADES: I get hit, and then I wait a little, and call 495 people to witness; then, after waiting another second, I go to law.

SOCRATES: Come on then, lay down your cloak.

STREPSIADES: Have I done something wrong?

SOCRATES: No, it is the custom to undress before entering.

STREPSIADES: But I'm not going in to search your house for stolen goods.

Σω.   κατάθου· τί ληρεῖς;

Στ.   εἰπὲ δή νύν μοι τοδί·   500
ἦν ἐπιμελὴς ὦ καὶ προθύμως μανθάνω,
τῷ τῶν μαθητῶν ἐμφερὴς γενήσομαι;

Σω.   οὐδὲν διοίσεις Χαιρεφῶντος τὴν φύσιν.

Στ.   οἴμοι κακοδαίμων, ἡμιθνὴς γενήσομαι.

Σω.   οὐ μὴ λαλήσεις, ἀλλ' ἀκολουθήσεις ἐμοὶ   505
ἀνύσας τι δευρὶ θᾶττον;

Στ.   εἰς τὼ χεῖρέ νυν
δός μοι μελιτοῦτταν πρότερον, ὡς δέδοικ' ἐγὼ
εἴσω καταβαίνων ὥσπερ εἰς Τροφωνίου.

Σω.   χώρει· τί κυπτάζεις ἔχων περὶ τὴν θύραν;

Χο.   ἀλλ' ἴθι χαίρων τῆς ἀνδρείας   510
      οὕνεκα ταύτης.
εὐτυχία γένοιτο τάν-
      θρώπῳ, ὅτι προήκων
εἰς βαθὺ τῆς ἡλικίας
      νεωτέροις τὴν φύσιν αὑ-   515
      τοῦ πράγμασιν χρωτίζεται
      καὶ σοφίαν ἐπασκεῖ.

ὦ θεώμενοι, κατερῶ πρὸς ὑμᾶς ἐλευθέρως
τἀληθῆ, νὴ τὸν Διόνυσον τὸν ἐκθρέψαντά με.
οὕτω νικήσαιμί τ' ἐγὼ καὶ νομιζοίμην σοφός,   520
ὡς ὑμᾶς ἡγούμενος εἶναι θεατὰς δεξιοὺς
καὶ ταύτην σοφώτατ' ἔχειν τῶν ἐμῶν κωμῳδιῶν
πρώτους ἠξίωσ' ἀναγεῦσ' ὑμᾶς, ἣ παρέσχε μοι

520 νικήσαιμί τ' ἐγὼ Bentley: νικήσαιμ' ἔγωγε codd.

58

SOCRATES: Put it down; what are you blethering about?   500

STREPSIADES [*taking off his cloak and shoes*]: Well, tell me
this: if I am attentive and a keen student, which of your disciples
will I come to resemble?

SOCRATES: In your essential features you will be no different from Chaerephon.

STREPSIADES: God help me, I'll look half a corpse!

SOCRATES [*at the door*]: Will you stop chattering, and hurry   505
up and follow me quickly in here?

STREPSIADES: Well, first of all give me a honey-cake in my
hands, because I'm frightened of going down inside there, like into
the cave of Trophonius.

SOCRATES: Move! Why do you keep hanging round the door?   *
[*They go inside, Socrates taking in Strepsiades' cloak and shoes.*]

CHORUS-LEADER: Go, and good luck to you in return   510
               for the courage you have shown.

CHORUS: May good fortune attend
               the man, because, though advanced
               deep into old age,
               he is dipping himself in the dye   515
               of revolutionary new ideas
               and pursuing knowledge.

CHORUS-LEADER: Spectators, I shall be frank and tell you
the truth, I swear it by Dionysus who nurtured me to manhood. So   520
may I be victorious, so may I be thought a true artist, I took you
for an intelligent audience and this for the most intellectual of my
comedies, and therefore saw fit to give you the first taste of it, a
play that cost me a great deal of labour; and then I retired defeated   524-5

59

ἔργον πλεῖστον· εἶτ' ἀνεχώρουν ὑπ' ἀνδρῶν φορτικῶν
ἡττηθείς, οὐκ ἄξιος ὤν. ταῦτ' οὖν ὑμῖν μέμφομαι   525
τοῖς σοφοῖς, ὧν οὔνεκ' ἐγὼ ταῦτ' ἐπραγματευόμην.
ἀλλ' οὐδ' ὣς ὑμῶν ποθ' ἑκὼν προδώσω τοὺς δεξιούς.
ἐξ ὅτου γὰρ ἐνθάδ' ὑπ' ἀνδρῶν, οὓς ἡδὺ καὶ λέγειν,
ὁ σώφρων τε χὡ καταπύγων ἄριστ' ἠκουσάτην,
κἀγώ—παρθένος γὰρ ἔτ' ἦ, κοὐκ ἐξῆν πώ μοι τεκεῖν—   530
ἐξέθηκα, παῖς δ' ἑτέρα τις λαβοῦσ' ἀνείλετο,
ὑμεῖς δ' ἐξεθρέψατε γενναίως κἀπαιδεύσατε,
ἐκ τούτου μοι πιστὰ παρ' ὑμῶν γνώμης ἔσθ' ὅρκια.
νῦν οὖν Ἠλέκτραν κατ' ἐκείνην ἥδ' ἡ κωμῳδία
ζητοῦσ' ἦλθ', ἤν που 'πιτύχῃ θεαταῖς οὕτω σοφοῖς·   535
γνώσεται γάρ, ἤνπερ ἴδῃ, τἀδελφοῦ τὸν βόστρυχον.
ὡς δὲ σώφρων ἐστὶ φύσει σκέψασθ'· ἥτις πρῶτα μὲν
οὐδὲν ἦλθε ῥαψαμένη σκυτίον καθειμένον,
ἐρυθρὸν ἐξ ἄκρου, παχύ, τοῖς παιδίοις ἵν' ᾖ γέλως·
οὐδ' ἔσκωψεν τοὺς φαλακρούς, οὐδὲ κόρδαχ' εἵλκυσεν·   540
οὐδὲ πρεσβύτης ὁ λέγων τἄπη τῇ βακτηρίᾳ
τύπτει τὸν παρόντ', ἀφανίζων πονηρὰ σκώμματα·
οὐδ' εἰσῇξε δᾷδας ἔχουσ', οὐδ' "ἰοὺ ἰού" βοᾷ·
ἀλλ' αὑτῇ καὶ τοῖς ἔπεσιν πιστεύουσ' ἐλήλυθεν.
κἀγὼ μὲν τοιοῦτος ἀνὴρ ὢν ποιητὴς οὐ κομῶ,   545
οὐδ' ὑμᾶς ζητῶ 'ξαπατᾶν δὶς καὶ τρὶς ταῦτ' εἰσάγων,

527 ὑμῶν RV<u>n</u>: ὑμᾶς A.
528 οὓς Blaydes: οἷς codd.
530 ἦ Dindorf: ἦν codd.: so also 1402.
533 ὑμῶν V3^s: ὑμῖν codd.
534 Ἠλέκτραν Νθ^2 λ$_Σ$Νp1Vs1 : Ἠλέκτρα RVEKθ^1 λ$_Σ$ΕΜ.
538 σκυτίον X Ln5: σκύτινον RV<u>n</u> Suda.

60

undeservedly by vulgar men. For that I hold you intelligent people
to blame, for whose sake I was taking all that trouble. But even so,
I will never willingly desert the bright ones among you. For since
the time when in this place my virtuous boy and my buggered boy
were extremely well spoken of by certain men whom it is a pleasure even to mention, and I (being still unmarried and not yet sup-   530
posed to give birth) exposed the child, another girl picked it up,
and you generously reared it and educated it — since that time I
have held sworn pledges of your good opinion. So now, like Electra
of old, this comedy has come seeking and hoping somewhere to   535
find spectators as intelligent; for she will recognize, if she sees it,
the lock of her brother's hair. Look at the modesty of her nature.
First of all, she hasn't come with a dangling bit of stitched leather,
red at the end and thick, to give the children a laugh; nor has she   540
made fun of men who are bald, nor danced a cordax; nor does an
old man, the one with the leading part, conceal bad jokes by hitting whoever is around with his stick; nor does this comedy rush on
stage with torches, nor cry "help, help"; no, she has come trusting
in herself and in her script. And I myself, being a poet of the same   545
stamp, do not give myself *h*airs, nor try to cheat you by presenting
the same things a second and a third time; rather I always apply my

ἀλλ' ἀεὶ καινὰς ἰδέας εἰσφέρων σοφίζομαι,
οὐδὲν ἀλλήλαισιν ὁμοίας καὶ πάσας δεξιάς·
ὃς μέγιστον ὄντα Κλέων' ἔπαισ' εἰς τὴν γαστέρα,
κοὐκ ἐτόλμησ' αὖθις ἐπεμπηδῆσ' αὐτῷ κειμένῳ.   550
οὗτοι δ', ὡς ἅπαξ παρέδωκεν λαβὴν Ὑπέρβολος,
τοῦτον δείλαιον κολετρῶσ' ἀεὶ καὶ τὴν μητέρα.
Εὔπολις μὲν τὸν Μαρικᾶν πρώτιστον παρείλκυσεν
* ἐκστρέψας τοὺς ἡμετέρους Ἱππέας κακὸς κακῶς,
προσθεὶς αὐτῷ γραῦν μεθύσην τοῦ κόρδακος οὕνεχ', ἣν   555
Φρύνιχος πάλαι πεποίηχ', ἣν τὸ κῆτος ἤσθιεν.
εἶθ' Ἕρμιππος αὖθις ἐποίησεν εἰς Ὑπέρβολον,
ἄλλοι τ' ἤδη πάντες ἐρείδουσιν εἰς Ὑπέρβολον,
τὰς εἰκοὺς τῶν ἐγχέλεων τὰς ἐμὰς μιμούμενοι.
ὅστις οὖν τούτοισι γελᾷ, τοῖς ἐμοῖς μὴ χαιρέτω·   560
* ἢν δ' ἐμοὶ καὶ τοῖσιν ἐμοῖς εὐφραίνησθ' εὑρήμασιν,
εἰς τὰς ὥρας τὰς ἑτέρας εὖ φρονεῖν δοκήσετε.

ὑψιμέδοντα μὲν θεῶν   (στρ.
    Ζῆνα τύραννον εἰς χορὸν
    πρῶτα μέγαν κικλήσκω·   565
τόν τε μεγασθενῆ τριαίνης ταμίαν,
    γῆς τε καὶ ἁλμυρᾶς θαλάσ-
    σης ἄγριον μοχλευτήν·
καὶ μεγαλώνυμον ἡμέτερον πατέρ',
    Αἰθέρα σεμνότατον, βιοθρέμμονα πάντων·   570
τόν θ' ἱππονώμαν, ὃς ὑπερ-
    λάμπροις ἀκτῖσιν κατέχει
    γῆς πέδον, μέγας ἐν θεοῖς
    ἐν θνητοῖσί τε δαίμων.

ὦ σοφώτατοι θεαταί, δεῦρο τὸν νοῦν προσέχετε·   575
ἠδικημέναι γὰρ ὑμῖν μεμφόμεσθ' ἐναντίον.

skills to introducing new forms of comedy, quite different one from another and every one full of ingenuity. When Cleon was almighty, I hit him in the stomach; I did not have the hardihood to jump on him again when he was down. But these fellows, from the moment Hyperbolus let them get a hold of him, have been incessantly trampling on the poor chap and his mother as well. First of all Eupolis hauled his *Maricas* on to the stage, serving a vile rehash of my *Knights* like the vile fellow he is, and adding on a drunken old woman for the sake of the cordax, the woman presented years ago by Phrynichus, the one the sea-monster tried to devour. Then Hermippus again wrote about Hyperbolus, and now all the others are piling into Hyperbolus, copying my similes about eels. Well, whoever laughs at them, let him not enjoy my work; but if you take pleasure in me and my poetic inventions, you will be thought by future ages to have been wise.

CHORUS: The most high ruler of the gods,
          Zeus the great sovereign,
          I call first to my dance;
          and the Warden of the Trident, great and mighty,
          him who savagely upheaves
          the earth and the briny sea;
          and our own greatly renowned father,
          the Sky, most revered, who nourishes all living
             things;
          and the Charioteer who fills
          with his brilliant rays
          the expanse of the earth, a great Power
          among gods and mortals.

CHORUS-LEADER: Spectatórs, let your wisdom pay attention to us; for you have wronged us, and we reproach you to your faces.

πλεῖστα γὰρ θεῶν ἁπάντων ὠφελούσαις τὴν πόλιν
δαιμόνων ἡμῖν μόναις οὐ θύετ' οὐδὲ σπένδετε,
αἵτινες τηροῦμεν ὑμᾶς. ἦν γὰρ ᾖ τις ἔξοδος
μηδενὶ ξὺν νῷ, τότ' ἢ βροντῶμεν ἢ φακάζομεν.   580
εἶτα τὸν θεοῖσιν ἐχθρὸν βυρσοδέψην Παφλαγόνα
ἡνίχ' ᾑρεῖσθε στρατηγόν, τὰς ὀφρῦς ξυνήγομεν
κἀποιοῦμεν δεινά, βροντὴ δ' ἐρράγη δι' ἀστραπῆς,
ἡ σελήνη δ' ἐξέλειπεν τὰς ὁδούς, ὁ δ' ἥλιος
τὴν θρυαλλίδ' εἰς ἑαυτὸν εὐθέως ξυνελκύσας   585
οὐ φανεῖν ἔφασκεν ὑμῖν, εἰ στρατηγήσοι Κλέων.
ἀλλ' ὅμως εἵλεσθε τοῦτον. φασὶ γὰρ δυσβουλίαν
τῇδε τῇ πόλει προσεῖναι· ταῦτα μέντοι τοὺς θεούς,
ἅττ' ἂν ὑμεῖς ἐξαμάρτητ', ἐπὶ τὸ βέλτιον τρέπειν.
ὡς δὲ καὶ τοῦτο ξυνοίσει, ῥᾳδίως διδάξομεν.   590
ἢν Κλέωνα τὸν λάρον δώρων ἑλόντες καὶ κλοπῆς
εἶτα φιμώσητε τούτου τῷ ξύλῳ τὸν αὐχένα,
αὖθις εἰς τἀρχαῖον ὑμῖν, εἴ τι κἀξημάρτετε,
ἐπὶ τὸ βέλτιον τὸ πρᾶγμα τῇ πόλει ξυνοίσεται.

ἀμφί μοι αὖτε, Φοῖβ' ἄναξ   (ἀντ.
    Δήλιε, Κυνθίαν ἔχων   596
    ὑψικέρατα πέτραν·
ἤ τ' Ἐφέσου μάκαιρα πάγχρυσον ἔχεις
    οἶκον, ἐν ᾧ κόραι σε Λυ-
    δῶν μεγάλως σέβουσιν·   600
ἤ τ' ἐπιχώριος ἡμετέρα θεός,
    αἰγίδος ἡνίοχος, πολιοῦχος Ἀθάνα·
Παρνασσίαν θ' ὃς κατέχων

584 ἐξέλειπεν U al.: ἐξέλιπε RVθ<u>ⁿ'</u>: ἐκλέλοιπε θ.

64

Though we benefit your city more than any other god, nevertheless
to us alone of the gods you make no sacrifice or libation, us who
constantly watch over you. If there is a military expedition which
is senseless, then we either thunder or rain. Then again, when you   580
were about to elect as general the god-hated tanner Paphlagon, we
contracted our brows and made loud complaint: amid the lightning
came the burst of thunder, the moon took to forsaking her path,
and the sun at once retracted his wick into his orb and said that he   585
wouldn't give you light if Cleon was to be general. But you elected
him just the same: they say that ill-advised decisions are endemic
to this city — but also that whatever mistakes you make, the gods
make them turn out for the best. And we can easily explain to you   590
how this mistake too can redound to your advantage. If you con-
vict that seagull Cleon of bribery and theft, and then clap his neck
in the stocks, then even though you *have* made a mistake, you will
find things back as they were before, with all turning out for the
best for the city.

    CHORUS: Grant me thy presence too, Phoebus, lord   595
            of Delos, who dwellest on Cynthus'
            high rocky peak;
            and thou, blest Lady, who dwellest in Ephesus'
            house of gold, wherein the daughters of the Lydians
            greatly revere thee;   600
            and our own native Goddess,
            mistress of the aegis, Athena guardian of the city;
            and he who haunts Parnassus' rock

πέτραν σὺν πεύκαις σελαγεῖ
Βάκχαις Δελφίσιν ἐμπρέπων,   605
κωμαστὴς Διόνυσος.

ἡνίχ' ἡμεῖς δεῦρ' ἀφορμᾶσθαι παρεσκευάσμεθα,
ἡ Σελήνη ξυντυχοῦσ' ἡμῖν ἐπέστειλεν φράσαι
πρῶτα μὲν χαίρειν 'Αθηναίοισι καὶ τοῖς ξυμμάχοις·
εἶτα θυμαίνειν ἔφασκε· δεινὰ γὰρ πεπονθέναι,   610
ὠφελοῦσ' ὑμᾶς ἅπαντας οὐ λόγοις ἀλλ' ἐμφανῶς·
πρῶτα μὲν τοῦ μηνὸς εἰς δᾶδ' οὐκ ἔλαττον ἢ δραχμήν,
ὥστε καὶ λέγειν ἅπαντας ἐξιόντας ἑσπέρας
"μὴ πρίῃ, παῖ, δᾷδ', ἐπειδὴ φῶς Σεληναίης καλόν."
ἄλλα τ' εὖ δρᾶν φησιν· ὑμᾶς δ' οὐκ ἄγειν τὰς ἡμέρας   615
οὐδὲν ὀρθῶς, ἀλλ' ἄνω τε καὶ κάτω κυδοιδοπᾶν·
ὥστ' ἀπειλεῖν φησιν αὐτῇ τοὺς θεοὺς ἑκάστοτε,
ἡνίκ' ἂν ψευσθῶσι δείπνου κἀπίωσιν οἴκαδε
τῆς ἑορτῆς μὴ τυχόντες κατὰ λόγον τῶν ἡμερῶν.
κᾆθ', ὅταν θύειν δέῃ, στρεβλοῦτε καὶ δικάζετε·   620
πολλάκις δ' ἡμῶν ἀγόντων τῶν θεῶν ἀπαστίαν,
ἡνίκ' ἂν πενθῶμεν ἢ τὸν Μέμνον' ἢ Σαρπηδόνα,
σπένδεθ' ὑμεῖς καὶ γελᾶτ'· ἀνθ' ὧν λαχὼν 'Υπέρβολος
τῆτες ἱερομνημονεῖν κἄπειθ' ὑφ' ἡμῶν τῶν θεῶν
τὸν στέφανον ἀφῃρέθη· μᾶλλον γὰρ οὕτως εἴσεται   625
κατὰ σελήνην ὡς ἄγειν χρὴ τοῦ βίου τὰς ἡμέρας.

Σω. μὰ τὴν 'Αναπνοήν, μὰ τὸ Χάος, μὰ τὸν 'Αέρα,
οὐκ εἶδον οὕτως ἄνδρ' ἄγροικον οὐδαμοῦ

604   πεύκαις Rn: πεύκηις V: πευκη Π7.
615   ὑμᾶς δ' οὐκ Lpc: ὑμᾶς κοὐκ codd.: κουκ[υμας Π7.
619   for the non-aspiration of ἑορτῆς cf. Threatte i 500:
        εορτης Π7: ἑορτῆς codd.
628   οὐδαμοῦ Π7 V Suda: οὐδένα Rn.

66

and blazes with pine-torches,
conspicuous among the Delphian bacchants,   605
the reveller Dionysus.

CHORUS-LEADER: When we were ready to set out on our
journey here, the Moon happened to meet us and instructed us first
of all to convey her greetings to the Athenians and their allies; and   610
then she said she was annoyed, because she had been shamefully
treated despite being of benefit to you all not with mere words but
with plain deeds. First of all, she saves you at least a drachma a
month in torches, so that you all say when you go out in the even-
ing, "Don't buy a torch, boy; the light of Selene does fine." And   615
there are other ways in which she says she benefits you; but you
don't keep the calendar right, you make topsy-tu y havoc of it.
The result is, she says, that the gods are always making threats
against her, when they are cheated of a dinner and go off home not
having had their due festival according to the reckoning of the days.
Then again, when you ought to be sacrificing, you are applying tor-   620
ture and giving judgement; and many a time, when we gods are holding a solemn fast while we mourn Memnon or Sarpedon, you are
pouring libations and laughing. That is why Hyperbolus, after being
chosen by lot this year to be sacred remembrancer, then had his
garland taken away by us gods. That way he will know better that   625
you should reckon the days of your life in accordance with the moon.

SOCRATES [*coming out of the school*]: By Respiration, by
Void, by Air, I've never seen anywhere a man so rustic and clueless,

οὐδ' ἄπορον οὐδὲ σκαιὸν οὐδ' ἐπιλήσμονα·
ὅστις σκαλαθυρμάτι' ἄττα μικρὰ μανθάνων   630
ταῦτ' ἐπιλέλησται πρὶν μαθεῖν. ὅμως γε μὴν
αὐτὸν καλῶ θύραζε δευρὶ πρὸς τὸ φῶς.
ποῦ Στρεψιάδης; ἔξει τὸν ἀσκάντην λαβών;

Στ.   ἀλλ' οὐκ ἐῶσί μ' ἐξενεγκεῖν οἱ κόρεις.

Σω.   ἀνύσας τι κατάθου, καὶ πρόσεχε τὸν νοῦν.

Στ.   ἰδού.   635

Σω.   ἄγε δή, τί βούλει πρῶτα νυνὶ μανθάνειν
      ὧν οὐκ ἐδιδάχθης πώποτ' οὐδέν; εἰπέ μοι.
*   πότερον περὶ μέτρων ἢ περὶ ἐπῶν ἢ ῥυθμῶν;

Στ.   περὶ τῶν μέτρων ἔγωγ'· ἔναγχος γάρ ποτε
      ὑπ' ἀλφιταμοιβοῦ παρεκόπην διχοινύκου.   640

Σω.   οὐ τοῦτ' ἐρωτῶ σ', ἀλλ' ὅ τι κάλλιστον μέτρον
      ἡγεῖ, πότερον τὸ τρίμετρον ἢ τὸ τετράμετρον.

Στ.   ἐγὼ μὲν οὐδὲν πρότερον ἡμιέκτεω.

Σω.   οὐδὲν λέγεις, ὦνθρωπε.

Στ.   περίδου νυν ἐμοί,
      εἰ μὴ τετράμετρόν ἐστιν ἡμιέκτεων.   645

Σω.   ἐς κόρακας· ὡς ἄγροικος εἶ καὶ δυσμαθής.
      τάχα δ' ἂν δύναιο μανθάνειν περὶ ῥυθμῶν.

Στ.   τί δέ μ' ὠφελήσουσ' οἱ ῥυθμοὶ πρὸς τἄλφιτα;

Σω.   πρῶτον μὲν εἶναι κομψὸν ἐν ξυνουσίᾳ

640   διχοινύκου Blaydes: διχοινύκῳ codd., Tzetzes.
647   τάχα δ' Thom.: ταχὺ δ' λΣEM: ταχύ γ' codd.

68

so stupid and forgetful. He's been trying to acquire some little   630
hen-scratches of knowledge, and he's forgotten them before he's
learned them. All the same I'll call him out here into the light.
[*Calling within*] Where's Strepsiades? Will you come out, bringing
your bed with you?

      STREPSIADES [*coming out, carrying bed*]: The bugs aren't
letting me bring it out.

      SOCRATES: Hurry up and put it down, and pay attention   635
to me.

      STREPSIADES: There you are.

      SOCRATES: Come on now, tell me, what do you want to
begin now by learning, of all the things that you were never taught
before at all? About measures, or words, or rhythms?   *

      STREPSIADES: Measures for me, please. The other day a
corn-dealer cheated me out of two quarts.   640

      SOCRATES: I'm not asking you about that; I'm asking you
what you consider the best measure aesthetically — the three-
measure or the four-measure?

      STREPSIADES: I think the gallon measure is second to none.

      SOCRATES: You're talking nonsense, man.

      STREPSIADES: Will you bet me, then, that a gallon doesn't   645
consist of four measures?

      SOCRATES: Oh, to hell with you, you dimwitted rustic!
Perhaps though you might be able to learn about rhythms.

      STREPSIADES: But how will rhythms help me get my daily
groats?

      SOCRATES: Well, for a start, it'll make you seem refined in

ἐπαΐειν θ' ὁποῖός ἐστι τῶν ῥυθμῶν 650
κατ' ἐνόπλιον χὥποῖος αὖ κατὰ δάκτυλον.

Στ. κατὰ δάκτυλον; νὴ τὸν Δί', ἀλλ' οἶδ'.

Σω.   εἰπὲ δή. 652

Στ. πρὸ τοῦ μέν, ἐπ' ἐμοῦ παιδὸς ὄντος, οὑτοσί. 654

Σω. ἀγρεῖος εἶ καὶ σκαιός.

Στ.   οὐ γάρ, ὦζυρέ, 655
τούτων ἐπιθυμῶ μανθάνειν οὐδέν.

Σω.   τί δαί;

Στ. ἐκεῖν' ἐκεῖνο, τὸν ἀδικώτατον λόγον.

Σω. ἀλλ' ἕτερα δεῖ σε πρότερα τούτου μανθάνειν,
τῶν τετραπόδων ἅττ' ἐστὶν ὀρθῶς ἄρρενα.

Στ. ἀλλ' οἶδ' ἔγωγε τἄρρεν', εἰ μὴ μαίνομαι· 66(
κριός, τράγος, ταῦρος, κύων, ἀλεκτρυών.

< Σω.

Στ.   ἀλεκτρυών.>

Σω. ὁρᾷς ἃ πάσχεις; τήν τε θήλειαν καλεῖς
ἀλεκτρυόνα καὶ ταὐτὸ καὶ τὸν ἄρρενα.

650 ἐπαΐειν θ' Blaydes, cf. Σ^{RVEMNp1}: ἐπαΐειντ R^{pc}: ἐπαΐοντ'
     ἐπαΐειν Choeroboscus: εἶτ' ἐπαΐειν Vn.
[653] τίς ἄλλος ἀντὶ τουτουὶ (τουι θ^1) τοῦ δακτύλου; codd.: del
     Dover.
661 lacuna posited by Bentley: perh. e.g. <(Σω.) τὰ δὲ θήλε';
     (Στ.) οἶς, αἴξ, βοῦς, κύων, ἀλεκτρυών.>
663 καὶ ταὐτὸ Hermann: κατ' αὐτὸ VE^{ac}: κατὰ ταὐτὸ RV^sNθ^{ac}: κα
     ταὐτὸν E^{pc}Kθ^{pc}: καταταυτὸν ^λΣ^E.

company, and be aware what kind of rhythm is enoplian and what 650
kind is digital.

STREPSIADES: Digital? But, by Zeus, I know that.

SOCRATES: Then tell me.

STREPSIADES: Well, in the old days, in my boyhood, it was
this [*sticking out his middle finger at Socrates*].

SOCRATES: You're a stupid peasant. 655

STREPSIADES: The thing is, you silly man, that I don't wish
to learn *any* of these things.

SOCRATES: What then?

STREPSIADES: That other thing, that — that supremely
Wrongful Argument.

SOCRATES: But there are other things you must learn before
that, such as which of the quadrupeds are properly called masculine.

STREPSIADES: Well, I know which are masculine, if I've not 660
lost my wits: ram, he-goat, bull, dog, fowl.

<SOCRATES: And feminine are —?

STREPSIADES: Ewe, she-goat, cow, bitch, fowl.>

SOCRATES: Do you see what you're doing? You call the
female "fowl", and the male as well you call the same thing.

Στ. πῶς δή, φέρε;

Σω.   πῶς; ἀλεκτρυὼν κἀλεκτρυών.

Στ. νὴ τὸν Ποσειδῶ. νῦν δὲ πῶς με χρὴ καλεῖν;   665

Σω. ἀλεκτρύαιναν, τὸν δ' ἕτερον ἀλέκτορα.

Στ. ἀλεκτρύαιναν; εὖ γε, νὴ τὸν 'Αέρα·
     ὥστ' ἀντὶ τούτου τοῦ διδάγματος μόνου
     διαλφιτώσω σου κύκλῳ τὴν κάρδοπον.

Σω. ἰδοὺ μάλ' αὖθις· τοῦθ' ἕτερον. τὴν κάρδοπον   670
     ἄρρενα καλεῖς θήλειαν οὖσαν.

Στ.   τῷ τρόπῳ;
     ἄρρενα καλῶ 'γὼ κάρδοπον;

Σω.   μάλιστά γε,
     ὥσπερ γε καὶ Κλεώνυμον.

Στ.   πῶς δή; φράσον.

Σω. ταὐτὸν δύναταί σοι κάρδοπος Κλεωνύμῳ.

Στ. ἀλλ', ὦγάθ', οὐδ' ἦν κάρδοπος Κλεωνύμῳ,   675
     ἀλλ' ἐν θυείᾳ στρογγύλῃ γ' ἀνεμάττετο.
     ἀτὰρ τὸ λοιπὸν πῶς με χρὴ καλεῖν;

Σω.   ὅπως;
     τὴν καρδόπην, ὥσπερ καλεῖς τὴν Σωστράτην.

Στ. τὴν καρδόπην, θήλειαν;

Σω.   ὀρθῶς γὰρ λέγεις.

Στ. ἐκεῖνο δ' ἦν ἂν "καρδόπη Κλεωνύμη";   680

680 Κλεωνύμη Ct3: Κλεωνύμη codd.

72

STREPSIADES: How do you mean, please?

SOCRATES: How do I mean? "Fowl" and "fowl".

STREPSIADES: By Poseidon, so I do. What should I really 665
call it?

SOCRATES: "Fowless", and the other one "fowler".

STREPSIADES: "Fowless"? By Air, that's a good one. In
fact, for that piece of instruction alone I'll fill the whole surface of
your *cardopus* with groats.

SOCRATES: There you go again; that's another one. You 670
speak of a *cardopus*, calling it masculine when it's feminine.

STREPSIADES: What do you mean? I call a *cardopus*
masculine?

SOCRATES: You certainly do, just like *Cleonymus.*

STREPSIADES: In what way? Tell me.

SOCRATES: You give the same treatment to *cardopus* that
is given to *Cleonymus.*

STREPSIADES: But, my good man, Cleonymus never had a 675
cardopus at all — the kneading he did was done in a round mortar.
What should I call it in future, though?

SOCRATES: What should you call it? *Cardopé*, just as you
say *Sostraté.*

STREPSIADES: *Cardopé*, feminine?

SOCRATES: That's correct.

STREPSIADES: And what I said would then have been 680
"Cleonymé never had a *cardopé*"?

Σω. ἔτι δέ γε περὶ τῶν ὀνομάτων μαθεῖν σε δεῖ,
ἅττ' ἄρρεν' ἐστίν, ἅττα δ' αὐτῶν θήλεα.

Στ. ἀλλ' οἶδ' ἔγωγ' ἃ θήλε' ἐστίν.

Σω.   εἰπὲ δή.

Στ. Λύσιλλα, Φίλιννα, Κλειταγόρα, Δημητρία.

Σω. ἄρρενα δὲ ποῖα τῶν ὀνομάτων;

Στ.   μυρία·   685
Φιλόξενος, Μελησίας, 'Αμυνίας.

Σω. ἀλλ', ὦ πόνηρε, ταῦτά γ' ἔστ' οὐκ ἄρρενα.

Στ. οὐκ ἄρρεν' ὑμῖν ἐστιν;

Σω.   οὐδαμῶς γ', ἐπεὶ
πῶς ἂν καλέσειας ἐντυχὼν 'Αμυνίᾳ;

Στ. ὅπως ἄν; ὡδί· "δεῦρο δεῦρ', 'Αμυνία."   690

Σω. ὁρᾷς; γυναῖκα τὴν 'Αμυνίαν καλεῖς.

Στ. οὔκουν δικαίως, ἥτις οὐ στρατεύεται;
ἀτὰρ τί ταῦθ' ἃ πάντες ἴσμεν μανθάνω;

Σω. οὐδέν, μὰ Δί'. ἀλλὰ κατακλινεὶς δευρὶ—

Στ.   τί δρῶ;

Σω. ἐκφρόντισόν τι τῶν σεαυτοῦ πραγμάτων.   695

681 ἔτι δέ γε θ^1: ἔτι γε RVE^{ac}: ἔτι Κ: ἔτ' ἔτι γε E^{pc}N: ἔτι
δή γε Tricl. (whence θ^2).
686 'Αμυνίας RV^{s}n, Libanius: so all codd. 689, 690, 691:
'Αμεινίας V.
688 ὑμῖν θ^{pc}: ἡμῖν RVθ^{ac}n'.

SOCRATES [*ignoring this*]: But you still have to learn about names, which of them are masculine and which feminine.

STREPSIADES: Well, I know which are feminine.

SOCRATES: Tell me then.

STREPSIADES: Lysilla, Philinna, Cleitagora, Demetria.

SOCRATES: And which names are masculine? 685

STREPSIADES: Loads of them — Philoxenus, Melesias, Amynias.

SOCRATES: But those aren't masculine, you fool.

STREPSIADES: You don't regard them as masculine?

SOCRATES: Certainly not; consider, if you happened to see Amynias, how would you call him?

STREPSIADES: How? Like this: "Come here, come here, 690 Amynia".

SOCRATES: Do you see? you're calling *her* a woman, "Amynia".

STREPSIADES: And doesn't she deserve it, for not doing her military service? But why should I be learning these things, which we all know?

SOCRATES: Never mind that now. Just lie down here [*indicating the bed*] and —

STREPSIADES: Do what?

SOCRATES: Think out one of your own problems. 695

Στ. μὴ δῆθ', ἱκετεύω, 'νταῦθά γ'· ἀλλ', εἴπερ γε χρή,
     χαμαί μ' ἔασον αὐτὰ ταῦτ' ἐκφροντίσαι.

Σω. οὐκ ἔστι παρὰ ταῦτ' ἄλλα.

Στ.   κακοδαίμων ἐγώ·
     οἵαν δίκην τοῖς κόρεσι δώσω τήμερον.   699

Χο. φρόντιζε δὴ καὶ διάθρει,   (στρ.
     πάντα τρόπον τε σαυτὸν
     στρόβει πυκνώσας· ταχὺς δ', ὅταν εἰς ἄπορον
     πέσῃς, ἐπ' ἄλλο πήδα
     νόημα φρενός· ὕπνος δ' ἀπέ-   705
     στω γλυκύθυμος ὀμμάτων—

Στ. ἀτταταῖ ἀτταταῖ.

Χο. τί πάσχεις; τί κάμνεις;

Στ. ἀπόλλυμαι δείλαιος· ἐκ τοῦ σκίμποδος
     δάκνουσί μ' ἐξέρποντες οἱ Κορίνθιοι,   710
     καὶ τὰς πλευρὰς δαρδάπτουσιν
         καὶ τὴν ψυχὴν ἐκπίνουσιν
         καὶ τοὺς ὄρχεις ἐξέλκουσιν
         καὶ τὸν πρωκτὸν διορύττουσιν,
     καί μ' ἀπολοῦσιν.   715

Χο. μή νυν βαρέως ἄλγει λίαν.

Στ. καὶ πῶς; ὅτε μου
     φροῦδα τὰ χρήματα, φροῦδη χροιά,
     φροῦδη ψυχή, φροῦδη δ' ἐμβάς·

696 'νταῦθά γ' Dobree: σ' ἐνταῦθ' RVEθ: σ' ἐνθάδ' KN $^{\lambda}\Sigma^{U}$.
696 εἴπερ γε N: εὖ γε RVn̲'.
712, 713 in this order n̲: in reverse order RV.

76

STREPSIADES: Please, I beg of you, not there! If I really
must, let me do the same thinking-out on the ground.

SOCRATES: There is no alternative.

STREPSIADES [*getting into the bed*]: God help me, how the
bugs are going to take it out on me today!

[*Socrates goes inside.*]

CHORUS: Now think and perpend,   700
           twist and twirl yourself every way,
           and concentrate your mind; and rapidly, when you come
           to a dead end, jump to another
           mental idea; and let sleep   705
           that delights the soul be far from your eyes —

STREPSIADES [*in torment*]: Aah, aah!

CHORUS: What ails thee, what pains thee?

STREPSIADES: I'm in agony, I'm perishing — being bitten   709
by these Tom Tugs creeping out of the bed;   710
           they're devouring my ribs,
           they're draining my life-blood,
           they're pulling out my balls,
           they're tunnelling through my arse,
           and they'll be the death of me.   715

CHORUS: Yet grieve thou not too sore.

STREPSIADES:
           Some advice! when I
           have lost my money, lost my suntan,
           lost my life-blood, and lost my shoes;

καὶ πρὸς τούτοις ἔτι τοῖσι κακοῖς   720
φρουρᾶς ᾄδων
ὀλίγου φροῦδος γεγένημαι.

Σω. οὗτος, τί ποιεῖς; οὐχὶ φροντίζεις;

Στ.   ἐγώ;
νὴ τὸν Ποσειδῶ.

Σω.   καὶ τί δῆτ' ἐφρόντισας;

Στ. ὑπὸ τῶν κόρεων εἴ μού τι περιλειφθήσεται.   725

Σω. ἀπολεῖ κάκιστ'.

Στ.   ἀλλ', ὦγαθ', ἀπόλωλ' ἀρτίως.

Χο. οὐ μαλθακιστέ', ἀλλὰ περικαλυπτέα.
ἐξευρετέος γὰρ νοῦς ἀποστερητικὸς
κἀπαιόλημ'.

Στ.   οἴμοι, τίς ἂν δῆτ' ἐπιβάλοι
ἐξ ἀρνακίδων γνώμην ἀποστερητρίδα;   730

Σω. φέρε νυν ἀθρήσω πρῶτον, ὅ τι δρᾷ, τουτονί.
οὗτος, καθεύδεις;

Στ.   μὰ τὸν Ἀπόλλω 'γὼ μὲν οὔ.

Σω. ἔχεις τι;

Στ.   μὰ Δί' οὐ δῆτ' ἔγωγ'.

Σω.   οὐδὲν πάνυ;

Στ. οὐδέν γε, πλὴν ἢ τὸ πέος ἐν τῇ δεξιᾷ.

720 ἔτι V<u>n</u>: ἐπι R.
728 ἐξευρετέος N Suda^rell·: ἐξευρητέος RVE Suda^GMpc : εὑρητέος Kθ.

78

and then on top of all these miseries   720
here I am whistling in the dark
within an ace of being lost once and for all!

SOCRATES [*coming out*]: Here, you, what are you doing?   *
Aren't you thinking?

STREPSIADES: What, me? Yes, I am, I swear.

SOCRATES: And what have you thought of?

STREPSIADES: Whether there'll be anything left of me when   725
the bugs have finished.

SOCRATES: Oh, to hell with you! [*He goes inside.*]

STREPSIADES [*calling after him*]: I'm in hell right now, mate!

CHORUS-LEADER: You must not be soft, you must cover
right up; for you have to think up a defraudative idea, a piece of
chicanery.

STREPSIADES: Ah, if only instead of lambskins someone   730
would throw over me a lovely bit of . . . fraudulent ingenuity!

SOCRATES; [*coming out*]: All right, let me see first of all
what this fellow's doing. [*To Strepsiades*] Hey, you, are you
asleep?

STREPSIADES [*uncovering his head*]: By Apollo, not me.

SOCRATES: Have you managed to get hold of anything?

STREPSIADES: No, I really haven't.

SOCRATES: Nothing at all?

STREPSIADES: Nothing — except I've got hold of my cock
in my right hand.

Σω. οὐκ ἐγκαλυψάμενος ταχέως τι φροντιεῖς; 735

Στ. περὶ τοῦ; σὺ γάρ μοι τοῦτο φράσον, ὦ Σώκρατες.

Σω. αὐτὸς ὅ τι βούλει πρῶτον ἐξευρεῖν λέγε.

Στ. ἀκήκοας μυριάκις ἁγὼ βούλομαι·
περὶ τῶν τόκων, ὅπως ἂν ἀποδῶ μηδενί.

Σω. ἴθι νυν καλύπτου, καὶ σχάσας τὴν φροντίδα 740
λεπτὴν κατὰ μικρὸν περιφρόνει τὰ πράγματα,
ὀρθῶς διαιρῶν καὶ σκοπῶν.

Στ.   οἴμοι τάλας.

Σω. ἔχ' ἀτρέμα· κἂν ἀπορῇς τι τῶν νοημάτων,
ἀφεὶς ἄπελθε, κᾆτα τῇ γνώμῃ πάλιν
κίνησον αὖθις αὐτὸ καὶ ζυγώθρισον. 745

Στ. ὦ Σωκρατίδιον φίλτατον.

Σω.   τί, ὦ γέρον;

Στ. ἔχω τόκου γνώμην ἀποστερητικήν.

Σω. ἐπίδειξον αὐτήν.

Στ.   εἰπὲ δή νύν μοι—

Σω.   τὸ τί;

Στ. γυναῖκα φαρμακίδ' εἰ πριάμενος Θετταλην
καθέλοιμι νύκτωρ τὴν σελήνην, εἶτα δὴ 750
αὐτὴν καθείρξαιμ' εἰς λοφεῖον στρογγύλον,

737 πρῶτον ἐξευρεῖν P14, Tzetzes in Σ^U: πρῶτος ἐξευρεῖν n:
      πρῶτος ἐξευρὼν RV.
744 τῇ γνώμῃ Reiske: τὴν γνώμην codd.

SOCRATES: Cover up, will you, and think of something, fast.   735
STREPSIADES: What about? You tell me that, Socrates.

SOCRATES: You say yourself what is the first thing you want
to discover.

STREPSIADES: You've heard a million times what I want.
About interest, so I won't have to pay it to anyone.

SOCRATES: Very well then, cover your head [*Strepsiades*   740 *
does so]; now slice your thought into minute parts and contemplate the subject piece by piece, investigating and analysing correctly.

STREPSIADES [*again in torment from the bugs*]: Aah! Help!

SOCRATES: Keep still; and if you reach an impasse with one
of your ideas, let it go and move away from it, and later on set it   745
back in motion again in your mind and weigh it in the balance.

STREPSIADES [*after an interval, getting out of bed*]: My
dearest sweet Socrates!

SOCRATES: What is it, old man?

STREPSIADES: I have a defraudative device for avoiding
interest.

SOCRATES: Let us hear it.

STREPSIADES: Well, tell me —

SOCRATES: What?

STREPSIADES: If I bought a Thessalian sorceress and had
her draw down the moon at night, and then shut it up in a round   750
case, like putting away a mirror, and then kept a close watch on it —

81

ὥσπερ κάτροπτον, κᾆτα τηροίην ἔχων—

Σω. τί δῆτα τοῦτ' ἂν ὠφελήσειέν σ';

Στ.   ὅ τι;
εἰ μηκέτ' ἀνατέλλοι σελήνη μηδαμοῦ,
οὐκ ἂν ἀποδοίην τοὺς τόκους.

Σω.   ὁτιὴ τί δή;   755

Στ. ὁτιὴ κατὰ μῆνα τἀργύριον δανείζεται.

Σω. εὖ γ'. ἀλλ' ἕτερον αὖ σοι προβαλῶ τι δεξιόν.
εἴ σοι γράφοιτο πεντετάλαντός τις δίκη,
ὅπως ἂν αὐτὴν ἀφανίσειας εἰπέ μοι.

Στ. ὅπως; ὅπως; οὐκ οἶδ'. ἀτὰρ ζητητέον.   760

Σω. μή νυν περὶ σαυτὸν ἴλλε τὴν γνώμην ἀεί,
ἀλλ' ἀποχάλα τὴν φροντίδ' εἰς τὸν ἀέρα,
λινόδετον ὥσπερ μηλολόνθην τοῦ ποδός.

Στ. ηὕρηκ' ἀφάνισιν τῆς δίκης σοφωτάτην,
ὥστ' αὐτὸν ὁμολογεῖν σέ μοι.

Σω.   ποίαν τινά;   765

Στ. ἤδη παρὰ τοῖσι φαρμακοπώλαις τὴν λίθον
ταύτην ἑόρακας, τὴν καλήν, τὴν διαφανῆ,
ἀφ' ἧς τὸ πῦρ ἅπτουσι;

Σω.   τὴν ὕαλον λέγεις;

Στ. ἔγωγε. φέρε, τί δῆτ' ἄν, εἰ ταύτην λαβών,
ὁπότ' ἐγγράφοιτο τὴν δίκην ὁ γραμματεύς,   770

---

752 κάτροπτον Dover: κάτοπτρον (-προν V^{ac}) codd.
770 ὁπότ' ἐγγράφοιτο Cobet: ὁπότε γράφοιτο codd.: ὁπόταν γράφοιτο
      Suda.

82

SOCRATES: Well, what good would that do you?

STREPSIADES: What good? If no moon were ever to rise 755
again anywhere, I'd never pay my interest.

SOCRATES: Why not?

STREPSIADES: Because money is lent out by the month.

SOCRATES: Very good. I'll set you another tricky problem.
Suppose a lawsuit was entered against you for five talents, tell me
how you'd dispose of it.

STREPSIADES: How? how? I don't know. I must think it 760
out.

SOCRATES: Now don't keep your thoughts wound closely
round you all the time, but pay your thought out a bit into the air,
like a cockchafer tethered by the leg with a thread.

STREPSIADES [*after an interval*]: I've found a really ingenious disposal method for that lawsuit, good enough to make even 765
you agree with me.

SOCRATES: What sort of method?

STREPSIADES: Have you ever seen that stone at the druggists', the beautiful transparent one they use to light fires?

SOCRATES: Do you mean glass?

STREPSIADES: I do. Well, look, what if I took that, and
when the clerk was getting the case entered on his list, if I was to 770

ἀπωτέρω στὰς ὧδε πρὸς τὸν ἥλιον
τὰ γράμματ' ἐκτήξαιμι τῆς ἐμῆς δίκης;

Σω. σοφῶς γε, νὴ τὰς Χάριτας.

Στ.   οἴμ', ὡς ἥδομαι
ὅτι πεντετάλαντος διαγέγραπταί μοι δίκη.

Σω. ἄγε δὴ ταχέως τουτὶ ξυνάρπασον.

Στ.   τὸ τί;   775

Σω. ὅπως ἀποστρέψαις ἂν ἀντιδικῶν δίκην,
μέλλων ὀφλήσειν, μὴ παρόντων μαρτύρων.

Στ. φαυλότατα καὶ ῥᾷστ'.

Σω.   εἰπὲ δή.

Στ.   καὶ δὴ λέγω.
εἰ πρόσθεν ἔτι μιᾶς ἐνεστώσης δίκης
πρὶν τὴν ἐμὴν καλεῖσθ' ἀπαγξαίμην τρέχων.   780

Σω. οὐδὲν λέγεις.

Στ.   νὴ τοὺς θεοὺς ἔγωγ', ἐπεὶ
οὐδεὶς κατ' ἐμοῦ τεθνεῶτος εἰσάξει δίκην.

Σω. ὑθλεῖς. ἄπερρ'· οὐκ ἂν διδαξαίμην σ' ἔτι.

Στ. ὁτιὴ τί; ναὶ πρὸς τῶν θεῶν, ὦ Σώκρατες.

Σω. ἀλλ' εὐθὺς ἐπιλήθει σύ γ' ἅττ' ἂν καὶ μάθῃς.   785
ἐπεὶ τί νυνὶ πρῶτον ἐδιδάχθης; λέγε.

Στ. φέρ' ἴδω, τί μέντοι πρῶτον ἦν; τί πρῶτον ἦν;
τίς ἦν ἐν ᾗ ματτόμεθα μέντοι τἄλφιτα;
οἴμοι, τίς ἦν;

Σω.   οὐκ ἐς κόρακας ἀποφθερεῖ,

84

stand some distance from him, like this, between him and the sun, and make the writing melt away where my case was?

SOCRATES: That's clever, by the Graces!

STREPSIADES: My goodness, I *am* pleased! I've struck out a five-talent lawsuit!

SOCRATES: Come on now, hurry up and get your teeth into this one. 775

STREPSIADES: What?

SOCRATES: How would you contest and rebut a case brought against you which you were on the point of losing, if you had no witnesses?

STREPSIADES: Child's play — easy as anything.

SOCRATES: Tell me.

STREPSIADES: All right, I am. Suppose that when there were still one case pending before mine was called on, I were to run off and hang myself? 780

SOCRATES: You're talking nonsense.

STREPSIADES: Heavens above, it's perfect sense; nobody's going to bring a case to court against me when I'm dead.

SOCRATES: You're drivelling. Get the hell out of here. I'm not going to teach you any more.

STREPSIADES: Why not? Do, Socrates, in the gods' name.

SOCRATES: But anything you do learn you forget right away. For instance, tell me, what was the first thing you were taught just now? 785

STREPSIADES: Let me see now, what *was* the first thing? what was first? what *was* that feminine thing that we knead groats in? God help me, what was it?

SOCRATES: Oh, away and to blazes with you, you stupid 790

ἐπιλησμότατον καὶ σκαιότατον γερόντιον;   790

Στ. οἴμοι· τί οὖν δῆθ' ὁ κακοδαίμων πείσομαι;
ἀπὸ γὰρ ὀλοῦμαι μὴ μαθὼν γλωττοστροφεῖν.
ἀλλ', ὦ Νεφέλαι, χρηστόν τι συμβουλεύσατε.

Χο. ἡμεῖς μέν, ὦ πρεσβῦτα, συμβουλεύομεν,
εἴ σού τις υἱός ἐστιν ἐκτεθραμμένος,   795
πέμπειν ἐκεῖνον ἀντὶ σαυτοῦ μανθάνειν.

Στ. ἀλλ' ἔστ' ἔμοιγ' υἱὸς καλός τε κἀγαθός·
ἀλλ' οὐκ ἐθέλει γὰρ μανθάνειν, τί ἐγὼ πάθω;

Χο. σὺ δ' ἐπιτρέπεις;

Στ.   εὐσωματεῖ γὰρ καὶ σφριγᾷ,
κἄστ' ἐκ γυναικῶν εὐπτέρων τῶν Κοισύρας.   800
ἀτὰρ μέτειμί γ' αὐτόν· ἢν δὲ μὴ 'θέλῃ,
οὐκ ἔσθ' ὅπως οὐκ ἐξελῶ 'κ τῆς οἰκίας.
ἀλλ' ἐπανάμεινόν μ' ὀλίγον εἰσελθὼν χρόνον.

Χο. ἆρ' αἰσθάνει πλεῖστα δι' ἡ-   (ἀντ.
μᾶς ἀγάθ' αὐτίχ' ἕξων   805
μόνας θεῶν; ὡς ἕτοιμος ὅδ' ἐστὶν ἅπαντα δρᾶν ὅσ' ἂν κελεύῃς.
σὺ δ' ἀνδρὸς ἐκπεπληγμένου
καὶ φανερῶς ἐπηρμένου
γνοὺς ἀπολάψεις ὅ τι πλεῖστον δύνασαι   810
ταχέως· φιλεῖ γάρ πως τὰ τοι-
αῦθ' ἑτέρᾳ τρέπεσθαι.

Στ. οὔτοι μὰ τὴν Ὁμίχλην ἔτ' ἐνταυθοῖ μενεῖς·
ἀλλ' ἔσθι' ἐλθὼν τοὺς Μεγακλέους κίονας.   815

800 τῶν <u>n'</u> Suda $^{\lambda}\Sigma^E$ $^{i}\Sigma^{VE}$: τῶν ἀπὸ K: om. R: καὶ V.

forgetful old nitwit! [*He turns his back on Strepsiades.*]

STREPSIADES: God help me, I'm lost — what's going to happen to me now? If I don't learn to be a verbal twister, that'll be the end of me. Please, Clouds, give me some good advice.

CHORUS-LEADER: Well, old man, our advice is, if you have a grown-up son, send him to be taught instead of you.   795

STREPSIADES: Well, I have a son, a fine upstanding fellow; but he doesn't want to go to school, so what am I supposed to do?

CHORUS-LEADER: And you let him get away with it?

STREPSIADES: Yes, because he's strong and lusty, and comes   800
of a high-flying race of women, the house of Coesyra. But I'm going for him; and if he refuses, then without fail I'll throw him out of the house. [*To Socrates*] Go in and wait for me a moment.

CHORUS [*as Strepsiades enters his own house*]:
>   Do you perceive that soon
>   you will have many blessings, thanks to us   805
>   alone of the gods? For this man is ready
>   to do whatever you bid him.

[*Turning to Socrates as he goes into the Reflectory*]
>   And you, aware that the man is moonstruck
>   and is plainly in great excitement,
>   will no doubt lap up as much as you can   810
>   quickly; for such things have a sort of habit
>   of turning out otherwise than expected.

[*Strepsiades comes out of his house, driving Pheidippides before him.*]

STREPSIADES: You shan't, by Mist, you shan't stay here any longer! Go and eat the columns of Megacles' mansion.   815

Φε. ὦ δαιμόνιε, τί χρῆμα πάσχεις, ὦ πάτερ;
     οὐκ εὖ φρονεῖς, μὰ τὸν Δία τὸν Ὀλύμπιον.

Στ. ἰδού γ' ἰδοὺ Δί' Ὀλύμπιον. τῆς μωρίας·
*   τὸν Δία νομίζειν, ὄντα τηλικουτουί.

Φε. τί δὲ τοῦτ' ἐγέλασας ἐτεόν;

Στ.   ἐνθυμούμενος   820
     ὅτι παιδάριον εἶ καὶ φρονεῖς ἀρχαϊκά.
     ὅμως γε μὴν πρόσελθ', ἵν' εἰδῇς πλείονα,
     καί σοι φράσω τι πρᾶγμ', ὃ μαθὼν ἀνὴρ ἔσει.
     ὅπως δὲ τοῦτο μὴ διδάξεις μηδένα.

Φε. ἰδού· τί ἐστιν;

Στ.   ὤμοσας νυνὶ Δία.   825

Φε. ἔγωγ'.

Στ.   ὁρᾷς οὖν ὡς ἀγαθὸν τὸ μανθάνειν;
     οὐκ ἔστιν, ὦ Φειδιππίδη, Ζεύς.

Φε.   ἀλλὰ τίς;

Στ. Δῖνος βασιλεύει, τὸν Δί' ἐξεληλακώς.

Φε. αἰβοῖ· τί ληρεῖς;

Στ.   ἴσθι τοῦθ' οὕτως ἔχον.

Φε. τίς φησι ταῦτα;

Στ.   Σωκράτης ὁ Μήλιος   830
     καὶ Χαιρεφῶν, ὃς οἶδε τὰ ψυλλῶν ἴχνη.

Φε. σὺ δ' εἰς τοσοῦτον τῶν μανιῶν ἐλήλυθας

823 ὃ Hermann: ὃ σὺ codd.

88

PHEIDIPPIDES: My dear father, what *is* wrong with you? You're not in your right mind, by Olympian Zeus you're not.

STREPSIADES: Just listen to that! Olympian Zeus! How stupid can you get — believing in Zeus at your age!

PHEIDIPPIDES: Why ever do you laugh like that?   820

STREPSIADES: To think that you're such a baby and your ideas so antiquated. All the same, come to me, if you want to know more, and I'll tell you something which when you've learnt, you'll be a man. But be sure not to divulge this to anyone.

PHEIDIPPIDES [*coming close to his father*]: Here I am. What   825
is it?

STREPSIADES [*in conspiratorial tones*]: You swore just now by Zeus.

PHEIDIPPIDES [*likewise*]: I did.

STREPSIADES: Now do you see what a fine thing learning is? Pheidippides, there is no Zeus.

PHEIDIPPIDES: Then who is there?

STREPSIADES: Vortex is king, having expelled Zeus.

PHEIDIPPIDES [*aloud*]: Ugh, what rubbish is this?

STREPSIADES: I assure you that's the way it is.

PHEIDIPPIDES: Who says so?   830

STREPSIADES: Socrates the Melian and Chaerephon, who knows all about the footsteps of fleas.

PHEIDIPPIDES: And you're so far gone in your madness that

ὥστ' ἀνδράσιν πείθει χολῶσιν;

Στ.   εὐστόμει,
καὶ μηδὲν εἴπῃς φλαῦρον ἄνδρας δεξιοὺς
καὶ νοῦν ἔχοντας· ὧν ὑπὸ τῆς φειδωλίας   835
ἀπεκείρατ' οὐδεὶς πώποτ' οὐδ' ἠλείψατο
οὐδ' εἰς βαλανεῖον ἦλθε λουσόμενος· σὺ δὲ
ὥσπερ τεθνεῶτος καταλόει μου τὸν βίον.
ἀλλ' ὡς τάχιστ' ἐλθὼν ὑπὲρ ἐμοῦ μάνθανε.

Φε. τί δ' ἂν παρ' ἐκείνων καὶ μάθοι χρηστόν τις ἄν;   840

Στ. ἄληθες; ὅσαπέρ ἐστιν ἀνθρώποις σοφά.
γνώσει δὲ σαυτὸν ὡς ἀμαθὴς εἶ καὶ παχύς.
ἀλλ' ἐπανάμεινόν μ' ὀλίγον ἐνταυθοῖ χρόνον.

Φε. οἴμοι, τί δράσω, παραφρονοῦντος τοῦ πατρός;
πότερον παρανοίας αὐτὸν εἰσαγαγὼν ἕλω,   845
ἢ τοῖς σοροπηγοῖς τὴν μανίαν αὐτοῦ φράσω;

Στ. φέρ' ἴδω, σὺ τοῦτον τίνα νομίζεις; εἰπέ μοι.

Φε. ἀλεκτρυόνα.

Στ.   καλῶς γε· ταυτηνὶ δὲ τί;

Φε. ἀλεκτρυόν'.

* Στ.   ἄμφω ταὐτό; καταγέλαστος εἶ.

838 καταλόει μου Bekker: καταλούει μου vel sim. RVθ²n' Suda,
     Choeroboscus: μου καταλούει θ¹.
841 ὅσαπέρ ἐστιν Eᵖᶜ: ὅσαπέρ ἐστ' ἐν Eᵃᶜθ: ὅσαπερ N: ὅσα πάρεστιν
     R: ὅσα πάρεστ' VK.
847 τοῦτον θ: τουτονὶ RVn', whence τί for τίνα Reisig.
849 ταὐτό Vs1: ταὐτὸν RVn': ταὐτὰ K.

90

you take the word of men who've got the bile-sickness?

STREPSIADES: Mind what you say, and don't slander men of ingenuity and intelligence, men who are so thrifty that none of them has ever cut his hair or anointed himself, or gone to a bath-house to wash — whereas *you* squander my livelihood by washing yourself as if I were dead. Now go as quickly as you can and study instead of me. 835

PHEIDIPPIDES: But what that's any use could anyone *learn* from these people? 840

STREPSIADES: You ask that? All human wisdom; and you'll realise how stupid and thick *you* are. Look, wait for me here a moment. [*He goes inside.*]

PHEIDIPPIDES [*to himself*]: Heavens, what am I to do? because my father's out of his mind. Shall I take him to court and get him adjudged insane, or shall I tell the coffin-makers of his afflic-tion? 845

STREPSIADES [*returning with a slave who carries a cock and a hen*]: Let me see; tell me, what are you accustomed to call this?

PHEIDIPPIDES: A fowl.

STREPSIADES: Good; and this one?

PHEIDIPPIDES: A fowl.

STREPSIADES: Both the same? You *are* making yourself

μή νυν τὸ λοιπόν, ἀλλὰ τήνδε μὲν καλεῖν   850
ἀλεκτρύαιναν, τουτονὶ δ' ἀλέκτορα.

Φε. ἀλεκτρύαιναν; ταῦτ' ἔμαθες τὰ δεξιὰ
εἴσω παρελθὼν ἄρτι παρὰ τοὺς γηγενεῖς;

Στ. χἅτερά γε πόλλ'· ἀλλ' ὅ τι μάθοιμ' ἑκάστοτε
ἐπελανθανόμην ἂν εὐθὺς ὑπὸ πλήθους ἐτῶν.   855

Φε. διὰ ταῦτα δὴ καὶ θοἰμάτιον ἀπώλεσας;

Στ. ἀλλ' οὐκ ἀπολώλεκ', ἀλλὰ καταπεφρόντικα.

Φε. τὰς δ' ἐμβάδας ποῖ τέτροφας, ὦνόητε σύ;

Στ. ὥσπερ Περικλέης εἰς τὸ δέον ἀπώλεσα.
ἀλλ' ἴθι, βάδιζ', ἴωμεν. εἶτα τῷ πατρὶ   860
πιθόμενος ἐξάμαρτε. κἀγώ τοί ποτε
οἶδ' ἐξέτει σοι τραυλίσαντι πιθόμενος·
ὃν πρῶτον ὀβολὸν ἔλαβον ἡλιαστικόν,
τούτου 'πριάμην σοι Διασίοις ἁμαξίδα.

Φε. ἦ μὴν σὺ τούτοις τῷ χρόνῳ ποτ' ἀχθέσει.   865

Στ. εὖ γ', ὅτι ἐπείσθης. δεῦρο δεῦρ', ὦ Σώκρατες,
ἔξελθ'· ἄγω γάρ σοι τὸν υἱὸν τουτονί,
ἄκοντ' ἀναπείσας.

Σω.   νηπύτιος γάρ ἐστ' ἔτι
καὶ τῶν κρεμαστῶν οὐ τρίβων τῶν ἐνθάδε.

855 ἐτῶν Κ: τῶν ἐτῶν RVn'.
861 πιθόμενος Bentley: πειθόμενος codd., Eustathius.
862 πιθόμενος θ^{2pc}: πειθόμενος RVθ^{1}n' Suda, Zonaras.
869 κρεμαστῶν Σ^{RV} 869, Σ^{VM} 870: κρεμαστρῶν Σ^{RE} 870: κρεμαθρῶν
       sim. codd. Suda ^{i}Σ^{EM} 869 ^{λ}Σ^{Np1} 869 Σ^{Np5} 870, Σ Wasps 14
       Eustathius.

92

ridiculous. Now don't do that in future, but call this one a "fowl- 850
ess" and that one a "fowler".

PHEIDIPPIDES: "Fowless"? Are those the pearls of wisdom
you picked up on your recent entry into the house of those Children of Earth?

STREPSIADES: Yes, and much else too; but every time I
learnt anything, I'd forget it right away because I was too old. 855

PHEIDIPPIDES: Oh, *that's* why you've lost your cloak, is it?

STREPSIADES: I haven't lost it, I've invested it in knowledge.

PHEIDIPPIDES: And what have you done with your shoes,
you fathead?

STREPSIADES: I lost them "for essential purposes", as
Pericles would have put it. But come on, move, let's go. So *do* 860
wrong, at your father's request. I know, I tell you, that once I
complied with your request when you were a lisping six-year-old:
the first obol of jury pay I received, I used it to buy you a toy cart
for the Diasia.

PHEIDIPPIDES [*reluctantly following him towards the Reflec-*
tory]: I swear the time will come when you'll be sorry for this. 865

STREPSIADES: Good for you, you've obeyed me. Come
here, come here, Socrates, come outside! [*Socrates does so.*] I
bring you my son here; I talked him into coming, though he didn't
want to.

SOCRATES: No, he's still an infant, and doesn't know the
ropes and lashings here.

Φε. αὐτὸς τρίβων εἴης ἄν, εἰ κρέμαιό γε.   870

Στ. οὐκ ἐς κόρακας; καταρᾷ σὺ τῷ διδασκάλῳ;

Σω. ἰδοὺ κρέμαι'· ὡς ἠλίθιον ἐφθέγξατο
     καὶ τοῖσι χείλεσιν διερρυηκόσιν.
     πῶς ἂν μάθοι ποθ' οὗτος ἀπόφευξιν δίκης
     ἢ κλῆσιν ἢ χαύνωσιν ἀναπειστηρίαν;   875
     καίτοι ταλάντου γ' αὐτ' ἔμαθεν Ὑπέρβολος.

Στ. ἀμέλει, δίδασκε· θυμόσοφός ἐστιν φύσει.
     εὐθύς γέ τοι παιδάριον ὂν τυννουτονὶ
     ἔπλαττεν ἔνδον οἰκίας ναῦς τ' ἔγλυφεν
     ἁμαξίδας τε συκίνας ἠργάζετο   880
     κἀκ τῶν σιδίων βατράχους ἐποίει πῶς δοκεῖς.
     ὅπως δ' ἐκείνω τὼ λόγω μαθήσεται,
     τὸν κρείττον', ὅστις ἐστί, καὶ τὸν ἥττονα,
     ὃς τἄδικα λέγων ἀνατρέπει τὸν κρείττονα·
     ἐὰν δὲ μή, τὸν γοῦν ἄδικον πάσῃ τέχνῃ.   885

Σω. αὐτὸς μαθήσεται παρ' αὐτοῖν τοῖν λόγοιν·
     ἐγὼ δ' ἀπέσομαι.

Στ.   τοῦτό νυν μέμνησ', ὅπως
     πρὸς πάντα τὰ δίκαι' ἀντιλέγειν δυνήσεται.

ΚΡΕΙΤΤΩΝ ΛΟΓΟΣ
     χώρει δευρί, δεῖξον σαυτὸν
     τοῖσι θεαταῖς, καίπερ θρασὺς ὤν.   890

---

872 κρέμαι' (-αιο) Md1[1]: κρέμαιό γ' RVn Md1[2]: γε κρέμαι' Reisig.
876 ταλάντου γ' αὐτ' Reisig: γε ταλάντου τοῦτ' RV: ταλάντου
     τοῦτ' n Suda.
880 συκίνας Naber: σκυτίνας codd. Suda.

PHEIDIPPIDES: Hang *you* on the end of a wope and you'd   870
weceive a good lashing yourself!

STREPSIADES: Damn you to blazes, how dare you curse
your teacher?

SOCRATES: Listen to his "weceive"! What a babyish pronunciation he gave it, with his lips sagging apart! How is he ever
going to learn effective forensic defence, or the summons, or per-   875
suasion by bombast? And yet Hyperbolus did learn them, for a
talent.

STREPSIADES: Oh, don't worry, teach him. He's naturally
gifted. At any rate, right from the start, when he was a little boy
that high, he made clay houses at home and carved out boats, and   880
made carts of figwood and frogs of pomegranate peel, you can't
think how cleverly. And make sure he learns those two Arguments,
the Better, whatever that may be, and the Worse, which can plead
an unjust cause and overthrow the Better; or if not both, then at   885
least and at all costs the Wrongful one.

SOCRATES: He will learn himself from the Arguments in
person; I shall not be there.

STREPSIADES [*as Socrates goes inside*]: Remember this
now, that he must be able to argue against every kind of justified
claim.

[*The Better Argument comes out of the Reflectory.*]

BETTER ARGUMENT [*to Worse Argument, who is still
inside*]: Come here, show yourself to the audience – though you're   890
brazen enough for that anyway.

ΗΤΤΩΝ ΛΟΓΟΣ
    ἴθ' ὅπου χρῄζεις· πολὺ γὰρ μᾶλλόν σ'
    ἐν τοῖς πολλοῖσι λέγων ἀπολῶ.

Κρ.   ἀπολεῖς σύ; τίς ὤν;

Ητ.   λόγος.

Κρ.   ἥττων γ' ὤν.

Ητ.   ἀλλά σε νικῶ τὸν ἐμοῦ κρείττω
    φάσκοντ' εἶναι.

Κρ.   τί σοφὸν ποιῶν;   8

Ητ.   γνώμας καινὰς ἐξευρίσκων.

Κρ.   ταῦτα γὰρ ἀνθεῖ διὰ τουτουσὶ
    τοὺς ἀνοήτους.

Ητ.   οὔκ, ἀλλὰ σοφούς.

Κρ.   ἀπολῶ σε κακῶς.

Ητ.   εἰπέ, τί ποιῶν;

Κρ.   τὰ δίκαια λέγων.   9

Ητ.   ἀλλ' ἀνατρέψω γ' αὔτ' ἀντιλέγων·
    οὐδε γὰρ εἶναι πάνυ φημὶ Δίκην.

Κρ.   οὐκ εἶναι φής;

Ητ.   φέρε γάρ, ποῦ 'στιν;

Κρ.   παρὰ τοῖσι θεοῖς.

Ητ.   πῶς δῆτα Δίκης οὔσης ὁ Ζεὺς
    οὐκ ἀπόλωλεν τὸν πατέρ' αὑτοῦ   ς
    δήσας;

Κρ.   αἰβοῖ, τουτὶ καὶ δὴ

WORSE ARGUMENT [*strolling out after him*] : Go wherever you like. Speaking in public I'll be all the more certain to destroy you.

BETTER ARGUMENT: You destroy me? Who do you think you are?

WORSE ARGUMENT: An Argument.

BETTER ARGUMENT: Yes, but an Inferior one.

WORSE ARGUMENT: Yes, but I'll defeat you who vaunt yourself Better than me. 894-5 *

BETTER ARGUMENT: Oh, what'll you do that's so clever?

WORSE ARGUMENT: Devise a new set of principles.

BETTER ARGUMENT: Yes, that's all the rage now, thanks to these fools [*indicating the audience*].

WORSE ARGUMENT: Not fools, but intelligent people.

BETTER ARGUMENT: I'll massacre you.

WORSE ARGUMENT: Tell me, how will you do it?

BETTER ARGUMENT: By putting my just case. 900

WORSE ARGUMENT: But I'll overthrow it by counter-argument. I say that Justice simply doesn't exist.

BETTER ARGUMENT: You say she doesn't exist?

WORSE ARGUMENT: Well then, where is she?

BETTER ARGUMENT: She dwells with the gods.

WORSE ARGUMENT: Then if Justice exists, how come Zeus hasn't been destroyed for imprisoning his father? 905

BETTER ARGUMENT: Ugh, this really gets worse and worse. Give me a basin!

χωρεῖ τὸ κακόν. δότε μοι λεκάνην.

Ητ.   τυφογέρων εἶ κἀνάρμοστος.

Κρ.   καταπύγων εἶ κἀναίσχυντος.

Ητ.   ῥόδα μ' εἴρηκας.

Κρ.   καὶ βωμολόχος.   910

Ητ.   κρίνεσι στεφανοῖς.

Κρ.   καὶ πατραλοίας.

Ητ.   χρύσῳ πάττων μ' οὐ γιγνώσκεις.

Κρ.   οὐ δῆτα πρὸ τοῦ γ', ἀλλὰ μολύβδῳ.

Ητ.   νῦν δέ γε κόσμος τοῦτ' ἐστίν ἐμοί.

Κρ.   θρασὺς εἶ πολλοῦ.

Ητ.   σὺ δέ γ' ἀρχαῖος.   915

Κρ.   διὰ σὲ δὲ φοιτᾶν
οὐδεὶς ἐθέλει τῶν μειρακίων·
καὶ γνωσθήσει ποτ' Ἀθηναίοις
οἷα διδάσκεις τοὺς ἀνοήτους.

Ητ.   αὐχμεῖς αἰσχρῶς.

Κρ.   σὺ δέ γ' εὖ πράττεις·   920
καίτοι πρότερόν γ' ἐπτώχευες,
Τήλεφος εἶναι Μυσὸς φάσκων,
ἐκ πηριδίου
γνώμας τρώγων Πανδελετείους.

918   καὶ N: om. RVn'.
924   -ειους Suda^GMpc, Tricl.: -ίους Rn Suda^rell.: -ίας V.

WORSE ARGUMENT: You're senile and out of touch.

BETTER ARGUMENT: You're a shameless faggot.

WORSE ARGUMENT: Your words are like roses! 910

BETTER ARGUMENT: And an impudent trickster.

WORSE ARGUMENT: You're crowning me with lilies!

BETTER ARGUMENT: And a father-beater.

WORSE ARGUMENT: You don't realize it, but you're spangling me with gold.

BETTER ARGUMENT: Those names weren't gold in the old days, they were lead.

WORSE ARGUMENT: But now I regard them as an honour.

BETTER ARGUMENT: You're thoroughly brazen. 915

WORSE ARGUMENT: And you're thoroughly archaic.

BETTER ARGUMENT: It's because of you that none of the young lads is prepared to go to school; and one day the Athenians will realise what sort of teaching the silly fools get from you.

WORSE ARGUMENT: You're repulsively dirty. 920

BETTER ARGUMENT: While *you're* thriving — though you *used* to be a beggar, claiming to be the Mysian Telephus and nibbling Pandeletean maxims from a little bag.

Ητ.   ὤμοι σοφίας—

Κρ.   ὤμοι μανίας—   925

Ητ.   ἧς ἐμνήσθης.

Κρ.   —τῆς σῆς, πόλεως θ'
ἥτις σε τρέφει
λυμαινόμενον τοῖς μειρακίοις.

Ητ.   οὐχὶ διδάξεις τοῦτον Κρόνος ὤν.

Κρ.   εἴπερ γ' αὐτὸν σωθῆναι χρὴ   930
καὶ μὴ λαλιὰν μόνον ἀσκῆσαι.

Ητ.   δεῦρ' ἴθι, τοῦτον δ' ἔα μαίνεσθαι.

Κρ.   κλαύσει, τὴν χεῖρ' ἢν ἐπιβάλλῃς.

Χο.   παύσασθε μάχης καὶ λοιδορίας.
ἀλλ' ἐπίδειξαι σύ τε τοὺς προτέρους   935
ἅττ' ἐδίδασκες, σύ τε τὴν καινὴν
παίδευσιν, ὅπως ἂν ἀκούσας σφῷν
ἀντιλεγόντοιν κρίνας φοιτᾷ.

Κρ.   δρᾶν ταῦτ' ἐθέλω.

Ητ.   κἄγωγ' ἐθέλω.

Χο.   φέρε δή, πότερος λέξει πρότερος;   940

Ητ.   τούτῳ δώσω·
κᾆτ' ἐκ τούτων ὧν ἂν λέξῃ
ῥηματίοισιν καινοῖς αὐτὸν
καὶ διανοίαις κατατοξεύσω·

925-6   are thus arranged in RV (perhaps implying that the two speak
        simultaneously): in n̲ ἧς ἐμνήσθης precedes ὤμοι μανίας.
933   ἐπιβάλλ- N: ἐπιβάλ- RVn̲'.

100

WORSE ARGUMENT: Oh, the cleverness —   925

BETTER ARGUMENT: Oh, the lunacy —

WORSE ARGUMENT: — of what you've mentioned!

BETTER ARGUMENT: — of you, and of a city that feeds you
while you corrupt its youth!

WORSE ARGUMENT: You're not going to educate this boy,
you Cronus!

BETTER ARGUMENT: Yes, I am, if he's to be saved, and not   930
to study mere idle blabber.

WORSE ARGUMENT [to Pheidippides]: Come here and leave
him to his raving.

BETTER ARGUMENT: I'll make you howl if you lay a hand
on him!

CHORUS-LEADER: Stop your wrangling and abuse. Rather   935
give an exposition, you [to Better Argument] of the teaching you
gave to the men of old, and you of the new education, so that he
may hear both your opposing arguments, make his decision, and
join the appropriate school.

BETTER ARGUMENT: I am willing to do that.

WORSE ARGUMENT: And I am willing too.

CHORUS-LEADER: All right then, which of you will speak   940
first?

WORSE ARGUMENT: I'll concede my opponent that right;
and then, on the basis of what he says, I'll shoot him down with
deft new phrases and ideas; and the end will be that if he utters so   945

τὸ τελευταῖον δ', ἢν ἀναγρύξῃ,   945
τὸ πρόσωπον ἅπαν καὶ τὠφθαλμὼ
κεντούμενος, ὥσπερ ὑπ' ἀνθρηνῶν,
ὑπὸ τῶν γνωμῶν ἀπολεῖται.

Χο. νῦν δείξετον τὼ πισύνω   (στρ.
     τοῖς περιδεξίοισιν   950
     λόγοισι καὶ φροντίσι καὶ
     γνωμοτύποις μερίμναις
*   ὁπότερος αὐτοῖν †λέγων ἀμείνων†
     φανήσεται. νῦν γὰρ ἅπας
     ἐνθάδε κίνδυνος ἀνεῖται σοφίας,   955
     ἧς πέρι τοῖς ἐμοῖς φίλοις
     ἐστὶν ἀγὼν μέγιστος.

ἀλλ', ὦ πολλοῖς τοὺς πρεσβυτέρους ἤθεσι χρηστοῖς στεφανώσας,
ῥῆξον φωνὴν ᾗτινι χαίρεις, καὶ τὴν σαυτοῦ φύσιν εἰπέ.   960

Κρ. λέξω τοίνυν τὴν ἀρχαίαν παιδείαν ὡς διέκειτο,
*   ὅτ' ἐγὼ τὰ δίκαια λέγων ἤνθουν καὶ σωφροσύνη 'νενόμιστο.
     πρῶτον μὲν ἔδει παιδὸς φωνὴν γρύξαντος μηδέν' ἀκοῦσαι·
     εἶτα βαδίζειν ἐν ταῖσιν ὁδοῖς εὐτάκτως εἰς κιθαριστοῦ
     τοὺς κωμήτας γυμνοὺς ἀθρόους, κεἰ κριμνώδη κατανείφοι.   965
     εἶτ' αὖ προμαθεῖν ᾆσμ' ἐδίδασκεν, τὼ μηρὼ μὴ ξυνέχοντας,
     ἢ "Παλλάδα περσέπολιν δεινὰν" ἢ "τηλέπορόν τι βόαμα",
     ἐντειναμένους τὴν ἁρμονίαν ἣν οἱ πατέρες παρέδωκαν.
     εἰ δέ τις αὐτῶν βωμολοχεύσαιτ' ἢ κάμψειέν τινα καμπήν,   969

953 †λέγων ἀμείνων† codd.: ἀμείνων Wilamowitz: perh. e.g. <περιὼν>.
954 φανήσεται Rθ[1]n': γενήσεται V: γε φανήσεται θ[2].
967 περσέπολιν A Σ[K], Aristides: περσέπτολιν RVn Σ[RVEM], Stobaeus:
     Σ[U] exhibits both forms.

102

much as a grunt, then stung by my arguments, as if by hornets,
all over his face and eyes, he will perish.

      CHORUS: Now these two will show, who trust
                 in their ultra-clever   950
                 arguments and thoughts and
                 phrase-coining cogitations,
                 which of them will prove himself
                 <superior>. For now everything
                 is at stake here for Learning,   955
                 in regard to which, for my friends,
                 this is the crunch.

      CHORUS-LEADER [*to Better Argument*] : Now, you who
adorned the men of old with abundance of virtuous disposition,
utter forth a sound, that in which you rejoice, and describe your   960
own nature.

      BETTER ARGUMENT: Very well, I will describe how the
old education was managed, in the days when I and my just cause
flourished and it was the done thing to be decent. First of all, it
was the rule that not a sound should be heard from a boy, not a
grunt; then, the boys of the neighbourhood had to walk through   964-5
the streets to the music-master's together and in good order, and
without cloaks, even if it was snowing as thick as barley groats.
Then again he would teach them to learn a song by heart, and not
to keep their thighs together while doing so — a song such as "Pallas
the terrible, sacker of cities" or "A strain that sounds afar", singing it in the mode their fathers handed down. And if any of them   969
played the clown or introduced some convolution such as the mod-   971

οἵας οἱ νῦν, τὰς κατὰ Φρῦνιν ταύτας τὰς δυσκολοκάμπτους,   971
ἐπετρίβετο τυπτόμενος πολλὰς ὡς τὰς Μούσας ἀφανίζων.
ἐν παιδοτρίβου δὲ καθίζοντας τὸν μηρὸν ἔδει προβαλέσθαι
*   τοὺς παῖδας, ὅπως τοῖς ἔξωθεν μηδὲν δείξειαν ἀπηνές·
*   εἶτ' αὖ πάλιν αὖθις ἀνισταμένους συμψῆσαι, καὶ προνοεῖσθαι 975
εἴδωλον τοῖσιν ἐρασταῖσιν τῆς ἥβης μὴ καταλείπειν.
ἠλείψατο δ' ἂν τοὐμφαλοῦ οὐδεὶς παῖς ὑπένερθεν τότ' ἄν, ὥστε
τοῖς αἰδοίοισι δρόσος καὶ χνοῦς ὥσπερ μήλοισιν ἐπήνθει·
οὐδ' ἂν μαλακὴν φυρασάμενος τὴν φωνὴν πρὸς τὸν ἐραστὴν
αὐτὸς ἑαυτὸν προαγωγεύων τοῖς ὀφθαλμοῖς ἐβάδιζεν.   980
οὐδ' ἀνελέσθαι δειπνοῦντ' ἐξῆν κεφάλαιον τῆς ῥαφανῖδος,
οὐδ' ἄννηθον τῶν πρεσβυτέρων ἁρπάζειν οὐδὲ σέλινον,
οὐδ' ὀψοφαγεῖν, οὐδὲ κιχλίζειν, οὐδ' ἴσχειν τὼ πόδ' ἐναλλάξ.

Ητ.   ἀρχαῖά γε καὶ Διπολιώδη καὶ τεττίγων ἀνάμεστα
καὶ Κηδείδου καὶ Βουφονίων.

Κρ.   ἀλλ' οὖν ταῦτ' ἐστὶν ἐκεῖνα,   985
ἐξ ὧν ἄνδρας Μαραθωνομάχας ἡμὴ παίδευσις ἔθρεψεν.
σὺ δὲ τοὺς νῦν εὐθὺς ἐν ἱματίοισι διδάσκεις ἐντετυλίχθαι·
ὥστε μ' ἀπάγχεσθ', ὅταν, ὀρχεῖσθαι Παναθηναίοις δέον αὐτούς,
τὴν ἀσπίδα τῆς κωλῆς προέχων ἀμελῇ τῆς Τριτογενείης.

[970] was a line quoted by the Suda (χ296) which Valckenaer inserted
      here: it is absent from mss., papyri, ancient quotations,
      and Suda δ1650, κ2647.

975 ἀνισταμένους n̲ Suda, Stobaeus:]νους Π8:]νοις Π8 : ἀνιστά-
     μενον RV.

982 ἄννηθον Dindorf: ἄνηθον RV Suda, Stobaeus:]θον Π8: ἂν
     ἄνηθον n̲.

985 Κηδ- Π8² Suda^V, cf. IG i² 770.3, Et. Mag. 166.4, Photius:
     Κηθ- ^iHesychius: Κειδ- Stobaeus: Κηκ- (Κικ- Ε ^λΣΕ, Κυκ-
     Ν) Π8¹ codd. Suda^rell. ΣRVVs1 λΣΕ λSuda.

989 τῆς codd. Stobaeus: τις Ct1^ac.

erns use, those annoying twists in the style of Phrynis, he was
thrashed hard and often for disfiguring the music. At the gymna-
stic trainer's the boys, when they sat down, had to cover themselves
with their thighs, so as not to expose to the onlookers anything that
was — cruel; and then, when they stood up again, they had to smooth   975
the sand down, and take care not to leave behind for their lovers the
impress of their manhood. In those days, too, no boy would anoint
himself below the navel, and so on their private parts there was a
coat of dewy down like on quinces; nor would he water down his
voice to speak tenderly to his lover, and walk along making eyes and   980
being his own pimp. Nor was he allowed when dining to pick up a
head of the radish, nor to snatch his elders' dill or celery, nor to eat
dainties, nor to giggle, nor to have his legs crossed.   *

    WORSE ARGUMENT: What antiquated rot, smelling of the
Dipolieia, and crawling with cicadas, Cedeides and ritual bovicide!   985

    BETTER ARGUMENT: But what matters is that these are the
ways in which my education bred the men who fought at Marathon.
While *you* teach the young of today to swaddle themselves in cloaks
right from the start; which makes me choke with rage, when they
have to dance at the Panathenaea, and one of them holds his shield
in front of his ham, caring nothing for Tritogeneia. So, my lad,   990

πρὸς ταῦτ', ὦ μειράκιον, θαρρῶν ἐμὲ τὸν κρείττω λόγον αἱροῦ·
κἀπιστήσει μισεῖν ἀγορὰν καὶ βαλανείων ἀπέχεσθαι,   991
καὶ τοῖς αἰσχροῖς αἰσχύνεσθαι, κἄν σκώπτῃ τίς σε φλέγεσθαι,
καὶ τῶν θάκων τοῖς πρεσβυτέροις ὑπανίστασθαι προσιοῦσιν,
καὶ μὴ περὶ τοὺς σαυτοῦ γονέας σκαιουργεῖν, ἄλλο τε μηδὲν
*   αἰσχρὸν ποιεῖν, ὅ τι τῆς Αἰδοῦς μέλλει τἄγαλμ' †ἀναπλήσειν†·
μηδ' εἰς ὀρχηστρίδος εἰσᾴττειν, ἵνα μὴ πρὸς ταῦτα κεχηνὼς   996
μήλῳ βληθεὶς ὑπὸ πορνιδίου τῆς εὐκλείας ἀποθραυσθῇς·
μηδ' ἀντειπεῖν τῷ πατρὶ μηδέν, μηδ' Ἰαπετὸν καλέσαντα
μνησικακῆσαι τὴν ἡλικίαν, ἐξ ἧς ἐνεοττοτροφήθης.

Ητ.   εἰ ταῦτ', ὦ μειράκιον, πείσει τούτῳ, νὴ τὸν Διόνυσον   1000
τοῖς Ἱπποκράτους υἱέσιν εἴξεις, καί σε καλοῦσι βλιτομάμμαν.

Κρ.   ἀλλ' οὖν λιπαρός γε καὶ εὐανθὴς ἐν γυμνασίοις διατρίψεις,
οὐ στωμύλλων κατὰ τὴν ἀγορὰν τριβολεκτράπελ', οἷάπερ οἱ νῦν,
οὐδ' ἑλκόμενος περὶ πραγματίου γλισχραντιλογεξεπιτρίπτου·
*   ἀλλ' εἰς Ἀκαδημείαν κατιὼν ὑπὸ ταῖς μορίαις ἀποθρέξει   1005
στεφανωσάμενος καλάμῳ γλαυκῷ μετὰ σώφρονος ἡλικιώτου,
μίλακος ὄζων καὶ ἀπραγμοσύνης καὶ λεύκης φυλλοβολούσης,
ἦρος ἐν ὥρᾳ χαίρων, ὁπόταν πλάτανος πτελέᾳ ψιθυρίζῃ.
ἢν ταῦτα ποιῇς ἁγὼ φράζω
καὶ πρὸς τούτοισιν ἔχῃς τὸν νοῦν,   1010

995   μέλλει Σ^V Suda Σ(i)^E: μέλλεις codd. Suda, ^{i}Σ(ii)^E, Stobaeus.
995   †ἀναπλήσειν† RVEKΘ^1 Suda, Stobaeus: ἀναπλάσειν ΝΘ^2: ἀναπλάσσειν
        Thom.: perh. παλάξειν (παλάσσειν Kock), cf. Σ^E μολύνειν.
1005 ἀποθρ- Rn' Suda, Stobaeus, Σ Soph. O.C. 701: ὑποθρ- E:
        καταθρ- V.
1006 γλαυκῷ Cantarella: om. RV: λευκῷ n Suda, Stobaeus.
1010 τούτοισιν ἔχῃς Bergk: τουτοι[Π8: τούτοις (ταύτης θ^{ac})
        προσέχῃς codd.

choose me, the Better Argument, with confidence; and you will
know to hate the Agora and shun the bath-houses, and to be
ashamed of what is shameful, and to flare up when someone makes
fun of you, and to give up seats to your elders when they approach,
and not to act rudely towards your own parents, nor to do anything   995
else disgraceful that would <defile> the statue of Honour; nor to
rush into a dancing-girl's house, lest while you're panting after that
sort of thing you may have an apple thrown at you by a little whore
and so have your good name shattered; nor to contradict your
father in anything, nor to call him Iapetus and so cast his years in
his teeth, those years which were spent in rearing you from a nest-
ling.

    WORSE ARGUMENT: If you follow this advice of his, my   1000
lad, then, by Dionysus, you'll become like the sons of Hippocrates,
and they'll call you a pap-sucker.

    BETTER ARGUMENT: But you'll be spending your time in
gymnasia, with a gleaming, blooming body, not in outlandish chatter on thorny subjects in the Agora like the present generation, nor
in being dragged into court over some sticky, contentious, damnable
little dispute; no, you will go down to the Academy, and under the   1005 *
sacred olive-trees, wearing a chaplet of green reed, you will start a
race together with a good decent companion of your own age, fragrant with green-brier and catkin-shedding poplar and freedom from
cares, delighting in the season of spring, when the plane tree whispers to the elm.

    If you do these things I tell you, and bend your efforts to them,   1010

ἕξεις ἀεὶ
στῆθος λιπαρόν, χροιὰν λαμπράν,
ὤμους μεγάλους, γλῶτταν βαιάν,
πυγὴν μεγάλην, πόσθην μικράν.
ἢν δ' ἅπερ οἱ νῦν ἐπιτηδεύῃς,   1015
πρῶτα μὲν ἕξεις
χροιὰν ὠχράν, ὤμους μικρούς,
στῆθος λεπτόν, γλῶτταν μεγάλην,
πυγὴν μικράν, κωλῆν μεγάλην,
ψήφισμα μακρόν· καί σ' ἀναπείσει
τὸ μὲν αἰσχρὸν ἅπαν καλὸν ἡγεῖσθαι,   1020
τὸ καλὸν δ' αἰσχρόν,
καὶ πρὸς τούτοις τῆς Ἀντιμάχου
καταπυγοσύνης ἀναπλήσει.

Χο. ὦ καλλίπυργον σοφίαν   (ἀντ.
       κλεινοτάτην ἐπασκῶν,   1025
     ὡς ἡδύ σου τοῖσι λόγοις
       σῶφρον ἔπεστιν ἄνθος.
*   εὐδαίμονές γ' ἦσαν ἄρ' οἱ
       ζῶντες τότ' ἐπὶ τῶν προτέρων.
     πρὸς τάδε σ', ὦ κομψοπρεπῆ μοῦσαν ἔχων,   1030
     δεῖ σε λέγειν τι καινόν, ὡς
       ηὐδοκίμηκεν ἀνήρ.

     δεινῶν δέ σοι βουλευμάτων ἔοικε δεῖν πρὸς αὐτόν,
     εἴπερ τὸν ἄνδρ' ὑπερβαλεῖ καὶ μὴ γέλωτ' ὀφλήσεις.   1035

1028 γ' Blaydes: δ' codd.
1030 τάδε σ' Hall & Geldart: οὖν τάδ' codd.

108

you will always have a shining breast, a bright skin, big shoulders,
a minute tongue, a big rump and a small prick. But if you follow   1015
the practices of the youth of today, for a start you'll have a pale
skin, small shoulders, a skinny chest, a big tongue, a small rump, a
big ham and a long . . . winded decree; and he [*indicating the Worse
Argument*] will talk you into believing whatever is foul to be fair,   1020
and whatever is fair foul; and on top of that he will infect you with
the faggotry of Antimachus.

      CHORUS: You who perfect yourself in wisdom,
               wisdom the glorious, the fair and lofty,   1025
               how sweet on your words
               is the bloom of virtue!
               Happy indeed, I see, were they   *
               who lived then, in the time of the men of old.

[*To the Worse Argument*]

               In answer to this, you with your refined and   1030
                  plausible art
               will have to say something novel; for
               the man has won great credit.

     CHORUS-LEADER: It seems you will need some clever
schemes against him, if you are going to overcome the man and not   1035
be a laughing-stock.

Ητ. καὶ μὴν πάλαι γ' ἐπνιγόμην τὰ σπλάγχνα κἀπεθύμουν
ἄπαντα ταῦτ' ἐναντίαις γνώμαισι συνταράξαι.
ἐγὼ γὰρ ἥττων μὲν λόγος δι' αὐτὸ τοῦτ' ἐκλήθην
ἐν τοῖσι φροντισταῖσιν, ὅτι πρώτιστος ἐπενόησα
τοῖσιν νόμοις καὶ ταῖς δίκαις τἀναντί' ἀντιλέξαι.   1040
καὶ τοῦτο πλεῖν ἢ μυρίων ἔστ' ἄξιον στατήρων,
αἱρούμενον τοὺς ἥττονας λόγους ἔπειτα νικᾶν.
σκέψαι δὲ τὴν παίδευσιν, ᾗ πέποιθεν, ὡς ἐλέγξω·
ὅστις σε θερμῷ φησι λοῦσθαι πρῶτον οὐκ ἐάσειν.
καίτοι τίνα γνώμην ἔχων ψέγεις τὰ θερμὰ λουτρά;   1045

Κρ. ὁτιὴ κάκιστόν ἐστι καὶ δειλὸν ποιεῖ τὸν ἄνδρα.

Ητ. ἐπίσχες· εὐθὺς γάρ σε μέσον ἔχω λαβὴν ἄφυκτον.
καί μοι φράσον· τῶν τοῦ Διὸς παίδων τίν' ἄνδρ' ἄριστον
ψυχὴν νομίζεις, εἰπέ, καὶ πλείστους πόνους πονῆσαι;

Κρ. ἐγὼ μὲν οὐδέν' Ἡρακλέους βελτίον' ἄνδρα κρίνω.   1050

Ητ. ποῦ ψυχρὰ δῆτα πώποτ' εἶδες Ἡράκλεια λουτρά;
καίτοι τίς ἀνδρειότερος ἦν;

Κρ.   ταῦτ' ἐστὶ ταῦτ' ἐκεῖνα,
ἃ τῶν νεανίσκων ἀεὶ δι' ἡμέρας λαλούντων
πλῆρες τὸ βαλανεῖον ποιεῖ, κενὰς δὲ τὰς παλαίστρας.

Ητ. εἶτ' ἐν ἀγορᾷ τὴν διατριβὴν ψέγεις· ἐγὼ δ' ἐπαινῶ.   1055
εἰ γὰρ πονηρὸν ἦν, Ὅμηρος οὐδέποτ' ἂν ἐποίει
τὸν Νέστορ' ἀγορητὴν ἄν, οὐδὲ τοὺς σοφοὺς ἄπαντας.

1036 πάλαι γ' Thom.: ἔγωγ' RV: πάλαι γ' ἔγωγ' E^{pc}N: πάλ' ἔγωγ'
      vel sim. E^{ac}Kθ: πάλαι 'γὼ Bentley.
1046 δειλὸν Thom.: δειλότατον codd.
1047 λαβὴν W.H. Thompson: λαβὼν codd. Suda.

110

WORSE ARGUMENT: Well, actually I've been choking in my insides for some time with eagerness to make mincemeat of all this by counter-arguments. For it was for just this reason that I got the name of Worse Argument among the men of thought, because I was the first who conceived the notion of arguing in contradiction to established values and justified pleas. [*To Pheidippides*] And that is worth more than ten thousand staters, to be able to choose the inferior case and yet win. Look at the way I shall examine the education in which he puts his trust. He says that first of all he won't let you bathe in hot water. Now [*to Better Argument*] on what principle do you base your objection to hot baths? 1045

BETTER ARGUMENT: That they are a most unmanly thing, and make the man who takes them a coward.

WORSE ARGUMENT: Hold it! Right away I've got you held round the waist in a grip you can't escape. Now tell me: of the sons of Zeus, whom do you consider to have been the greatest-hearted man, tell me, and to have performed the most labours?

BETTER ARGUMENT: For my part, I reckon no man superior to Heracles. 1050

WORSE ARGUMENT: Well then, where have you ever seen Heraclean baths that were cold? And yet who was more manly than he?

BETTER ARGUMENT: That — that's the stuff that the young men are always blabbering about all day, which makes the bath-house full and the wrestling-schools empty.

WORSE ARGUMENT: Then you object to their frequenting the Agora; I, on the contrary, commend it. If it were something wicked, Homer would never have described Nestor and indeed all his men of wisdom as "agoretes". Well, from there I shall proceed 1055

111

ἄνειμι δῆτ' ἐντεῦθεν εἰς τὴν γλῶτταν, ἣν ὁδὶ μὲν
οὔ φησι χρῆναι τοὺς νέους ἀσκεῖν· ἐγὼ δέ φημι.
καὶ σωφρονεῖν αὖ φησι χρῆναι· δύο κακὼ μεγίστω.   1060
ἐπεὶ σὺ διὰ τὸ σωφρονεῖν τῷ πώποτ' εἶδες ἤδη
ἀγαθόν τι γενόμενον; φράσον, καί μ' ἐξέλεγξον εἰπών.

Κρ.   πολλοῖς. ὁ γοῦν Πηλεὺς ἔλαβεν διὰ τοῦτο τὴν μάχαιραν.

Ητ.   μάχαιραν; ἀστεῖόν γε κέρδος ἔλαβεν ὁ κακοδαίμων.
      Ὑπέρβολος δ' οὐκ τῶν λύχνων πλεῖν ἢ τάλαντα πολλὰ   1065
      εἴληφε διὰ πονηρίαν, ἀλλ' οὐ μὰ Δί' οὐ μάχαιραν.

Κρ.   καὶ τὴν Θέτιν γ' ἔγημε διὰ τὸ σωφρονεῖν ὁ Πηλεύς.

Ητ.   κᾆτ' ἀπολιποῦσά γ' αὐτὸν ᾤχετ'· οὐ γὰρ ἦν ὑβριστής,
      οὐδ' ἡδὺς ἐν τοῖς στρώμασιν τὴν νύκτα παννυχίζειν·
      γυνὴ δὲ σιναμωρουμένη χαίρει. σὺ δ' εἶ Κρόνιππος.   1070
      σκέψαι γάρ, ὦ μειράκιον, ἐν τῷ σωφρονεῖν ἅπαντα
      ἄνεστιν, ἡδονῶν θ' ὅσων μέλλεις ἀποστερεῖσθαι·
      παίδων, γυναικῶν, κοττάβων, ὄψων, πότων, καχασμῶν.
      καίτοι τί σοι ζῆν ἄξιον, τούτων ἐὰν στερηθῇς;
      εἶέν. πάρειμ' ἐντεῦθεν εἰς τὰς τῆς φύσεως ἀνάγκας.   1075
      ἥμαρτες, ἠράσθης, ἐμοίχευσάς τι, κᾆτ' ἐλήφθης·
      ἀπόλωλας· ἀδύνατος γὰρ εἶ λέγειν. ἐμοὶ δ' ὁμιλῶν
      χρῶ τῇ φύσει, σκίρτα, γέλα, νόμιζε μηδὲν αἰσχρόν.
      μοιχὸς γὰρ ἦν τύχῃς ἁλούς, τάδ' ἀντερεῖς πρὸς αὐτόν,
      ὡς οὐδὲν ἠδίκηκας· εἶτ' εἰς τὸν Δί' ἐπανενεγκεῖν,   1080
      κἀκεῖνος ὡς ἥττων ἔρωτός ἐστι καὶ γυναικῶν·

1064 γε VEK: γε τὸ N: τὸ Rθ.
1066 εἴληφε was aspirated in Attic: see Threatte
      i 463.
1073 καχασμῶν R: κιχλισμῶν V<u>n</u> Σ^{RV}.
1076 τι κᾆτ' Bentley: τι κατ- (τί δή· κατ- θ^2 Tricl.) codd.

112

to the tongue, which my opponent says it is not right for the young
to train: I say it is right. And again, he says one should be modest: 1060
that makes two pernicious evils. For [*to Better Argument*] who is
there that you have ever yet seen to derive any benefit from being
modest? Say who, and by naming him refute me.

BETTER ARGUMENT: Plenty of people. For example, Peleus got his knife because of that.

WORSE ARGUMENT: A knife? A charming profit the poor
devil made! Now Hyperbolus from the lamp market has made a   1065
whole load of talents by being wicked, but never a knife, by Zeus,
no!

BETTER ARGUMENT: And also Peleus got to marry Thetis
because of his virtue.

WORSE ARGUMENT: Yes, and then she left him and went
away, because he wasn't wanton and wasn't an enjoyable partner for
an all-night session under the covers. A woman enjoys being mauled.   1070
Your're just a hulking old Cronus. [*To Pheidippides*] Look, my lad, at
all that virtue entails, and all the pleasures you'll be deprived of:
boys, women, cottabus, good food, drink, laughter. How can life
be worth living for you if you're deprived of these? Very well; I   1075
will go on from there to the demands of nature. You've erred,
you've fallen in love, you've had a bit of an affair, and then you've
been caught. You're done for, because you're not able to argue.
But if you become my pupil you can indulge your nature, leap and
laugh, think nothing shameful. If by chance you are taken in adultery, this is what you will reply to the husband: that you have done   1080
nothing wrong. Then transfer the responsibility to Zeus, saying
that even he is a slave to love and women, and how can you, a

καίτοι σὺ θνητὸς ὢν θεοῦ πῶς μεῖζον ἂν δύναιο;

Κρ. τί δ', ἢν ῥαφανιδωθῇ πιθόμενός σοι τέφρᾳ τε τιλθῇ;
ἕξει τινὰ γνώμην λέγειν τὸ μὴ εὐρύπρωκτος εἶναι;

Ητ. ἢν δ' εὐρύπρωκτος ᾖ, τί πείσεται κακόν;   1085

Κρ. τί μὲν οὖν ἂν ἔτι μεῖζον πάθοι τούτου ποτέ;

Ητ. τί δῆτ' ἐρεῖς, ἢν τοῦτο νικηθῇς ἐμοῦ;

Κρ. σιγήσομαι· τί δ' ἄλλο;

Ητ.   φέρε δή μοι φράσον·
συνηγοροῦσιν ἐκ τίνων;

Κρ. ἐξ εὐρυπρώκτων.

Ητ.   πείθομαι.   1090
τί δαί; τραγῳδοῦσ' ἐκ τίνων;

Κρ. ἐξ εὐρυπρώκτων.

Ητ.   εὖ λέγεις.
δημηγοροῦσι δ' ἐκ τίνων;

Κρ. ἐξ εὐρυπρώκτων.

Ητ.   ἆρα δῆτ'
ἔγνωκας ὡς οὐδὲν λέγεις;   1095
καὶ τῶν θεατῶν ὁπότεροι
πλείους σκόπει.

Κρ.   καὶ δὴ σκοπῶ.

Ητ. τί δῆθ' ὁρᾷς;

Κρ. πολὺ πλείονας, νὴ τοὺς θεούς,

1083 πιθόμενός θ: πειθόμενός RVEK: πυθόμενός N.

114

mortal, be stronger than a god?

BETTER ARGUMENT: But what if, as a result of following your advice, he gets the radish treatment and is plucked and singed with ashes? Will he have any argument he can use to save himself from being wide-arsed?

WORSE ARGUMENT: And if he does become wide-arsed, how will that harm him? 1085

BETTER ARGUMENT: You mean, what further misfortune could he ever suffer that would be greater than that?

WORSE ARGUMENT: Well, what will you say if I confute you on this point?

BETTER ARGUMENT: I'll remain silent; what else?

WORSE ARGUMENT: Come on then, tell me: from what type of person do advocates come?

BETTER ARGUMENT: From the wide-arsed. 1090

WORSE ARGUMENT: I agree. Again, from what type do tragedians come?

BETTER ARGUMENT: From the wide-arsed.

WORSE ARGUMENT: Quite right. And from what type do politicians come?

BETTER ARGUMENT: From the wide-arsed.

WORSE ARGUMENT: Then do you realize that you were talking nonsense? Again, look and see which are in the majority among the audience. 1095

BETTER ARGUMENT: There, I'm looking.

WORSE ARGUMENT: Well, what do you see?

BETTER ARGUMENT: That, heavens above! the wide-arsed

τοὺς εὐρυπρώκτους. τουτονὶ
γοῦν οἶδ' ἐγὼ κἀκεινονὶ
καὶ τὸν κομήτην τουτονί.   1100

Ητ. τί δῆτ' ἐρεῖς;

Κρ. ἡττήμεθ'. ὦ κινούμενοι,
πρὸς τῶν θεῶν δέξασθέ μου
θοἰμάτιον, ὡς
ἐξαυτομολῶ πρὸς ὑμᾶς.

Ητ. τί δῆτα; πότερα τοῦτον ἀπάγεσθαι λαβὼν   1105
βούλει τὸν υἱόν, ἢ διδάσκω σοι λέγειν;

Στ. δίδασκε καὶ κόλαζε, καὶ μέμνησ' ὅπως
εὖ μοι στομώσεις αὐτόν, ἐπὶ μὲν θάτερα
οἷον δικιδίοις, τὴν δ' ἑτέραν αὐτοῦ γνάθον
στόμωσον οἵαν εἰς τὰ μείζω πράγματα.   1110

Ητ. ἀμέλει, κομιεῖ τοῦτον σοφιστὴν δεξιόν.

Φε. ὠχρὸν μὲν οὖν, οἶμαί γε, καὶ κακοδαίμονα.

* Χο. χωρεῖτέ νυν. οἶμαι δέ σοι
ταῦτα μεταμελήσειν.

τοὺς κριτὰς ἃ κερδανοῦσιν, ἤν τι τόνδε τὸν χορὸν   1115
ὠφελῶσ' ἐκ τῶν δικαίων, βουλόμεσθ' ἡμεῖς φράσαι.
πρῶτα μὲν γάρ, ἢν νεᾶν βούλησθ' ἐν ὥρᾳ τοὺς ἀγρούς,
ὕσομεν πρώτοισιν ὑμῖν, τοῖσι δ' ἄλλοις ὕστερον.
* εἶτα τὸν καρπόν τε καὶ τὰς ἀμπέλους φυλάξομεν,
ὥστε μήτ' αὐχμὸν πιέζειν μήτ' ἄγαν ἐπομβρίαν.   1120

1109 οἷον ⁱΣ(i)ⱽ: οἵαν codd. Suda ⁱΣREMNp1Np5 λΣEMNp5 ⁱΣ(ii)ⱽ.
1116 ἡμεῖς RV: ὑμεῖς K: ὑμῖν Εθ: ἡμῖν Ν.
1119 τε καὶ τὰς Coraes: τεκούσας τὰς Ν: τεκούσας RVn'.

are the *vast* majority. At any rate, I know *that* one is, and that one over there, and that one with the long hair. 1100

WORSE ARGUMENT: Well, what are you going to say?

BETTER ARGUMENT: We are defeated. Here, you buggers, please for heaven's sake take my cloak; I'm deserting to your camp! [*He throws his cloak to the Worse Argument and rushes into the Reflectory.*]

WORSE ARGUMENT [*to Strepsiades*]: Well, how about it? 1105 Do you want to take this son of yours away, or shall I teach him oratory for you?

STREPSIADES: Teach him and chastise him, and remember to give him a sharp edge, with one side adapted to small lawsuits, while the other side of his jaws you should whet to serve for weight- 1110 ier affairs.

WORSE ARGUMENT: Don't worry, you'll receive him back a skilled sophist.

PHEIDIPPIDES [*aside*]: More like a god-forsaken paleface, I should think.

CHORUS: Now go your way.

[*The Worse Argument leads Pheidippides into the Reflectory; the Chorus turn towards Strepsiades, who is entering his own house.*]
But I think that you
will come to regret this.

CHORUS-LEADER: We wish to tell you how the judges 1115 will benefit, if they do this chorus a service as by rights they should. First of all, if you wish to plough and sow your fields in season, we shall rain on you first and on everyone else later. Then we shall pro- *
tect your crops and your vines, so that they are not damaged either 1120 by drought or by excessive rain. But if anyone who is a mortal

117

ἢν δ' ἀτιμάσῃ τις ἡμᾶς θνητὸς ὢν οὔσας θεάς,
προσεχέτω τὸν νοῦν, πρὸς ἡμῶν οἷα πείσεται κακά,
λαμβάνων οὔτ' οἶνον οὔτ' ἄλλ' οὐδὲν ἐκ τοῦ χωρίου·
ἡνίκ' ἂν γὰρ αἵ τ' ἐλαῖαι βλαστάνωσ' αἵ τ' ἄμπελοι,
ἀποκεκόψονται· τοιαύταις σφενδόναις παιήσομεν.   1125
ἢν δὲ πλινθεύοντ' ἴδωμεν, ὕσομεν καὶ τοῦ τέγους
τὸν κέραμον αὐτοῦ χαλάζαις στρογγύλαις συντρίψομεν.
κἂν γαμῇ ποτ' αὐτὸς ἢ τῶν ξυγγενῶν ἢ τῶν φίλων,
ὕσομεν τὴν νύκτα πᾶσαν· ὥστ' ἴσως βουλήσεται
κἂν ἐν Αἰγύπτῳ τυχεῖν ὢν μᾶλλον ἢ κρῖναι κακῶς.   1130

Στ. πέμπτη, τετράς, τρίτη, μετὰ ταύτην δευτέρα·
εἶθ', ἣν ἐγὼ μάλιστα πασῶν ἡμερῶν
δέδοικα καὶ πέφρικα καὶ βδελύττομαι,
εὐθὺς μετὰ ταύτην ἔσθ' ἕνη τε καὶ νέα.
πᾶς γάρ τις ὀμνύς, οἷς ὀφείλων τυγχάνω,   1135
θεύς μοι πρυτανεῖ' ἀπολεῖν μέ φησι κἀξολεῖν,
ἐμοῦ τε μέτρια καὶ δίκαι' αἰτουμένου,
"ὦ δαιμόνιε, τὸ μέν τι νυνὶ μὴ λάβῃς,
τὸ δ' ἀναβαλοῦ μοι, τὸ δ' ἄφες," οὔ φασίν ποτε
οὕτως ἀπολήψεσθ', ἀλλὰ λοιδοροῦσί με   1140
ὡς ἄδικός εἰμι, καὶ δικάσεσθαί φασί μοι.
νῦν οὖν δικαζέσθων· ὀλίγον γάρ μοι μέλει,
εἴπερ μεμάθηκεν εὖ λέγειν Φειδιππίδης.
τάχα δ' εἴσομαι κόψας τὸ φροντιστήριον.
παῖ, ἠμί, παῖ παῖ.

Σω.   Στρεψιάδην ἀσπάζομαι.   1145

1124 ἡνίκ' ἂν U al.: ἡνίκα RVn.
1137 τε μέτρια Green: μέτριά τε codd.
1141 δικάσεσθαι θ: δικάσασθαι RVn'.

118

dishonours us who are goddesses, let him pay attention and hear what evil he will suffer at our hands: he will get neither wine nor anything else from his land; for when the olives and vines are sprouting, the shoots will be cut off, such will be the sling-shots with which we'll smite them. And if we see him making bricks, we will rain, and shatter the tiling of his roof with round hailstones. And if at any time he himself, or one of his relations or friends, is getting married, we shall rain the whole night long; so that perhaps he will wish even to find himself in Egypt rather than having given a wrong verdict. 1125

1130

[*Strepsiades comes out of his house.*]

STREPSIADES [*counting on his fingers*]: Twenty-sixth, twenty-seventh, twenty-eighth, then twenty-ninth; then comes the day that I dread above all days, that makes me shudder, that turns my stomach — for right after that comes Old-and-New Day. For everyone to whom I find myself in debt swears that he will lodge a deposit against me and crush and destroy me; and when I make modest and fair requests of them — "My dear sir, this sum don't insist on receiving now, this one put off, please, this one wipe out" — they say they'll never accept that kind of payment, and instead abuse me as dishonest and say they'll sue me. Well, now let them sue; little do I care, if Pheidippides has really learned to be a good speaker. I'll soon know, if I knock at the Reflectory. [*Doing so*] Boy, I say! boy, boy! 1135

1140

1145

SOCRATES [*coming to the door*]: Greeting, Strepsiades.

Στ. κἄγωγέ σ'. ἀλλὰ τουτονὶ πρῶτον λαβέ·
     χρὴ γὰρ ἐπιθαυμάζειν τι τὸν διδάσκαλον.
     καί μοι τὸν υἱόν, εἰ μεμάθηκε τὸν λόγον
     ἐκεῖνον, εἴφ', ὃν ἀρτίως εἰσήγαγες.

Σω. μεμάθηκεν.

Στ.   εὖ γ', ὦ παμβασίλει' Ἀπαιόλη.   1150

Σω. ὥστ' ἀποφύγοις ἂν ἥντιν' ἂν βούλῃ δίκην.

Στ. κεἰ μάρτυρες παρῆσαν ὅτ' ἐδανειζόμην;

Σω. πολλῷ γε μᾶλλον, κἂν παρῶσι χίλιοι.

Στ. βοάσομαι τἄρα τὰν ὑπέρτονον
        βοάν. ἰώ, κλάετ', ὠβολοστάται,   1155
     αὐτοί τε καὶ τἀρχαῖα καὶ τόκοι τόκων.
     οὐδὲν γὰρ ἄν με φλαῦρον ἐργάσαισθ' ἔτι·
     οἷος ἐμοὶ τρέφεται
     τοῖσδ' ἐνὶ δώμασι παῖς,
     ἀμφήκει γλώττῃ λάμπων,   1160
     πρόβολος ἐμός, σωτὴρ δόμοις, ἐχθροῖς βλάβη,
     λυσανίας πατρῴων μεγάλων κακῶν·
        ὃν κάλεσον τρέχων ἔνδοθεν ὡς ἐμέ.
     ὦ τέκνον, ὦ παῖ, ἔξελθ' οἴκων·   1165
     ἄιε σοῦ πατρός.

Σω. ὅδ' ἐκεῖνος ἀνήρ.

Στ. ὦ φίλος, ὦ φίλος.

Σω. ἄπιθί σφε λαβών.

1157 ἐργάσαισθ' M: ἐργάσεσθ' RVE^{ac}Kθ Suda^{rell.}: ἐργάσησθ' E^{pc}N:
        ἐργάσασθ' Suda^{GVM}.
1169 σφε λαβών Sommerstein: σὺ λαβών n̲: λαβὼν τὸν υἱόν σου RV.

120

STREPSIADES: The same to you. But please accept this first
of all [*giving him a present*] ; one must in some way pay one's
respects to the teacher. And tell me if my son has learnt that Argument, the one you brought on stage a little while ago.

SOCRATES: He has.   1150

STREPSIADES: Almighty Fraud, how splendid!

SOCRATES: So you'll be able to defend sucessfully any lawsuit
you like.

STREPSIADES: Even if there were witnesses present when I
borrowed the money?

SOCRATES: Much more than that: even if there are a thousand
of them.

STREPSIADES:

        Then I will shout an exceeding great
        shout. Oho! lament, ye moneylenders,   1155 *
        yourselves, your principal, and the interest on your
            interest!
        For no more can you do me any harm,
        such is the son that is being reared
        for me within these halls,
        gleaming with two-edged tongue,   1160
        a bulwark to me, a saviour to my house, a bane to
            my foes,
        who will dispel the grief of his father's great troubles.
        Run and call him to me from within.

[*Socrates goes inside.*]

        My child, my son, come forth from the house;   1165
        hearken to thy father.

SOCRATES [*bringing Pheidippides out*] :

        Here is the man you seek.

STREPSIADES:

        Beloved, beloved!

SOCRATES:

        Take him and depart.

Στ. ἰὼ ἰώ, τέκνον.   1170

*   ἰοὺ ἰού.

ὡς ἥδομαί σου πρῶτα τὴν χροιὰν ἰδών.

νῦν μέν γ' ἰδεῖν εἶ πρῶτον ἐξαρνητικὸς

κἀντιλογικός, καὶ τοῦτο τοὐπιχώριον

ἀτεχνῶς ἐπανθεῖ, τὸ "τί λέγεις σύ;" καὶ δοκεῖν

ἀδικοῦντ' ἀδικεῖσθαι, καὶ κακουργοῦντ', οἶδ' ὅτι.   1175

νῦν οὖν ὅπως σώσεις μ', ἐπεὶ κἀπώλεσας.   1177

Φε. φοβεῖ δὲ δὴ τί;

Στ.   τὴν ἕνην τε καὶ νέαν.

Φε. ἕνη γάρ ἐστι καὶ νέα τις ἡμέρα;

Στ. εἰς ἥν γε θήσειν τὰ πρυτανεῖά φασί μοι.   1180

Φε. ἀπολοῦσ' ἄρ' αὖθ' οἱ θέντες· οὐ γάρ ἔσθ' ὅπως
μί' ἡμέρα γένοιτ' ἂν ἡμέραι δύο.

Στ. οὐκ ἂν γένοιτο;

Φε.   πῶς γάρ; εἰ μή πέρ γ' ἅμα
αὑτὴ γένοιτ' ἂν γραῦς τε καὶ νέα γυνή.

Στ. καὶ μὴν νενόμισταί γ'.

Φε.   οὐ γάρ, οἶμαι, τὸν νόμον   1185
ἴσασιν ὀρθῶς ὅ τι νοεῖ.

Στ.   νοεῖ δὲ τί;

Φε. ὁ Σόλων ὁ παλαιὸς ἦν φιλόδημος τὴν φύσιν.

1170 V adds ἰώ before ἰοὺ ἰού (sic).

[1176] ἐπὶ τοῦ προσώπου τ' ἐστὶν Ἀττικὸν βλέπος vel sim. codd.
         Suda, Σ^{RVE} Wealth 342, Gregory of Corinth: del. Dover:
         possibly an author's variant for 1173-5 (cf. on 653).

122

STREPSIADES: Hurrah, hurrah, my child! 1170

[*Socrates goes in, leaving Strepsiades with his son.*]

STREPSIADES: Wowee! How delighted I am right away to see the colour of your skin! Now the first glance shows you to be traversive and contradictive, and that national look absolutely blooms on your face, the "what-do-you-mean?" look, the wronged 1175 look when you're in the wrong, even when you're committing felony, I'm certain. Now then see that you save me, since it was you that ruined me.

PHEIDIPPIDES: And what may you be afraid of?

STREPSIADES: Old-and-New Day.

PHEIDIPPIDES: You mean there's a day that's both old and new?

STREPSIADES: Yes, that's the day when they say they'll 1180 lodge their deposits against me.

PHEIDIPPIDES: Then those who do so will lose their deposits; for there's no way that one day can come to be two days.

STREPSIADES: It can't?

PHEIDIPPIDES: How could it? Unless it's possible for the same person to be an old crone and a young woman at the same time.

STREPSIADES: And yet that's the practice. 1185

PHEIDIPPIDES: The thing is, I think, that they don't know what the law properly means.

STRPSIADES: Well, what does it mean?

PHEIDIPPIDES: Old Solon was by disposition a friend of the people.

Στ. τουτὶ μὲν οὐδέν πω πρὸς ἔνην τε καὶ νέαν.

Φε. ἐκεῖνος οὖν τὴν κλῆσιν εἰς δύ' ἡμέρας
     ἔθηκεν, εἴς γε τὴν ἔνην τε καὶ νέαν,   1190
     ἵν' αἱ θέσεις γίγνοιντο τῇ νουμηνίᾳ.

* Στ. ἵνα δὴ τί τὴν ἔνην προσέθηκ';

Φε.   ἵν', ὦ μέλε,
     παρόντες οἱ φεύγοντες ἡμέρᾳ μιᾷ
     πρότερον ἀπαλλάττοινθ' ἑκόντες, εἰ δὲ μή,
     ἕωθεν ὑπανιῷντο τῇ νουμηνίᾳ.   1195

Στ. πῶς οὐ δέχονται δῆτα τῇ νουμηνίᾳ
     ἀρχαὶ τὰ πρυτανεῖ', ἀλλ' ἔνῃ τε καὶ νέᾳ;

Φε. ὅπερ οἱ προτένθαι γὰρ δοκοῦσί μοι παθεῖν·
     ὅπως τάχιστα τὰ πρυτανεῖ' ὑφελοίατο,
     διὰ τοῦτο προυτένθευσαν ἡμέρᾳ μιᾷ.   1200

Στ. εὖ γ'. ὦ κακοδαίμονες, τί κάθησθ' ἀβέλτεροι,
     ἡμέτερα κέρδη τῶν σοφῶν, ὄντες λίθοι,
     ἀριθμός, πρόβατ' ἄλλως, ἀμφορῆς νενημένοι;
     ὥστ' εἰς ἐμαυτὸν καὶ τὸν υἱὸν τουτονὶ
     ἐπ' εὐτυχίαισιν ᾀστέον μούγκώμιον.   1205
     "μάκαρ ὦ Στρεψίαδες,
     αὐτός τ' ἔφυς ὡς σοφὸς
        χοῖον τὸν υἱὸν τρέφεις,"
     φήσουσι δή μ' οἱ φίλοι
        χοἰ δημόται
     ζηλοῦντες, ἡνίκ' ἂν σὺ νι-   1210

1198 παθεῖν n, Athenaeus: ποεῖν RV.
1203 νενημένοι Bentley: νενησμένοι codd. Suda.

124

STREPSIADES: So far that's nothing to do with Old-and-New Day.

PHEIDIPPIDES: So he fixed the summons for two days, namely Old Day and New Day, so that the lodging of the deposits should take place on the New Moon. 1189-1190

STREPSIADES: And why did he name Old Day as well?

PHEIDIPPIDES: In order, my good fellow, that the defendants might appear one day in advance and settle the case voluntarily, and if they did not, might be made to feel a bit uneasy on the morning of the New Moon. 1195

STREPSIADES: Then why do the magistrates not accept deposits on the New Moon, but only on Old-and-New Day?

PHEIDIPPIDES: I think they're in the same position as the Tasters: in order to embezzle the deposits as soon as possible, they've been tasting them one day early. 1200

STREPSIADES: Splendid! [*To the audience*] You poor fools, why are you sitting there like dunces, ripe for fleecing by us intellectuals? You're stones, ciphers, mere sheep, a heap of earthenware! — Now I ought to sing a song of praise to myself and my son here over this good fortune. 1205

"O blest Strepsiades,
how clever you are yourself
and what a son you're bringing up!"
— so my friends and my fellow-demesmen
will say of me
in envy, when you win 1210

κᾆς λέγων τὰς δίκας.
ἀλλ' εἰσάγων σε βούλομαι
πρῶτον ἑστιᾶσαι.

ΧΡΗΣΤΗΣ Α
εἶτ' ἄνδρα τῶν αὑτοῦ τι χρὴ προϊέναι;
οὐδέποτέ γ', ἀλλὰ κρεῖττον εὐθὺς ἦν τότε   1215
ἀπερυθριᾶσαι μᾶλλον ἢ σχεῖν πράγματα,
ὅτε τῶν ἐμαυτοῦ γ' ἕνεκα νυνὶ χρημάτων
ἕλκω σε κλητεύσοντα, καὶ γενήσομαι
ἐχθρὸς ἔτι πρὸς τούτοισιν ἀνδρὶ δημότῃ.
ἀτὰρ οὐδέποτέ γε τὴν πατρίδα καταισχυνῶ   1220
ζῶν, ἀλλὰ καλοῦμαι Στρεψιάδην—

Στ.   τίς οὑτοσί;

Χρ.ᵅ —εἰς τὴν ἕνην τε καὶ νέαν.

Στ.   μαρτύρομαι
ὅτι εἰς δύ' εἶπεν ἡμέρας.   τοῦ χρήματος;

Χρ.ᵅ τῶν δώδεκα μνῶν, ἃς ἔλαβες ὠνούμενος
τὸν ψαρὸν ἵππον.

Στ.   ἵππον;   οὐκ ἀκούετε;   1225
ὃν πάντες ὑμεῖς ἴστε μισοῦνθ' ἱππικήν.

Χρ.ᵅ καὶ νὴ Δί' ἀποδώσειν γ' ἐπώμνυς τοὺς θεούς.

Στ.   μὰ τὸν Δί' οὐ γάρ πω τότ' ἐξηπίστατο
Φειδιππίδης μοι τὸν ἀκατάβλητον λόγον.

Χρ.ᵅ νῦν δὲ διὰ τοῦτ' ἔξαρνος εἶναι διανοεῖ;   1230

1228   μὰ τὸν Tricl.: μὰ FVn: νὴ τὸν θ²: RVEKθ add τὸ χρέος at the
start of the line, assigning it to the creditor.

126

my lawsuits with your speeches.
But first of all I want to take you inside
and feast you.

[*Strepsiades and Pheidippides go into their house. Presently one of Strepsiades' creditors arrives, accompanied by a friend as witness.*]

FIRST CREDITOR: So ought a man to throw some of his own money away? Never; it would have been better to refuse unblush- 1215 ingly right from the start rather than give myself trouble, seeing that now I'm dragging you here to witness a summons over money that's mine, and what is more, in addition to that I'm going to make an enemy of a fellow-demesman. But never while I live shall I disgrace 1220 my country; [*raising his voice*] I summon Strepsiades —

STREPSIADES [*coming out*]: Who's here?

FIRST CREDITOR: — to appear on Old-and-New Day.

STREPSIADES [*to the audience*]: I call you to witness that he summoned me for two different days. [*To the Creditor*] What is it about?

FIRST CREDITOR: The twelve minas that you borrowed when you bought the dark-grey horse. 1225

STREPSIADES: "Horse"! Hark at him! Me, who you all know loathes everything to do with horses!

FIRST CREDITOR: And also, by Zeus, you swore by the gods that you would pay.

STREPSIADES: Ah, well, at that time, I tell you, my Pheidippides didn't yet know the invincible Argument.

FIRST CREDITOR: And now because of that you intend to 1230 deny the debt?

Στ. τί γὰρ ἄλλ' ἂν ἀπολαύσαιμι τοῦ μαθήματος;

Χρ.^α καὶ ταῦτ' ἐθελήσεις ἀπομόσαι μοι τοὺς θεούς,
ἵν' ἂν κελεύσω 'γώ σε;

Στ.   τοὺς ποίους θεούς;

Χρ.^α τὸν Δία, τὸν Ἑρμῆν, τὸν Ποσειδῶ.

Στ.   νὴ Δία·
κἂν προσκαταθείην γ' ὥστ' ὀμόσαι τριώβολον.   1235

Χρ.^α ἀπόλοιο τοίνυν ἕνεκ' ἀναιδείας ἔτι.

Στ. ἁλσὶν διασμηχθεὶς ὄναιτ' ἂν οὑτοσί.

Χρ.^α οἴμ', ὡς καταγελᾷς.

Στ.   ἓξ χοᾶς χωρήσεται.

Χρ.^α οὗτοι, μὰ τὸν Δία τὸν μέγαν καὶ τοὺς θεούς,
ἐμοῦ καταπροίξει.

Στ.   θαυμασίως ἥσθην "θεοῖς",   1240
καὶ Ζεὺς γελοῖος ὀμνύμενος τοῖς εἰδόσιν.

Χρ.^α ἦ μὴν σὺ τούτων τῷ χρόνῳ δώσεις δίκην.
ἀλλ' εἴτ' ἀποδώσεις <μοι> τὰ χρήματ' εἴτε μή,
ἀπόπεμφον ἀποκρινάμενος.

Στ.   ἔχε νυν ἥσυχος·
ἐγὼ γὰρ αὐτίκ' ἀποκρινοῦμαί σοι σαφῶς.   1245

Χρ.^α τί σοι δοκεῖ δράσειν; ἀποδώσειν σοι δοκεῖ;

Στ. ποῦ 'σθ' οὗτος ἀπαιτῶν με τἀργύριον; λέγε,

1231 ἀλλ' ἂν Tricl.: ἄλλο γ' ἂν <u>n'</u>: ἄλλο γ' K: ἂν RV.
1243 ἀποδώσεις <μοι> K: ἀποδώσεις RVE^{ac}θ: γ' ἀποδώσεις E^{pc}N:
       ἀποδώσεις <δὴ> Ct1.

128

STREPSIADES: Why, what benefit will I otherwise get from his training?

FIRST CREDITOR: And you will be prepared to swear to this denial for me, in the name of the gods, in whatever place I may require?

STREPSIADES: Which gods?

FIRST CREDITOR: Zeus, Hermes and Poseidon.

STREPSIADES: By Zeus, yes! I'd even pay an extra three obols for the privilege of swearing.   1235

FIRST CREDITOR: Then may ruin yet fall on you for your shamlessness!

STREPSIADES [*ignoring this, and patting the creditor on his paunch*]: This could do with being rubbed down with salt.

FIRST CREDITOR: Damn you! such mockery!

STREPSIADES: It'll hold four gallons.

FIRST CREDITOR: By great Zeus and all the gods, you shan't get away with treating me like this.   1240

STREPSIADES [*laughing*]: That amuses me incredibly, "the gods", and swearing by Zeus is funny to us who know better.

FIRST CREDITOR: I swear the time will come when you'll get what you deserve for this. But at least let me leave with an answer, whether you're going to repay me my money or not.

STREPSIADES: Just wait; I'll give you a straight answer right away. [*He goes inside.*]   1245

FIRST CREDITOR [*to his witness*]: What do you think he's going to do? Do you think he's going to pay?

STREPSIADES [*coming out with a kneading-tray*]: Where's this man who's demanding his money from me? Tell me, what is this?

τουτὶ τί ἐστι;

Χρ.^α   τοῦθ' ὅ τι ἐστί; κάρδοπος.

Στ. ἔπειτ' ἀπαιτεῖς ἀργύριον, τοιοῦτος ὤν;
οὐκ ἂν ἀποδοίην οὐδ' ἂν ὀβολὸν οὐδενί,   1250
ὅστις καλέσειε κάρδοπον τὴν καρδόπην.

Χρ.^α οὐκ ἄρ' ἀποδώσεις;

Στ.   οὐχ ὅσον γ' ἔμ' εἰδέναι.
οὔκουν ἀνύσας τι θᾶττον ἀπολιταργιεῖς
ἀπὸ τῆς θύρας;

Χρ.^α   ἄπειμι· κᾆτ', εὖ ἴσθ' ὅτι,
θήσω πρυτανεῖ', ἢ μηκέτι ζῴην ἐγώ.   1255

Στ. προσαποβαλεῖς ἄρ' αὐτὰ πρὸς ταῖς δώδεκα.
καίτοι σε τοῦτό γ' οὐχὶ βούλομαι παθεῖν
ὁτιὴ 'κάλεσας εὐηθικῶς "τὴν κάρδοπον".

ΧΡΗΣΤΗΣ Β
ἰώ μού μοι.

Στ. ἔα·
τίς οὑτοσί ποτ' ἔσθ' ὁ θρηνῶν; οὔ τί που   1260
τῶν Καρκίνου τις δαιμόνων ἐφθέγξατο;

Χρ.^β τί δ', ὅστις εἰμί, τοῦτο βούλεσθ' εἰδέναι;
ἀνὴρ κακοδαίμων.

Στ.   κατὰ σεαυτόν νυν τρέπου.

Χρ.^β ὦ σκληρὲ δαῖμον, ὦ τύχαι θραυσάντυγες
ἵππων ἐμῶν· ὦ Παλλάς, ὥς μ' ἀπώλεσας.   1265

1249 ἀργύριον E^{ac}K: τἀργύριον RVE^{pc}Nθ.
1254 κᾆτ' εὖ Elmsley: καὶ τοῦτ' RVE^{pc}KN Suda: καίτοι γ' E^{ac}θ.
1263 σεαυτόν Tricl.: σαυτόν RV<u>n</u>: σαυτοῦ θ².

130

FIRST CREDITOR: What is that? A *cardopus*.

STREPSIADES: And you demand money, when you're such a fool as that? I wouldn't pay so much as an obol to anyone who called a *cardopé* a *cardopus*. 1250

FIRST CREDITOR: So you're not going to pay?

STREPSIADES: Not that I know of. So now will you hurry up and skip off, fastish, away from my door?

FIRST CREDITOR: I'm going; and then, I can assure you, I'll be lodging a deposit — else may I not live another moment. [*Exit,* 1255 *accompanied by the witness.*]

STREPSIADES [*calling after him*]: Then you'll be throwing that away as well as the twelve minas. And I really don't want that to happen to you just because you were silly enough to speak of a *cardopus*.

[*Enter another creditor, bruised and limping.*]

SECOND CREDITOR: Ah, woe is me!

STREPSIADES: Here, who on earth is this singing laments? 1260 It wasn't by any chance one of Carcinus' deities that gave tongue?

SECOND CREDITOR: Why do you wish to know who I am? I am a man accursed.

STREPSIADES: Then go away by yourself.

SECOND CREDITOR: "O cruel deity, O mishap that smashed my chariot-rail! O Pallas, how thou hast ruined me!" 1265

Στ. τί δαί σε Τληπόλεμός ποτ' εἴργασται κακόν;

Χρ.β μὴ σκῶπτέ μ', ὦ τᾶν, ἀλλά μοι τὰ χρήματα
τὸν υἱὸν ἀποδοῦναι κέλευσον ἅλαβεν,
ἄλλως τε μέντοι καὶ κακῶς πεπραγότι.

Στ. τὰ ποῖα ταῦτα χρήμαθ';

Χρ.β   ἀδανείσατο.   1270

Στ. κακῶς ἄρ' ὄντως εἶχες, ὥς γ' ἐμοὶ δοκεῖς.

Χρ.β ἵππους γ' ἐλαύνων ἐξέπεσον, νὴ τοὺς θεούς.

Στ. τί δῆτα ληρεῖς ὥσπερ ἀπ' ὄνου καταπεσών;

Χρ.β ληρῶ, τὰ χρήματ' ἀπολαβεῖν εἰ βούλομαι;

Στ. οὐκ ἔσθ' ὅπως σύ γ' αὖθις ὑγιανεῖς.

Χρ.β   τί δαί;   1275

Στ. τὸν ἐγκέφαλον ὥσπερ σεσεῖσθαί μοι δοκεῖς.

Χρ.β σὺ δέ, νὴ τὸν Ἑρμῆν, προσκεκλήσεσθαί γ' ἐμοί,
εἰ μὴ 'ποδώσεις τἀργύριον.

Στ.   κάτειπέ νυν·
πότερα νομίζεις καινὸν ἀεὶ τὸν Δία
ὕειν ὕδωρ ἑκάστοτ', ἢ τὸν ἥλιον   1280
ἕλκειν κάτωθεν ταὐτὸ τοῦθ' ὕδωρ πάλιν;

Χρ.β οὐκ οἶδ' ἔγωγ' ὁπότερον, οὐδέ μοι μέλει.

Στ. πῶς οὖν ἀπολαβεῖν τἀργύριον δίκαιος εἶ,
εἰ μηδὲν οἶσθα τῶν μετεώρων πραγμάτων;

1266 Τληπόλεμος R: Τληπόλεμος Vn Σ^RVENp1.
1275 αὖθις Hermann, ὑγιανεῖς Bergk: αὐτὸς ὑγιαίνεις codd. Suda.

STREPSIADES: Why, what harm has Tlempolemus done you?

SECOND CREDITOR: Don't make fun of me, my man; tell your son to pay me back the money he received — he should in any case, and particularly when I'm in distress.

STREPSIADES: What money is that?   1270

SECOND CREDITOR: The money he borrowed.

STREPSIADES: You really *are* in a bad way, if you want my opinion.

SECOND CREDITOR: Yes, indeed; I was driving a chariot and fell out.

STREPSIADES: Then why are you talking such nonsense, as if you'd fallen off a donkey?

SECOND CREDITOR: Is it nonsense to want to get my money back?

STREPSIADES: There's no chance of your regaining your   1275
sanity.

SECOND CREDITOR: Why not?

STREPSIADES: I think your brain has kind of had a shaking.

SECOND CREDITOR: And I think, by Hermes, that you're going to get a summons from me, if you don't repay the money.

STREPSIADES: Well, tell me: do you think that when Zeus rains, it is always new water every time, or do you think that the   1280
sun draws up again from down here the same water that fell before?

SECOND CREDITOR: I don't know which it is, and I don't care.

STREPSIADES: Then how can you be entitled to receive your money back, if you know nothing of meteorology?

Χρ^β. ἀλλ' εἰ σπανίζετ' ἀργυρίου, τὸν <γοῦν> τόκον   1285
ἀπόδοτε.

Στ.   τοῦτο δ' ἔσθ', ὁ τόκος, τί θηρίον;

* Χρ^β. τί δ' ἄλλο γ' ἢ κατα μῆνα καὶ καθ' ἡμέραν
πλέον πλέον τἀργύριον ἀεὶ γίγνεται,
ὑπορρέοντος τοῦ χρόνου;

Στ.   καλῶς λέγεις.
τί δῆτα; τὴν θάλατταν ἐσθ' ὅ τι πλείονα   1290
νυνὶ νομίζεις ἢ πρὸ τοῦ;

Χρ^β.   μὰ Δί', ἀλλ' ἴσην·
οὐ γὰρ δίκαιον πλεῖον' εἶναι.

Στ.   κᾆτα πῶς
αὕτη μέν, ὦ κακόδαιμον, οὐδὲν γίγνεται
ἐπιρρεόντων τῶν ποταμῶν πλείων, σὺ δὲ
ζητεῖς ποιῆσαι τἀργύριον πλέον τὸ σόν;   1295
οὐκ ἀποδιώξει σαυτὸν ἀπὸ τῆς οἰκίας;
φέρε μοι τὸ κέντρον.

Χρ^β.   ταῦτ' ἐγὼ μαρτύρομαι.

Στ. ὕπαγε. τί μέλλεις; οὐκ ἐλᾷς, ὦ σαμφόρα;

1285 σπανίζετ' ἀργυρίου Blaydes: σπανίζεις τἀργυρίου (ἀργ- N) c
1285 τὸν <γοῦν> Blaydes: μοι τὸν codd.
1296 ἀποδιώξει Elmsley: ἀποδιώξεις codd.
1296 ἀπὸ E^{ac}Κθ^{ac}: ἐκ RVE^{pc}Νθ^{pc}.
1298 σαμφόρα θ^s: σαπφόρα <u>n'</u>: Πασία RV.

SECOND CREDITOR: I tell you what: if you're short of money, at least pay me the interest. 1285

STREPSIADES: This "interest" — what kind of animal is it?

SECOND CREDITOR: What else but the fact that the money one owes gets constantly more and more, month by month and day by day, by the effluxion of time?

STREPSIADES: Quite correct. Now then, do you think that the sea is at all bigger now than it used to be? 1290

SECOND CREDITOR: Heavens, no, it's the same size; it would be against the laws of nature for it to be bigger.

STREPSIADES: In that case, you miserable fool, if the sea doesn't get any bigger with the influx of the rivers, what business have you trying to make your sum of money bigger? Will you kindly chase yourself away from the house? [*Calling within*] Fetch me the goad. 1295

SECOND CREDITOR: Witness!

STREPSIADES [*prodding him*]: Gee up! What are you waiting for? Get moving, you branded nag!

Χρ.^β ταῦτ' οὐχ ὕβρις δῆτ' ἐστίν;

Στ.   ἄξεις; ἐφιαλῶ

κεντῶν ὑπὸ τὸν πρωκτόν σε τὸν σειραφόρον.   1300

φεύγεις; ἔμελλόν σ' ἄρα κινήσειν ἐγὼ

αὐτοῖς τροχοῖς τοῖς σοῖσι καὶ ξυνωρίσιν.

Χο. οἷον τὸ πραγμάτων ἐρᾶν φλαύρων· ὁ γὰρ   (στρ.

     γέρων ὅδ' ἐρασθεὶς

ἀποστερῆσαι βούλεται   1305

     τὰ χρήμαθ' ἁδανείσατο.

κοὐκ ἔσθ' ὅπως οὐ τήμερον

λήψεταί τι πρᾶγμ', ὃ τοῦ-

τον ποιήσει τὸν σοφι-

στήν, ὧν πανουργεῖν ἤρξατ', ἐξ-

αίφνης †τι κακὸν λαβεῖν†.   1310

οἶμαι γὰρ αὐτὸν αὐτίχ' εὑρήσειν ὅπερ   (ἀντ.

     πάλαι ποτ' ἐπήτει,

εἶναι τὸν υἱὸν δεινόν οἱ

     γνώμας ἐναντίας λέγειν

τοῖσιν δικαίοις, ὥστε νι-   1315

κᾶν ἅπαντας, οἷσπερ ἂν

ξυγγένηται, κᾶν λέγῃ

παμπόνηρ'. ἴσως δ' ἴσως

βουλήσεται

κἄφωνον αὐτὸν εἶναι.   1320

Στ. ἰοὺ ἰού.

1299 ἐφ- van Leeuwen: ἐπ- codd.
1310 †τι κακὸν λαβεῖν† codd.: κακὸν λαβεῖν τι Hermann: καλόν γ'
     ὄνασθαι Dover: perh. e.g. <ἀποστραφῆναι>, cf. Peace 683.
1312 ἐπήτει Bergk: ἐπεζήτει RV: ἐζήτει n.

136

SECOND CREDITOR: This is sheer wanton outrage!

STREPSIADES: Move! I'm going to lay it on, and poke you   1300
up your thoroughbred arse. [*The creditor runs away.*] Running
away, are you? I *thought* I'd get you moving, with your wheels and
chariot-and-pairs and all. [*He goes inside.*]

CHORUS: What it is to be enamoured of evil things! For this
        old man has fallen in love with them,
        and now wants to evade payment   1305
        of the money he has borrowed.
        And it is certain that today
        he has something coming to him
        that will make this sophist
        all of a sudden < recoil   1310
        from > the villainy on which he has embarked.

        For I fancy he will shortly find, what
        he requested some time ago,
        that his son is skilled
        in arguing for opinions opposed
        to justice, so as to vanquish   1315
        every adversary with whom
        he may meet, even if his cause
        be utterly wicked; and perhaps, perhaps,
        he will actually wish
        for his son to be struck dumb.   1320

[*Strepsiades rushes out of his house, followed by Pheidippides.*]

STREPSIADES: Help, help! Neighbours, kinsmen, fellow-

ὦ γείτονες καὶ ξυγγενεῖς καὶ δημόται,
ἀμυνάθετέ μοι τυπτομένῳ πάσῃ τέχνῃ.
οἴμοι κακοδαίμων τῆς κεφαλῆς καὶ τῆς γνάθου.
ὦ μιαρέ, τύπτεις τὸν πατέρα;

Φε.   φήμ', ὦ πάτερ.   1325

Στ. ὁρᾶθ' ὁμολογοῦνθ' ὅτι με τύπτει;

Φε.   καὶ μάλα.

Στ. ὦ μιαρὲ καὶ πατραλοῖα καὶ τοιχωρύχε.

Φε. αὖθις με ταὐτὰ ταῦτα καὶ πλείω λέγε.
ἆρ' οἶσθ' ὅτι χαίρω πόλλ' ἀκούων καὶ κακά;

Στ. ὦ λακκόπρωκτε—

Φε.   πάττε πολλοῖς τοῖς ῥόδοις.   1330

Στ. τὸν πατέρα τύπτεις;

Φε.   κἀποφανῶ γε νὴ Δία
ὡς ἐν δίκῃ σ' ἔτυπτον.

Στ.   ὦ μιαρώτατε,
καὶ πῶς γένοιτ' ἂν πατέρα τύπτειν ἐν δίκῃ;

Φε. ἔγωγ' ἀποδείξω, καί σε νικήσω λέγων.

Στ. τουτὶ σὺ νικήσεις;

Φε.   πολύ γε καὶ ῥᾳδίως.   1335
ἑλοῦ δ' ὁπότερον τοῖν λόγοιν βούλει λέγειν.

Στ. ποίοιν λόγοιν;

Φε.   τὸν κρείττον' ἢ τὸν ἥττονα.

1329   is placed after 1330 by Suda λ59 (but in Suda μ1025, where
       1330 is not quoted, 1329 follows 1328).

138

demesmen, come to my aid, I implore you — I'm being assaulted!
Oh, my poor head, my poor cheeks! [*To Pheidippides*] You villain, 1325
do you strike your father?

    PHEIDIPPIDES: Yes, father, I do.

    STREPSIADES: Do you see? He admits he's been beating me.

    PHEIDIPPIDES: Just so.

    STREPSIADES: You villain, you father-beater, you felon!

    PHEIDIPPIDES: Do call me the same things again, and more.
Do you know I enjoy being called many foul names?

    STREPSIADES: You tank-arsed scoundrel — 1330

    PHEIDIPPIDES: Shower me with more of these roses.

    STREPSIADES: Do you strike your father?

    PHEIDIPPIDES: Yes, and what's more, by Zeus, I'll prove
that I was right to strike you.

    STREPSIADES: You utter villain! How can you say that
beating a father could be right?

    PHEIDIPPIDES: I'll show that it is, and vanquish you in argu-
ment.

    STREPSIADES: You'll vanquish me on *this*? 1335

    PHEIDIPPIDES: Decisively and with ease. Choose which of
the two Arguments you want to uphold.

    STREPSIADES: What do you mean, the two Arguments?

    PHEIDIPPIDES: The Better or the Worse.

Στ. ἐδιδαξάμην μέντοι σε νὴ Δί', ὦ μέλε,
τοῖσιν δικαίοις ἀντιλέγειν, εἰ ταῦτά γε
μέλλεις ἀναπείσειν, ὡς δίκαιον καὶ καλὸν   1340
τὸν πατέρα τύπτεσθ' ἐστὶν ὑπὸ τῶν υἱέων.

Φε. ἀλλ' οἴομαι μέντοι σ' ἀναπείσειν, ὥστε γε
οὐδ' αὐτὸς ἀκροασάμενος οὐδὲν ἀντερεῖς.

Στ. καὶ μὴν ὅ τι καὶ λέξεις ἀκοῦσαι βούλομαι.

Χο. σὸν ἔργον, ὦ πρεσβῦτα, φροντίζειν ὅπῃ   (στρ.
τὸν ἄνδρα κρατήσεις·   1346
ὡς οὗτος, εἰ μή τῳ 'πεπούθειν, οὐκ ἂν ἦν
οὕτως ἀκόλαστος.
ἀλλ' ἔσθ' ὅτῳ θρασύνεται· δῆλόν <γέ τοι>
τὸ λῆμα τάνθρώπου.   1350

ἀλλ' ἐξ ὅτου τὸ πρῶτον ἤρξαθ' ἡ μάχη γενέσθαι,
ἤδη λέγειν χρὴ πρὸς χορόν· πάντως δὲ τοῦτο δράσεις.

Στ. καὶ μὴν ὅθεν γε πρῶτον ἠρξάμεσθα λοιδορεῖσθαι
ἐγὼ φράσω. 'πειδὴ γὰρ εἰστιώμεθ', ὥσπερ ἴστε,
πρῶτον μὲν αὐτὸν τὴν λύραν λαβόντ' ἐγὼ 'κέλευσα   1355
ᾆσαι Σιμωνίδου μέλος, τὸν Κριόν, ὡς ἐπέχθη·
ὁ δ' εὐθέως ἀρχαῖον εἶν' ἔφασκε τὸ κιθαρίζειν
ᾄδειν τε πίνονθ' ὡσπερεὶ κάχρυς γυναῖκ' ἀλοῦσαν.

Φε. οὐ γὰρ τότ' εὐθὺς χρῆν σ' ἀράττεσθαί τε καὶ πατεῖσθαι,

1340 μέλλεις RVEK: μέλλεις μ' ΝΘ.
1347 'πεπούθειν Dawes: πεπούθει R ʸʳθ²: πέποιθεν or πέποιθ' V<u>n</u>.
1349 <γε> Tricl., <τοι> Hermann: om. codd.
1350 τὸ λῆμα Dover: τὸ λῆμ' (λῆμμ' R) ἐστὶ codd.
1359 ἀράττεσθαί Meineke: ἄρα τύπτεσθαι R<u>n</u>: ἀλλὰ τύπτεσθαι V.

140

STREPSIADES: I *have* had you taught all right, my good man, to argue against justice, if you're going to be able to make *this* claim 1340 convincing, that it's right and proper for a father to be beaten by his sons.

PHEIDIPPIDES: But I think I *shall* convince you, so much so that even you, when you've heard me, won't have a thing to say against it.

STREPSIADES: As a matter of fact I'd like to hear what *you'll* find to say.

CHORUS: It is up to you, old man, to think how 1345
           you can defeat him;
           for he, if he did not have something to rely on,
           would not have shown such effrontery.
           No, there is something that gives him confidence;
           at any rate the fellow's insolence is plain. 1350

CHORUS-LEADER [*to Strepsiades*]: Now you must tell the Chorus what the quarrel originally arose from. But you'll do that anyway.

STREPSIADES: I certainly will tell you what first caused us to begin using hard words. When we were feasting, which you know about, first of all I asked him to take his lyre and sing a song by 1355 Simonides, "How Sir Ram was shorn"; but he at once said that that was antiquated, playing the lyre and singing at a drinking party, like a woman grinding hulled barley.

PHEIDIPPIDES: Well, surely you should have been pounded and trampled right then — telling me to sing, as if you were enter- 1360

ᾄδειν κελεύονθ', ὡσπερεὶ τέττιγας ἑστιῶντα;   1360

Στ. τοιαῦτα μέντοι καὶ τότ' ἔλεγεν ἔνδον, οἷάπερ νῦν·
     καὶ τὸν Σιμωνίδην ἔφασκ' εἶναι κακὸν ποιητήν.
     κἀγὼ μόλις μέν, ἀλλ' ὅμως ἠνεσχόμην τὸ πρῶτον.
     ἔπειτα δ' ἐκέλευσ' αὐτὸν ἀλλὰ μυρρίνην λαβόντα
     τῶν Αἰσχύλου λέξαι τί μοι· κᾆθ' οὗτος εὐθὺς εἶπεν·   1365
     "ἐγὼ γὰρ Αἰσχύλον νομίζω πρῶτον ἐν ποιηταῖς—
     ψόφου πλέων, ἀξύστατον, στόμφακα, κρημνοποιόν."
     κἀνταῦθα πῶς οἴεσθέ μου τὴν καρδίαν ὀρεχθεῖν;
     ὅμως δὲ τὸν θυμὸν δακὼν ἔφην· "σὺ δ' ἀλλὰ τούτων
     λέξον τι τῶν νεωτέρων, ἅττ' ἐστὶ τὰ σοφὰ ταῦτα."   1370
     ὁ δ' εὐθὺς ἦκ' Εὐριπίδου ῥῆσίν τιν', ὡς ἐκίνει
     ἀδελφός, ὦλεξίκακε, τὴν ὁμομητρίαν ἀδελφήν.
     κἀγὼ οὐκέτ' ἐξηνεσχόμην, ἀλλ' εὐθέως ἀράττω
     πολλοῖς κακοῖς καἰσχροῖσι· κᾆτ' ἐντεῦθεν, οἷον εἰκός,
     ἔπος πρὸς ἔπος ἠρειδόμεσθ'· εἶθ' οὗτος ἐπαναπηδᾷ,   1375
     κἄπειτ' ἔφλα με κἀσπόδει κἄπνιγε κἀπέτριβεν.

Φε. οὔκουν δικαίως, ὅστις οὐκ Εὐριπίδην ἐπαινεῖς,
     σοφώτατον;

Στ.   σοφώτατόν γ' ἐκεῖνον, ὦ—τί σ' εἴπω;
     ἀλλ' αὖθις αὖ τυπτήσομαι.

Φε.   νὴ τὸν Δί', ἐν δίκῃ γ' ἄν.

1371 ἦκ' Sommerstein, cf. Wasps 562, Frogs 823: ἦσ' or ἦσεν RVn':
      om. N: ἦγ' Borthwick.

1373 εὐθέως ἀράττω (-άτω) Vb3: ευθεως αρράτω ?Π9 (with ταράττω in
      margin): εὐθέως ʸᵖΣᵁ: εὐθὺς ἐξαράττω RVn.

1376 κἀπέτριβεν Π9 n Suda: κἀπέθλιβεν RV.

1379 γ' ἄν RVEᵃᶜKN: γε Π9: γάρ EᵖᶜΘ.

142

taining cicadas!

STREPSIADES: That's just the sort of thing he was saying then inside, what he's saying now; and he also said that Simonides was a bad poet. I could only just endure it, but all the same I did endure it for the moment. Then I asked him at least to take a myrtle-branch and recite me something from the works of Aeschylus; 1365 and then he at once said, "Oh, yes, I regard Aeschylus as supreme among poets — at being full of noise, incoherent, a bombastic ranter and a creator of mountainous words." And how do you suppose my heart palpitated at that? But I bit back my rage and said, "All right, you recite something from these modern poets, that 1370 clever stuff, whatever it is." And he immediately loosed off a speech of Euripides, about how a brother, heaven forfend, was having it off with his sister by the same mother. Well, I could take it no longer, and I immediately piled into him with many hard and foul words; and after that, as you might expect, we attacked each other insult 1375 for insult. Then he jumps up; and he knocked me and banged me and choked me and pulverized me.

PHEIDIPPIDES: So wasn't I right to do so to one who won't praise Euripides, a man of genius?

STREPSIADES [*with angry sarcasm*]: Oh yes, a genius, you — what shall I call you? — [*Controlling himself*] No, I'll only be beaten all over again.

PHEIDIPPIDES: And, by Zeus, you'd deserve it.

Στ. καὶ πῶς δικαίως; ὅστις, ὦναίσχυντέ, σ' ἐξέθρεψα   1380
    αἰσθανόμενός σου πάντα τραυλίζοντος, ὅ τι νοοίης.
    εἰ μέν γε βρῦν εἴποις, ἐγὼ γνοὺς ἂν πιεῖν ἐπέσχον·
    μαμμᾶν δ' ἂν αἰτήσαντος, ἧκόν σοι φέρων ἂν ἄρτον·
    κακκᾶν δ' ἂν οὐκ ἔφθης φράσας, κἀγὼ λαβὼν θύραζε
    ἐξέφερον ἂν καὶ προυσχόμην σε. σὺ δ' ἐμὲ νῦν ἀπάγχων, 1385
    βοῶντα καὶ κεκραγόθ' ὅτι
        χεζητιῴην, οὐκ ἔτλης
        ἔξω 'ξενεγκεῖν, ὦ μιαρέ,
        θύραζέ μ', ἀλλὰ πνιγόμενος
        αὐτοῦ 'ποίησα κακκᾶν.   1390

Χο. οἶμαί γε τῶν νεωτέρων τὰς καρδίας   (ἀντ.
        πηδᾶν, ὅ τι λέξει.
    εἰ γὰρ τοιαῦτά γ' οὗτος ἐξειργασμένος
        λαλῶν ἀναπείσει,
    τὸ δέρμα τῶν γεραιτέρων λάβοιμεν ἂν   1395
        ἀλλ' οὐδ' ἐρεβίνθου.

    σὸν ἔργον, ὦ καινῶν ἐπῶν κινητὰ καὶ μοχλευτά,
    πειθώ τινα ζητεῖν, ὅπως δόξεις λέγειν δίκαια.

Φε. ὡς ἡδὺ καινοῖς πράγμασιν καὶ δεξιοῖς ὁμιλεῖν,
    καὶ τῶν καθεστώτων νόμων ὑπερφρονεῖν δύνασθαι.   1400
    ἐγὼ γάρ, ὅτε μὲν ἱππικῇ τὸν νοῦν μόνῃ προσεῖχον,
    οὐδ' ἂν τρί' εἰπεῖν ῥήμαθ' οἷός τ' ἦ πρὶν ἐξαμαρτεῖν·
    νυνὶ δ', ἐπειδή μ' οὑτοσὶ τούτων ἔπαυσεν αὐτός,
    γνώμαις δὲ λεπταῖς καὶ λόγοις ξύνειμι καὶ μερίμναις,
    οἶμαι διδάξειν ὡς δίκαιον τὸν πατέρα κολάζειν.   1405

1386 καὶ N: om. RVn'.
1401 τὸν νοῦν μόνῃ Bentley: μόνῃ τὸν νοῦν n: τὸν νοῦν μόνον R:
      τὸν νοῦν μου V.

STREPSIADES: What do you mean, I'd deserve it? I who 1380
brought you up, you shameless scoundrel, understanding the meaning of your every lisping utterance! If you said "bru", I'd understand and put a drink to your lips; if you asked for "mamma", I'd
come to you with bread; and no sooner did you say "kakka" than
I'd pick you up, carry you out of doors, and hold you out. Whereas 1385
just now, when you were throttling me, though I was shouting and
screaming that I wanted to crap, you couldn't bring yourself to carry
me out of doors, you villain, but you choked me until I did a 1390
kakka on the spot!

    CHORUS: I fancy that the hearts of the young
                  are throbbing to hear what he will say.
                  For if, after committing such an act,
                  he talks us into believing him right,
                  then for the skin of the elderly we'd give 1395
                  not a chickpea.

    CHORUS-LEADER: It's up to you, the shifter and upheaver
who uses new-fangled verbal tools, to find some means of persuasion to make it appear that what you say is right.

    PHEIDIPPIDES: How pleasant it is to be intimate with what
is new and clever, and to be able to look with scorn on established 1400
custom! In the days when I devoted my attention only to racing,
I was not able to say three words before making a blunder; but now,
since my opponent himself has made me stop all that, and I am familiar with subtle ideas, arguments and cogitations, I think I can show 1405
that it is right to chastise one's father.

Στ. ἵππευε τοίνυν νὴ Δί᾽· ὡς ἔμοιγε κρεῖττόν ἐστιν
 ἵππων τρέφειν τέθριππον ἢ τυπτόμενον ἐπιτριβῆναι.

Φε. ἐκεῖσε δ᾽ ὅθεν ἀπέσχισάς με τοῦ λόγου μέτειμι,
 καὶ πρῶτ᾽ ἐρήσομαί σε τουτί· παῖδά μ᾽ ὄντ᾽ ἔτυπτες;

Στ. ἔγωγέ σ᾽, εὐνοῶν γε καὶ κηδόμενος.

Φε.   εἰπὲ δή μοι,   1410
 οὐ κἀμὲ σοὶ δίκαιόν ἐστιν εὐνοεῖν ὁμοίως
 τύπτειν τ᾽, ἐπειδήπερ γε τοῦτ᾽ ἔστ᾽ εὐνοεῖν, τὸ τύπτειν;
 πῶς γὰρ τὸ μὲν σὸν σῶμα χρὴ πληγῶν ἀθῷον εἶναι,
 τοὐμὸν δὲ μή; καὶ μὴν ἔφυν ἐλεύθερός γε κἀγώ.
 "κλάουσι παῖδες, πατέρα δ᾽ οὐ κλάειν δοκεῖς;"   1415
 φήσεις νομίζεσθαι σὺ παιδὸς τοῦτο τοὔργον εἶναι·
 ἐγὼ δέ γ᾽ ἀντείποιμ᾽ ἂν ὡς δὶς παῖδες οἱ γέροντες·
 εἰκός τε μᾶλλον τοὺς γέροντας ἢ νέους τι κλάειν,
 ὅσῳπερ ἐξαμαρτάνειν ἧττον δίκαιον αὐτούς.

Στ. ἀλλ᾽ οὐδαμοῦ νομίζεται τὸν πατέρα τοῦτο πάσχειν.   1420

Φε. οὔκουν ἀνὴρ ὁ τὸν νόμον θεὶς τοῦτον ἦν τὸ πρῶτον,
 ὥσπερ σὺ κἀγώ, καὶ λέγων ἔπειθε τοὺς παλαιούς;
 ἧττόν τι δῆτ᾽ ἔξεστι κἀμοὶ καινὸν αὖ τὸ λοιπὸν
 θεῖναι νόμον τοῖς υἱέσιν, τοὺς πατέρας ἀντιτύπτειν;
 ὅσας δὲ πληγὰς εἴχομεν πρὶν τὸν νόμον τεθῆναι,   1425
 ἀφίεμεν, καὶ δίδομεν αὐτοῖς προῖκα συγκεκόφθαι.
 σκέψαι δὲ τοὺς ἀλεκτρυόνας καὶ τἆλλα τὰ βοτὰ ταυτί,
 ὡς τοὺς πατέρας ἀμύνεται· καίτοι τί διαφέρουσιν
 ἡμῶν ἐκεῖνοι, πλήν γ᾽ ὅτι ψηφίσματ᾽ οὐ γράφουσιν;

1410 γε Hermann: τε codd.
1412 γε E^2: om. RVKNΘ: [E^1].
1418 νέους Bentley: τους νέους RE^{pc}Θ: τους νεωτέρους VE^{ac}KN.

STREPSIADES: Stick to your horses then, in heaven's name; it's better for me to maintain a four-horse team than to be beaten and pulverized.

PHEIDIPPIDES: I shall go on to the point in the argument from which you made me break off, and first ask you this: did you beat me when I was a boy?

STREPSIADES: I did, out of benevolence and concern for 1410 your good.

PHEIDIPPIDES: Then tell me, is it not likewise right for me to be benevolent to you in the same way and beat you, seeing that that is what being benevolent to a person means — beating him? How can it be right for your body to be immune from blows and mine not? After all, I too am a free man born.

"The children howl; do you think the father shouldn't?" 1415 You will say that it is customary for this treatment to be reserved for children; but I would reply that the old are in a second childhood. And it is more reasonable that the old should be made to howl a bit rather than the young, inasmuch as it is less natural that they should go wrong.

STREPSIADES: But nowhere is it the law that a father should 1420 be so treated.

PHEIDIPPIDES: Well, wasn't it a man who made that law in the first place, a man like you or me, and didn't he persuade the men of old by argument to accept it? Is it then any less open to me in my turn to make a new law for sons in the future, that they should beat their fathers in return? All the blows we received before the 1425 law was made we wipe from the record, and we make it a concession to them that our having been thrashed hitherto shall remain without compensation. Consider fowls and those other animals, how they retaliate against their fathers; and after all, what difference is there between them and us, except that they don't propose decrees?

147

Στ. τί δῆτ', ἐπειδὴ τοὺς ἀλεκτρυόνας ἅπαντα μιμεῖ, 1430
οὐκ ἐσθίεις καὶ τὴν κόπρον κἀπὶ ξύλου καθεύδεις;

Φε. οὐ ταὐτόν, ὦ τᾶν, ἐστιν, οὐδ' ἂν Σωκράτει δοκοίη.

Στ. πρὸς ταῦτα μὴ τύπτ'· εἰ δὲ μή, σαυτόν ποτ' αἰτιάσει.

Φε. καὶ πῶς;

Στ.   ἐπεὶ σὲ μὲν δίκαιός εἰμ' ἐγὼ κολάζειν,
σὺ δ', ἢν γένηταί σοι, τὸν υἱόν.

Φε.   ἢν δὲ μὴ γένηται, 1435
μάτην ἐμοὶ κεκλαύσεται, σὺ δ' ἐγχανὼν τεθνήξεις.

Στ. ἐμοὶ μέν, ὦνδρες ἥλικες, δοκεῖ λέγειν δίκαια·
κἄμοιγε συγχωρεῖν δοκεῖ τούτοισι τἀπιεικῆ.
κλάειν γὰρ ἡμᾶς εἰκός ἐστ', ἢν μὴ δίκαια δρῶμεν.

Φε. σκέψαι δὲ χἀτέραν ἔτι γνώμην.

Στ.   ἀπὸ γὰρ ὀλοῦμαι. 1440

Φε. καὶ μὴν ἴσως γ' οὐκ ἀχθέσει παθὼν ἃ νῦν πέπονθας.

Στ. πῶς δή; δίδαξον γὰρ τί μ' ἐκ τούτων ἔτ' ὠφελήσεις.

Φε. τὴν μητέρ' ὥσπερ καὶ σὲ τυπτήσω.

Στ.   τί φής, τί φὴς σύ;
τοῦθ' ἕτερον αὖ μεῖζον κακόν.

Φε.   τί δ', ἢν ἔχων τὸν ἥττω
λόγον σε νικήσω λέγων 1445

1436 τεθνήξεις Dawes: τεθνήξει or -ῃ codd. Suda, Zonaras.

1437-9 should possibly be deleted as a remnant of an alternative
     draft for the transition to the revised ending.

1442 ἔτ' ὠφελήσεις Dover: ἐπωφελήσεις RVE^{pc}Nθ: ὠφελήσεις E^{ac}K.

STREPSIADES: Well then, if you're following the example 1430
of fowls in everything, why don't you also eat the dung and sleep on
a wooden perch?

PHEIDIPPIDES: It's not the same thing, my good man, nor
would Socrates think it was.

STREPSIADES: Well, in that case don't beat me; if you do,
you'll blame yourself one day.

PHEIDIPPIDES: Oh, why?

STREPSIADES: Because I, as things stand, have the right to
chastise you, and you to chastise your son, if you have one. 1435

PHEIDIPPIDES: But if I don't have one, I'll have howled all
for nothing, and there you'll be, dead, having had the last laugh on
me!

STREPSIADES [*to the old men in the audience*]: To me,
friends and contemporaries, it seems that what he says is right, and
I think we should concede to this generation what is reasonable. It's
only fair that we should get a hiding if we do wrong.

PHEIDIPPIDES: Now consider another further point. 1440

STREPSIADES: No, it'll be the death of me.

PHEIDIPPIDES: On the contrary, perhaps you won't be so
sorry to have suffered what you've suffered.

STREPSIADES: How do you mean? Explain in what way
you can still bring some good to me out of this.

PHEIDIPPIDES: I'll beat mother, just as I did you.

STREPSIADES: What's this, what's this you say? This is a
second and greater piece of wickedness.

PHEIDIPPIDES: Well, what if with the Worse Argument I
defeat you on the proposition that it's right to beat one's mother? 1445

149

τὴν μητέρ' ὡς τύπτειν χρεών;

Στ. τί δ' ἄλλο γ' ἤ, ταῦτ' ἢν ποιῇς,
οὐδέν σε κωλύσει σεαυ-
τὸν ἐμβαλεῖν εἰς τὸ βάραθρον
μετὰ Σωκράτους   1450
καὶ τὸν λόγον τὸν ἥττω;

ταυτὶ δι' ὑμᾶς, ὦ Νεφέλαι, πέπονθ' ἐγώ,
ὑμῖν ἀναθεὶς ἅπαντα τἀμὰ πράγματα.

Χο. αὐτὸς μὲν οὖν σαυτῷ σὺ τούτων αἴτιος,
στρέψας σεαυτὸν εἰς πονηρὰ πράγματα.   1455

Στ. τί δῆτα ταῦτ' οὔ μοι τότ' ἠγορεύετε,
ἀλλ' ἄνδρ' ἄγροικον καὶ γέροντ' ἐπήρατε;

Χο. ἀεὶ ποιοῦμεν ταῦθ' ἑκάστοθ', ὅντιν' ἂν
γνῶμεν πονηρῶν ὄντ' ἐραστὴν πραγμάτων,
ἕως ἂν αὐτὸν ἐμβάλωμεν εἰς κακόν,   1460
ὅπως ἂν εἰδῇ τοὺς θεοὺς δεδοικέναι.

Στ. ὤμοι, πονηρά γ', ὦ Νεφέλαι, δίκαια δέ·
οὐ γάρ με χρῆν τὰ χρήμαθ' ἁδανεισάμην
ἀποστερεῖν. νῦν οὖν ὅπως, ὦ φίλτατε,
τὸν Χαιρεφῶντα τὸν μιαρὸν καὶ Σωκράτη   1465
ἀπολεῖς μετ' ἐμοῦ 'λθών, οἵ σὲ κἄμ' ἐξηπάτων.

Φε. ἀλλ' οὐκ ἂν ἀδικήσαιμι τοὺς διδασκάλους.

Στ. ναὶ ναί· καταιδέσθητι πατρῷον Δία.

1447 ἤ, ταῦτ' ἢν Kock: ἢν ταύτην V: ἢν ταῦτα Νθ: ἢν ταυτὶ vel
       sim. REK.
1458 ἀεὶ n̲: ἡμεῖς RV.
1458 ὅντιν' ἂν Porson: ἄν τιν' οὖν E^{ac}K: ὅταν τινὰ RVE^{pc}Νθ.

150

STREPSIADES: What then? Just this: if you do that there'll be nothing to stop you throwing yourself into the Barathron along with Socrates and the Worse Argument. [*To the Chorus*] Clouds, this has come upon me because of you; I placed my whole fate in your hands.   1450

CHORUS-LEADER: No, you are responsible for bringing it on yourself, because you turned yourself towards evil actions.   1455

STREPSIADES: Then why didn't you tell me that at the time, instead of positively enticing an old rustic astray?

CHORUS-LEADER: This is what we always do on every occasion, whenever we find a man to be a lover of what is evil, until we   1460 cast him into misery, that he may learn to fear the gods.

STREPSIADES: Ah, Clouds! hard words, but they're fair: I ought not to have tried to evade payment of the money I borrowed. [*To Pheidippides*] Now, my dear, dear boy, come with me and let's   1465-6 murder that villain Chaerephon and Socrates, who have cheated both you and me.

PHEIDIPPIDES: But I couldn't wrong my teachers!

STREPSIADES: "Aye, aye: of Zeus Paternal stand in awe."

Φε. ἰδού γε Δία πατρῷον. ὡς ἀρχαῖος εἶ.
     Ζεὺς γάρ τίς ἐστιν;

Στ.   ἔστιν.

Φε.   οὐκ ἔστ', οὐκ, ἐπεὶ   1470
     Δῖνος βασιλεύει, τὸν Δί' ἐξεληλακώς.

Στ. οὐκ ἐξελήλακ', ἀλλ' ἐγὼ τοῦτ' ᾠόμην
     διὰ τουτονὶ τὸν δῖνον. οἴμοι δείλαιος,
     ὅτε καὶ σὲ χυτρεοῦν ὄντα θεὸν ἡγησάμην.

Φε. ἐνταῦθα σαυτῷ παραφρόνει καὶ φληνάφα.   1475

Στ. οἴμοι παρανοίας· ὡς ἐμαινόμην ἄρα,
     ὅτ' ἐξέβαλον καὶ τοὺς θεοὺς διὰ Σωκράτη.
     ἀλλ', ὦ φίλ' Ἑρμῆ, μηδαμῶς θύμαινέ μοι
     μηδέ μ' ἐπιτρίψῃς, ἀλλὰ συγγνώμην ἔχε
     ἐμοῦ παρανοήσαντος ἀδολεσχίᾳ·   1480
     καί μοι γενοῦ ξύμβουλος, εἴτ' αὐτοὺς γραφὴν
     διωκάθω γραψάμενος, εἴθ' ὅ τι σοι δοκεῖ.
     ὀρθῶς παραινεῖς οὐκ ἐῶν δικορραφεῖν,
     ἀλλ' ὡς τάχιστ' ἐμπιμπράναι τὴν οἰκίαν
     τῶν ἀδολεσχῶν. δεῦρο δεῦρ', ὦ Ξανθία·   1485
     κλίμακα λαβὼν ἔξελθε καὶ σμινύην φέρων,
     κἄπειτ' ἐπαναβὰς ἐπὶ τὸ φροντιστήριον
     τὸ τέγος κατάσκαπτ', εἰ φιλεῖς τὸν δεσπότην,
     ἕως ἂν αὐτοῖς ἐμβάλῃς τὴν οἰκίαν.
     ἐμοὶ δὲ δᾷδ' ἐνεγκάτω τις ἡμμένην,   1490

1477 ἐξέβαλον R^{ac}n̲ ^{λ}Σ^{θ}: ἐξέβαλε ^{λ}Σ^{E}: ἐξέβαλλον R^{pc}V.
1477 καὶ RVn̲': om. N ^{λ}Σ^{Εθ}.
1480 παρανοήσαντος n̲: παρανομήσαντος RV.
1484 ἐμπιμπράναι Brunck: πιμπράναι K: ἐμπιπράναι vel sim. RVn̲'.

152

PHEIDIPPIDES: Listen to that! Paternal Zeus! How old-fashioned you are! Is there any Zeus?   1470

STREPSIADES: There is.

PHEIDIPPIDES: There isn't, no there isn't, because Vortex is king, having expelled Zeus.

STREPSIADES: He hasn't expelled him; I thought he had, because of this vortex-cup [*pointing to a cup standing on a pillar in front of the Reflectory*]. Poor fool that I was, to take you, a piece of pottery, for a god!   *

PHEIDIPPIDES: You can rave and yammer here to yourself.   1475
[*He goes inside*].

STREPSIADES: My god, what insanity! How mad I see l was, when I actually discarded the gods because of Socrates! [*To the image of Hermes in front of his house*] Beloved Hermes, please don't be angry with me or crush me, but have mercy on me if I   1480
acted insanely because of their empty prattle; and be my counsellor, whether I should prosecute them by laying an indictment, or whatever you think best. [*He pauses for a reply.*] You advise me rightly — that I shouldn't cobble up lawsuits, but as quickly as possible set fire to the house of these prattlers. [*Calling within*] Come here,   1485
come here, Xanthias! come outside, and bring a ladder and a mattock, and then go up on top of the Reflectory and hack down the roof, if you love your master, until you bring the house down on them. [*The slave, having brought the implements out, climbs on to the roof and sets to work.*] And someone fetch me a lighted torch;   1490

κάγώ τιν' αὐτῶν τήμερον δοῦναι δίκην
ἐμοὶ ποιήσω, κεἰ σφόδρ' εἴσ' ἀλαζόνες.

Μα. ἰού ἰού.

Στ. σὸν ἔργον, ὦ δᾷς, ἰέναι πολλὴν φλόγα.

Μα. ἄνθρωπε, τί ποιεῖς;

Στ.   ὅ τι ποιῶ; τί δ' ἄλλο γ' ἢ   1495
διαλεπτολογοῦμαι ταῖς δοκοῖς τῆς οἰκίας;
ΧΑΙΡΕΦΩΝ
οἴμοι, τίς ἡμῶν πυρπολεῖ τὴν οἰκίαν;

Στ. ἐκεῖνος οὗπερ θοἰμάτιον εἰλήφατε.

Χα. ἀπολεῖς, ἀπολεῖς.

Στ.   τοῦτ' αὐτὸ γὰρ καὶ βούλομαι,
ἢν ἡ σμινύη μοι μὴ προδῷ τὰς ἐλπίδας,   1500
ἢ 'γὼ πρότερόν πως ἐκτραχηλισθῶ πεσών.

Σω. οὗτος, τί ποιεῖς ἐτεόν, οὑπὶ τοῦ τέγους;

Στ. ἀεροβατῶ καὶ περιφρονῶ τὸν ἥλιον.

Σω. οἴμοι τάλας, δείλαιος ἀποπνιγήσομαι.

Χα. ἐγὼ δὲ κακοδαίμων γε κατακαυθήσομαι.   1505

Στ. τί γὰρ μαθόντες τοὺς θεοὺς ὑβρίζετε,
καὶ τῆς Σελήνης ἐσκοπεῖσθε τὴν ἕδραν;
δίωκε, παῖε, βάλλε, πολλῶν οὕνεκα,

1506 μαθόντες RVE^{pc}Nθ: μαθόνθ' vel sim. E^{ac}K ^{γρ}θ.
1506 τοὺς θεοὺς RE^{pc}Nθ: εἰ τοὺς θεοὺς V: εἰς τοὺς θεοὺς ^{γρ}θ and
       (at end of line) E^{ac}K.
1506 ὑβρίζετε RVE^{pc}Nθ: ὑβρίζετον E^{ac}K ^{γρ}θ².
1507 ἐσκοπεῖσθε RVK^{pc}: ἐσκοπεῖσθον Eθ: ἐσκοπεῖτε K^{ac}N.

154

and I'll make someone here pay a penalty today for what they've done to me, no matter how big they talk. [*He is given a torch, and joins Xanthias on the roof.*]

A STUDENT [*inside*]: Help, help!

STREPSIADES: I bid you, torch, send forth abundant flame! [*He sets fire to the rafters.*]   *

STUDENT [*rushing outside, with others, and seeing Strepsiades*]: Here, man, what are you doing?   1495

STREPSIADES: What am I doing? What else but chopping logic with the rafters of your house?

CHAEREPHON [*appearing at an upper window*]: Help, who's putting our house to the flames?

STREPSIADES: The same man whose cloak you stole.

CHAEREPHON: You'll destroy us, you'll destroy us!

STREPSIADES: That's exactly what I want to do, if the mat-   1500
tock doesn't betray my hopes and I don't first fall somehow and break my neck.

SOCRATES [*coming out as smoke billows through the door*]: Here, you on the roof, what do you think you're doing?

STREPSIADES: I walk the air and descry the sun.

SOCRATES [*coughing*]: Help! wretched me! I'm going to choke!

CHAEREPHON [*still inside*]: But what about me, poor thing,   1505
I'll be burnt to death!

STREPSIADES [*descending to the ground, with Xanthias, while Chaerephon climbs dangerously down from his window*]: Well, what was your idea in wantonly flouting the gods and inspecting the seat of the Moon? Chase them, hit them, pelt them, for a hundred causes, but most of all remembering how they wronged

155

μάλιστα δ' εἰδὼς τοὺς θεοὺς ὡς ἠδίκουν.

Χο. ἡγεῖσθ' ἔξω· κεχόρευται γὰρ   1510
     μετρίως τό γε τήμερον ἡμῖν.

the gods! [*Socrates and his pupils flee, pursued by Strepsiades and Xanthias.*]

    CHORUS-LEADER [*to her companions*]: Lead the way out;   1510
for we have done enough singing and dancing for today. [*Exeunt.*]

7.   **it's not even possible ... to punish my slaves:** in wartime a discontented slave
      who ran away would be safe if he reached enemy territory: cf. *Peace* 451.
      The truce made between the Athenians and Spartans in spring 423 (a few
      days after the production of *Clouds*) included a provision that neither side
      was to receive deserters from the other "whether free men or slaves" (Thuc.
      4.118.6).

10.   **fleeced cloaks:** Greek *sisurā* means a cloak made of sheepskin or goatskin with
      the hair left on.

12.   **I just can't sleep ... with being bitten:** after this we expect "by bedbugs" (cf.
      37, 634, 699-726); what actually follows is a surprise.

13.   **expenses and mangers:** almost a hendiadys, = "the expense of keeping horses".

14.   **he wears his hair long:** this was fashionable among rich young men; cf. *Knights*
      580, 1121. Pheidippides wants to move in the highest social circles, but he
      cannot do so within his father's income.

17.   **when I see the moon in its twenties:** i.e. when the moon is twenty or more days
      old and the (lunar) month is nearing its end. The Greek plural *eikades* else-
      where, like the singular *eikas*, seem always to mean specifically the twentieth
      day of the month; here however the broader sense is required, since few people
      would feel confident in guessing the *exact* age of the moon merely from its
      shape.

*18. **the interest is mounting up:** interest was reckoned on a monthly basis (cf. 756),
      and the amount ultimately payable would therefore increase if a debt was not
      settled by the end of the month.

*21. **twelve minas:** a mina of silver was approximately 437 grams; one mina equalled
      100 drachmas.

*23. **the horse with the koppa brand:** the obsolete Greek letter *koppa* (ϙ) was used
      as a brand-mark to indicate the breed of a horse. Compare the similar use of

the letter *san* (122, *Knights* 603). For a detailed study of what is known abou Greek brand-marks on horses, see K. Braun, *MDAI(A)* 85 (1970) 256-267.

24. **I wish I'd had my eye knocked out**: the Greek for "I'd had knocked out" is *exekopēn*, which bears a punning resemblance to *koppatiās* "horse with a *koppa* brand".

25. **Philon, you're cheating**: Pheidippides is dreaming he is in a chariot-race. He calls out to another driver who is cutting in on him.

28. **war-chariots**: Greeks did not in historical times (except in Cyprus: Hdt. 5.113.1) use chariots in warfare, but there were races for "war-chariots" at festivals such as the Panathenaea (*IG* ii^2 2311.58; 2316.56-57; 2317.20). Probably the difference between a "war-chariot" and an ordinary racing chariot was that the former carried two men (originally, as in Homer, one to drive and one to fight).

29. **round enough bends**: lit. "many laps".

30. **what sad debt befell?**: Greek *ti khreos ebā me?*, adapted from a lyric passage of Euripides (fr. 1011) *ti khreos ebā dōma?* "what thing has befallen the house?" with a play on two senses of *khreos* (in poetry "thing", in normal language "debt").

31. **Amynias**: V has the different name "Ameinias", and this name is inscriptionally attested in classical Athens while "Amynias" is not. But (i) Aristophanic mss. elsewhere (686ff. and *Wasps* 74, 466, 1267) give uniformly "Amynias", (ii) V's reading could derive from the mention of Ameinias, archon in 423/2, in the scholia and one of the Hypotheses, (iii) if fourth-century Athenians could be called Amynander, Amynomachus and Amynomenus (*PA* 735, 741, 743; *IG* ii^2 1700.59; cf. also Amynon in *Eccl.* 365) we cannot say that a fifth century Athenian could not have been called Amynias.

31. **chariot-board**: the board on which the driver stood.

32. **let the horse have a roll**: the mention of a single horse suggests that Pheidippides' dream has shifted from chariot-driving to horse-riding. He is here giving orders to his groom: after its exercise, the horse is to be allowed to dry itself by rolling in the dust before returning to the stable.

33. **you've been rolling ... in my money**: lit. "you have rolled me out of my property", i.e. ruined me; for the metaphor cf. Plautus, *Menaechmi* 903 *quem ego hominem ... vita evolvam sua* "I'll roll that man out of his life", i.e. "I'll murder him".

* 34-
35. **distrain for their interest**: either these creditors have lent Strepsiades money on condition that they are entitled to distrain on his property if interest is not paid, or they are threatening legal proceedings with distraint to follow. See A.R.W. Harrison, *The Law of Athens II: Procedure* (Oxford, 1971) 188-9, 244-7.

160

36. **twisting and turning:** the verb *strephein* "twist" and its cognates are several times used in the play with reference to Strepsiades, whose name is derived from the verb and who is attempting to twist (cheat) his way out of debt. See 88, 434, 450, 776, 792, 1455.

37. **I'm getting bitten:** as at 12, we expect "by a bug".

*37. **deme official:** strictly "demarch", the annually-chosen chief official of each of the demes or districts of Attica. It is not clear what role he played in the procedure of distraint; but we know that when a debt *to the state* was unpaid it was the debtor's demarch who had the right to levy execution on his property, and possibly he could on request do the same for a judgement debt owed to an individual. See Harrison, op. cit. 189, 212.

39-40. **all these debts will be your headache:** when Pheidippides inherits his father's property, he will also inherit his father's debts.

41. **would that:** Greek *eith' ōphel'*, a tragic expression, made famous by the opening line of Euripides' *Medea* (cf. *Frogs* 1382).

44. **nice and mouldy ... as one pleased:** i.e. with no need to keep the house scrupulously clean or to sit and recline decorously (things about which, by inference, his present wife is punctilious).

45. **honey-bees and sheep and pressed olive:** from this and 50 we get a picture of Strepsiades before his marriage as a prosperous mixed farmer, keeping sheep, goats (71) and bees, and growing grapes, olives and figs.

46. **Megacles son of Megacles:** clearly a member of the aristocratic Alcmeonid family, in which the name Megacles was frequent; possibly meant for a specific contemporary Megacles son of Megacles (*PA* 9697), who held the office of secretary to the treasurers of Athena in 428/7 (*IG* i^2 237-9, 261-3; *SEG* xxiv 37). That the fictitious Strepsiades should be related by marriage to the real Megacles need be no more surprising than that the fictitious hero of *Thesm.* is related by marriage to the real Euripides.

48. **stuck-up snob:** Greek *semnēn*, which can be a commendatory epithet for a woman of stature, grace and good breeding (e.g. *Lys.* 1109, *Eccl.* 617, Xen. *Hell.* 5.4.4), but which here, in view of the words that accompany it and the whole picture of Strepsiades' wife, must suggest haughtiness and arrogance as it does in *Wasps* 627, *Frogs* 178, Eur. *Hipp.* 93-94.

*48. **Coesyrated:** i.e. like Coesyra, mother of the Megacles mentioned in the last note but one. She was a native of Eretria; she claimed to be descended from Zeus (so the scholia on 46), and her wealth and arrogance became proverbial. See J.K. Davies, *Athenian Propertied Families 600-300 B.C.* (Oxford, 1971) 380-2. Strepsiades' wife will have been a granddaughter of Coesyra (cf. 800).

50. **drying figs:** strictly, "a fig-drying rack".

51. **saffron:** Strepsiades' wife literally smelt of perfume; of deep kisses, extravagance, etc., she can have "smelt" only metaphorically. Saffron, placed be-

tween the literal and the figurative "smells", could in principle be either; in fact it is probably figurative, the reference being to the saffron-dyed dress (*krokōtos*) which Athenian women wore on festive occasions or when they wished to make themselves particularly attractive (cf. *Lys.* 44ff, 219, 645; *Thesm.* 253; *Eccl.* 879) but which was not suitable everyday wear for a farmer's wife.

52. **Colias and Genetyllis:** Colias was the name of a promontory near Phalerum where certain women's festivals were held (cf. *Lys.* 2); the Genetyllides were goddesses of procreation, who had a sanctuary there. See Paus. 1.1.5; Plut. *Sol.* 8.4. That the Genetyllides had erotic associations is clear from *Thesm.* 130 (and there, as here, there is mention of "deep kisses" in the immediate context), and probably the implication of the names here is not so much that Strepsiades' wife was fond of travelling to attend women's festivals as that she was oversexed.

54. **this cloak:** Strepsiades, as was normal, has been using his cloak as a blanket.

55. **you weave too close:** a current expression for "you are extravagant". The joke is that Strepsiades' cloak is actually old and full of holes; his wife's metaphorical "close weaving" has resulted in his having to go on wearing a garment that is now anything but close-woven.

56 - Strepsiades' concern to economize oil is further evidence of his financial diffi-
59. culties; he is as hard up as the old man in *Wasps* 249-253, who is trying to keep a family of three on his meagre pay as a juror.

63. **-hippus:** i.e. "horse". The mother wanted this element in her son's name not so much because it would sound aristocratic (many *-hippus* names were common among all classes) as because she wanted the boy to become a horseman and hoped that his *nomen* would prove an *omen*.

64. **Xanthippus** was a fairly common name, but had a strong aristocratic flavour. In particular, it had been borne by both the father (*PA* 11169) and the son (*PA* 11170) of Pericles, and might well therefore commend itself to the niece of Megacles who was Pericles' first cousin (his father Megacles and Pericles' mother Agariste being brother and sister: Hdt. 6.131.2).

64. **Chaerippus:** or, with *n*, "Charippus". Both names are found in the fifth century (for the latter cf. Andoc. 1.35 and also *IG* ii^2 1927.110.1, where the Charippus whose son and namesake was a public arbitrator about 325 — and hence then in his sixtieth year — must have been born about 415); neither seems to have any particular social cachet.

* 64. **Callippides:** as D.M. Lewis, *CR* 20 (1970) 288-9, points out, the one well-known Callippides at this period was a tragic actor, who won first prize for acting at the Lenaea in 418 (*IG* ii^2 2319.82-83) and on four other occasions (*IG* ii^2 2325.253). There is probably some comic point in the choice of his name here: perhaps the actor was notoriously of low birth, or perhaps the idea is

that such a name would be more likely to turn its bearer in the direction of the theatre than of the race-track.

65. **Pheidonides after his grandfather:** it was very common for boys to be named after their paternal grandfathers. In this case, oddly enough, we are told later that the grandfather's name was not Pheidonides but Pheidon (134); the same name, with and without the suffix -*idēs*, was often borne by different members of a family, but only rarely by grandfather and grandson (for an instance, though, see Davies, *Athenian Propertied Families* 32: Androcleides son of Androsthenes son of Androcles). Probably Ar. has been inconsistent; he is sometimes careless over names (a Sosias in the audience is addressed at *Wasps* 78, and at 136 it turns out that Sosias is the name of one of the characters who had then been on stage; the hero of *Birds* is called Stilbonides at 139, but Peisetaerus from 644). The meaning of Pheidonides is "Thrifty": Strepsiades wanted his son to take after himself, the economical and prosperous farmer, not after the family of Megacles.

* 67. **Pheidippides:** this name happens not to be attested at Athens, unless it was that of the herald sent to Sparta before the battle of Marathon in 490 (the mss. of Hdt. 6.105 are divided between "Pheidippides" and "Philippides"); but "Pheidippus" is common, and what is funny here is not the name itself but (i) the process by which it was arrived at and (ii) the fact, to which the description of the dispute compels attention, that the name is internally contradictory — thrift and horses do not go together.

69. **drive a chariot to the Acropolis:** either in the Panathenaic procession, or to dedicate a crown won at one of the panhellenic athletic festivals; "like Megacles" suggests the latter, since Megacles had won the chariot-race at Olympia in 436 (schol. Pind. *Pyth.* 7 inscr.)

74. **galloping consumption:** the phrase is due to Rogers. In Greek the affliction is called *hipperos*, a word coined from *hippos* "horse" and *ikteros* "jaundice" — Strepsiades' finances are looking jaundiced because of his son's mania for horses.

80. **my sweet little Pheidippides:** this renders the affectionate diminutive *Pheidippidion*. The use of such diminutives is a mannerism with Strepsiades: cf. 132, 223, 237, 746.

81. **kiss me and give me your right hand:** by so doing Pheidippides will (i) demonstrate his affection for his father (cf. *Frogs* 754-5, 788-9) and (ii) promise in advance to do whatever his father may require (cf. Soph. *Tr.* 1181-90).

88. **turn your way of life inside out:** the Greek verb *ekstrepson* continues the "twisting" theme which will come to be associated with Strepsiades' name (cf. on 36).

* 91. **now look over here:** by this point we must assume that the two men are *outside* their house, so presumably the beds have been removed from sight. Probably they were represented by the *ekkyklēma* platform, which will have been rolled out of the main door of the stage-house before the play began. Once father and son are both on their feet (after 82) the platform is withdrawn through the door, which is then closed; and in 91-94 the same door is identified as the entrance to the Reflectory. The door of Strepsiades' house (first used at 125) is represented by one of the flanking doors in the stage-house façade. See C.W. Dearden, *The Stage of Aristophanes* (London, 1976) 64-65.

92. **nice little door ... nice little house:** the diminutives (Greek *thurion, oikīdion*) do not necessarily imply that either door or house is actually small; Strepsiades is trying to convince Pheidippides, as one might try to convince a child, that there is no reason for him to be afraid of the house or what is inside it. Strepsiades not seldom talks to Pheidippides as if the latter were still a child: cf. 105, 823, 860ff, 878ff, 1380ff.

94. **Reflectory:** Greek *phrontistērion* "house of thinkers", coined on the model of e.g. *dikastērion* "lawcourt", *bouleutērion* "council-house", *telestērion* "hall of initiation" (at the Eleusinian Mysteries).

94. **spirits:** Greek *psūkhē* was regularly used by Socrates to mean a man's mind, personality, inner self, that part of the individual whose proper cultivation was in Socrates' view far more important than that of the body. But this was not a meaning the word had in normal usage, and Socrates' use of it was an invitation to jokes based on another meaning of *psūkhē*, namely "ghost". Thus in *Birds* 1553-64 Socrates is pictured as a necromancer, and here there is probably a suggestion that his pupils are like ghosts — which is true as the pupils are presented in this play, for they are thin, pale and weak.

95-96. **the sky is a baking-cover:** one way of making bread was to bake it under a dome-shaped cover, round the outside of which hot charcoal was heaped. The interior of the cover would first be pre-heated by burning the charcoal under it; it is to this stage of the process that the philosophers' model of the universe refers. See B.A. Sparkes, *JHS* 82 (1962) 128 and Plate IV.2. The "baking-cover theory" was ascribed by Cratinus (fr. 155) to the philosopher Hippon, and by Ar. elsewhere (*Birds* 1000-1) to the astronomer Meton; there is no mention of it in non-comic sources.

101. **reflective thinkers, fine upstanding people:** something of a paradox, since the power of speculative thought on "useless" subjects was not one of the qualities that normally caused a man to be admired, envied, and called *kalos kāgathos* as Strepsiades here calls the inmates of the Reflectory. On *kalos kāgathos* see K.J. Dover, *Greek Popular Morality in the Time of Plato and Aristotle* (Oxford, 1974) 41-45. Pheidippides' attitude to the philosophers is closer to that of the ordinary man, as evidenced in fourth- as well as fifth-century comedy.

*103. **the palefaces:** all Socrates' students are portrayed as pale and sickly (185-6, 718,

1112), but Pheidippides is perhaps thinking especially of Chaerephon, whom the comic poets call "yellow-faced" (*Wasps* 1413, Eupolis fr. 239) and "withered" (Ar. fr 377, Cratinus fr. 202).

*103. **the men with no shoes:** Socrates regularly went barefoot even in the coldest weather (363; Pl. *Symp.* 174a, 220b; Xen. *Mem.* 1.6.2), and in this play he makes his pupils do likewise (719, 858-9).

104. **Chaerephon** (*PA* 15203) was a close associate of Socrates for many years; it was he who asked the Delphic oracle whether any man was wiser than Socrates (Pl. *Apol.* 21a). He was well known for his pale, deathlike countanance (cf. 503-4) and was popularly called "the bat" (*Birds* 1296, 1564); cf. also last note but one. In addition he was satirized as a thief (Ar. fr. 291), a parasite (Eupolis fr. 165), and an informer (Ar. fr. 539); the last-named charge suggests that he took some part in public life, and he does seem to have been a convinced democrat, for unlike Socrates he went into exile when the Thirty assumed power in 404, returning at the restoration of democracy (Pl. loc. cit.) He died not long after, before Socrates' trial in 399.

106. **your father's groats:** barley groats was the main form of cereal bought to make food, so the phrase means "your father's daily bread", "your father's ability to buy food". So in *Knights* 1359 "there's no groats for you jurymen" means "you will not be paid and will therefore be unable to buy food".

109. **pheasants:** the pheasant was still a notable rarity in Greece; even two centuries later, in Ptolemaic Egypt, it was regarded as striking and unusual when a king bred pheasants for the table (Athenaeus 14.654b-c). Some ancient commentators believed that Greek *Phāsiānos* here did not mean "pheasant" but was the name of a breed of horse; but there is no actual evidence that any such breed existed.

109. **Leogoras** (*PA* 9075), the father of the orator Andocides, was a man of great wealth (despite the expenditure he lavished on his mistress Myrrhina: Eupolis fr. 44) and a lover of good food (*Wasps* 1269, Plato com. fr. 106); he was descended from one of the oldest families in Athens (Andoc. 1.147). He led an Athenian embassy to Perdiccas of Macedon in 426 (*IG* i² 57.51; cf. Andoc. 2.11). In 415 he was denounced on two charges of impiety (being party to the mutilation of the Hermae, and being present during a profanation of the Eleusinian Mysteries) but managed to avoid both trial and exile (Andoc. 1.17-22, 47-68); he died some time before 405, since on his death, Andocides being in exile for his part in the events of 415, his house was confiscated and given to the politician Cleophon (Andoc. 1.146).

112- The terminology of "the two Arguments" seems to be due to the sophist Prota-
115 goras, who said (fr. 6a D-K) that " there were two arguments about every matter, opposed to each other" and apparently claimed (Arist. *Rhet.* 1402a19ff) that it was always possible "to make the worse argument the better", i.e. to

make a convincing case for what seems prima facie the less plausible of two opposed theses. This claim was probably made in an epistemological rather than an ethical context, but it was popularly taken to mean that Protagoras, or the sophists generally, professed, and taught others, to be able to convince a jury or an assembly into giving a decision contrary to the merits of the case; and it is this skill – rhetoric – that Strepsiades wants his son to learn. In Pl. *Apol.* 18b, 19b, 23d Socrates complains of the way he has for many years been accused of "making the worse argument the better", a charge which he says is "always ready to hand to fling at any philosopher".

112. **they have in their house both the Arguments**: this expression, and the personification of the Worse Argument as an orator in 115, are the first foreshadowing of the appearance later in the play of the two Arguments in person.

113. **whatever that may be**: most likely this merely implies that Strepsiades does not fully understand the terminology or the concepts that lie behind it; he has only heard of the whole doctrine at second or third hand ("it's said" 112). Alternatively the phrase may be dismissive: it is only in the Worse Argument that Strepsiades is really interested (cf. 882-5 where the phrase "whatever that may be" recurs).

116. **Wrongful Argument**: this expression is used only by Strepsiades (cf. 657, 885); by using it he admits that his plan for avoiding payment of his debts is immoral and fraudulent.

120. **the Knights**: the rich young men who formed the Athenian cavalry; Pheidippides' equestrian interests will have led him to mix with them a great deal.

120. **with all the colour withered from my face**: cf. on 103.

122. **yoke-horse**: one of the two inner horses of a team of four, which were yoked to the chariot; the outer horses drew by traces.

122. **your san-branded thoroughbred**: cf. on 23. The brand-mark in this case is the Dorian letter *san* ($\wedge$).

124. **uncle**: actually great-uncle (cf. 46-47).

125. **horseless**: a surprise for "homeless". We might now have expected Pheidippides to leave for Megacles' house, confident he would be welcomed there; in fact he insolently re-enters the house of his father.

132. **Boy! Little boy!**: see on 80. The diminutive *paidion* appears once more in Ar. in the call of one knocking at a door (*Frogs* 37) and often in similar circumstances in Menander (e.g. *Dysk.* 459, 463, 498, 911f, 921); nevertheless in view of 80 and 223 it is probably intended here to be specially characteristic of Strepsiades.

133. **STUDENT**: one expects the door to be answered by a slave, but this person clearly is not one: he knows things that may be divulged only to students (140ff) and seems to have some authority over other members of the school (195ff). It would appear, in fact, that the school, which is too poor to feed

itself except by stealing (175ff), is also too poor to have any slaves; at 1145 Socrates answers the door himself.

133. **Oh, get stuffed!:** lit. "throw yourself to the crows".

134. **Cicynna:** a deme whose location is not certainly known, but which was probably (cf. *Lys.* 17.5) near Sphettus (see on 156) and belonged to the same tribe, Acamantis.

136. **kicked so hard at the door:** probably a ridiculous exaggeration; Dover well compares *Wealth* 1101 (where Carion asks "Was it you knocking so hard on the door?" when in fact by no means sure that there had been a knock at all) and suggest that Strepsiades' knock had actually been a timid and tentative one (compare his hesitations in 129-131).

138. **I live a long way off in the country:** yet for all dramatic purposes his house and that of Socrates are treated as adjacent. We cannot take the present line as meaning merely "my normal home is in the country" and suppose for instance that the war has driven Strepsiades to move to the city; for 1322 implies that he is living in his own deme of Cicynna. Rather we must suppose that for the purposes of the play the physical distance between Athens and Cicynna is simply ignored; Ar. plays similar tricks with topography in *Ach.*, where Dicaeopolis' house is in his own rural deme at 267 but apparently in the city for most of the rest of the play, and in *Peace* where the question how Trygaeus, in heaven, could so easily summon and receive the aid of a chorus of other mortal men is one that the audience is plainly not expected to raise.

139. **the thing that miscarried:** Strepsiades has almost certainly not understood the figurative use of "abortive"; throughout his time at the school he has great difficulty with figurative language and abstract concepts (see P. Green, *GRBS* 20 [1979] 15-25).

140. **it may not lawfully be divulged:** this is the first indication of Socrates' school being presented as a sort of secret society. The mention of "holy secrets" (lit. "mysteries") in 143 sharpens this notion to that of a secret *cult*-society, practising a novel mystery-religion and (as we shall see) rejecting Zeus and the other established gods in favour of novel deities of their own; it accords with this that Strepsiades must undergo a form of mystic initiation (254ff) before he may behold these deities. The picture is based partly on the actual existence in the past of such part-philosophical, part-religious secret societies (above all those of the Pythagoreans), partly perhaps on Socrates' use of the language of mystic initiation in speaking of philosophy (see A.W.H. Adkins, *Antichthon* 4 [1970] 13-24, who cites such Platonic passages as *Gorg.* 497c, *Meno* 76e, *Symp.* 209e, *Phdr.* 250b, *Tht.* 155e).

145- **could jump ... one had bitten:** or, with the bulk of the ms. tradition, "had
146 jumped ... it had bitten".

150. **both its feet:** the Greek has the dual number. Possibly the flea's long back legs are meant; but since Ar. can speak of a beetle as having two legs and two arms (*Peace* 7, 35) and since insect legs have no structure at all resembling the feet of mammals or birds, it is better not to demand an observationally adequate description but to suppose that Ar. used the dual here simply because one is accustomed to think of feet as two.

151. **Persian boots:** a common form of women's footwear (suitable therefore for a flea, since *psulla* "flea" is a feminine noun). The word "boots" is not in the Greek, but can be deduced from *Eccl.* 319, 346, where the "Persians" of the first passage are called *kothornoi* "boots" in the second and must have covered at least part of the calf.

152. **was measuring:** when Strepsiades' knock "aborted" the investigation (137).

156. **Chaerephon of Sphettus:** the deme of Sphettus was situated about eight miles south-east of Athens, a little to the east of Mount Hymettus; see A.G. Kalogeropoulou, *BCH* 93 (1969) 56-71. It is abnormal that Chaerephon's deme should be named only now, when the student has already mentioned him twice without it; either (i) the deme is mentioned only because it comically explains, via a pun on *sphēx* "wasp", why Chaerephon should be so interested in insects, or (ii) Ar. is parodying a common type of anecdote about the wise sayings of famous men, illustrated e.g. in [Pl.] *Theages* 128d-130e, and the student is made to tell the story in the way he always does regardless of the fact that he has just told another story about Chaerephon, or (iii) Chaerephon's name has supplanted someone else's in the text under the influence of 144ff. If there has been corruption, it would have been facilitated by similarity between the two names; the original name may thus perhaps have been that of Chaerecrates (*PA* 15131), Chaerephon's brother and like him a close associate of Socrates (Xen. *Mem.* 1.2.48), or of Cleitophon (*PA* 8546) son of Aristonymus, a character in Plato's *Republic* (1.328b, 340a-b). There is no independent evidence for the deme affiliation of any of these men.

163. **being a cavity adjacent to a narrow passage:** this refers to contemporary theories of hearing. Cf. Alcmaeon A5 and A6 D-K, from which it appears that Alcmaeon (whose date is uncertain, but who may belong to the mid-fifth century: see W.K.C. Guthrie, *A History of Greek Philosophy* i [Cambridge 1962] 357-8) held that the flow of air through the narrow outer-ear passage sets up a resonance in the adjacent middle-ear cavity, resulting in audible sound. Similarly, if the gnat is assumed to have a narrow intestine leading into a larger rectal cavity, the flow of air through the former can be supposed to result in sound being produced in the latter.

165. **the arsehole of gnats is a trumpet:** the tube of a Greek trumpet expanded into a broader chamber at the end remote from the mouthpiece, corresponding to the supposed rectum of the gnat.

166. **feat of evisceration:** Greek *dientereuma*, a word coined for the occasion, perhaps a blend of *di'enterou* "through the intestine" and *diereunēma* "investigation".

170. **spotted lizard** ... 173 **gecko:** the Greek words are respectively *askalabōtēs*, which seems to be a general name for any species of gecko (cf. Arist. *HA* 538a27, 599a31) and *galeōtēs*, which may be a synonym or may denote a particular species.

171- The story resembles one that was told about Thales (cf. 180): walking alone with
173. his eyes on the sky and his mind on an astronomical problem, he fell into a well (Pl. *Tht.* 174a).

173. **shat on him from the eaves:** cf. *Wasps* 202-6 where Xanthias, at work barricading the outside of a house-door, has earth or muck dropped on him from above, and Bdelycleon suggests a mouse might be responsible.

176. **groats:** see on 106.

177- Socrates is going to distract the students from their hunger by a geometrical dem-
178. onstration. Normally diagrams were drawn in the dust on the ground; here the table is used (with ash in lieu of dust), partly perhaps because the diagrams are to be a substitute dinner.

*178. **a faggot:** the Greek word is *diabētēs*, lit. "a bestrider". In geometry *diabētēs* means a pair of compasses, and the natural interpretation of 178, if we could ignore what follows in the next line, would be that Socrates bent a spit and took it to use as compasses. But what then is the connection between 177-8 and 179? Is it that Socrates suddenly abandons the attempt to satisfy his students with "food for thought" and instead procures the cost of a meal by stealing and selling a cloak? (For Socrates as a petty thief, cf. Eupolis fr. 361.) But the text does not say, as we would then expect, "a cloak" (*himation*) but "the cloak" or "his cloak" (*thoimation*) — the cloak of someone previously mentioned or assumed to be known. Who is this someone? I suggest that he lies hidden in a double meaning of the word *diabētēs*. When the audience first hear the word, they will take it to refer to the geometry lesson, according to the "natural interpretation" explained above; but as the sentence goes on, it becomes clear that *diabētēn labōn* "taking a *diabētēs*" goes not with what precedes but with what follows ("from the wrestling-school") and that *diabētēs* "a bestrider, one who spreads his legs" here denotes a youth addicted to passive homosexuality. Socrates' method of feeding himself and his students is to go to the wrestling-school, pick up a boy there, take him home, seduce and rob him (cf. *Frogs* 148), and sell his cloak to buy food. For the meaning assumed for *diabētēs* compare the use of *diabainein*, from which it is derived, in relation to a "young pathic" at *Wasps* 688, to a man with a "gaping arse" in *Knights* 77-78, and to a woman having intercourse in the "jockey" position in *Lys.* 60 (in *Thesm.* 153 it is envisaged that the passive homosexual Agathon might sometimes adopt the jockey position); for the connection between Socrates,

169

handsome boys, and wrestling-schools, see e.g. Plato's *Charmides* and *Lysis*; for the wrestling-school as a convenient place for man to meet boy, *Wasps* 1025 and *Peace* 762-3. The joke here lies in the sudden transition, within a sentence and via the stepping-stone of an ambiguous word, from a high-minded ignoring of the physical appetites to an ingenious and criminal system for satisfying hunger and sexual desire by the same process.

180. **Thales**, the founder of the Milesian school of philosophy, who lived in the first half of the sixth century, had acquired an almost legendary reputation for both theoretical and practical wisdom, and was credited with many achievements in applied science and even in politics and business (the stories are conveniently collected by Guthrie, *History of Greek Philosophy* i 50-52). Accordingly, to say that a man was comparable, let alone superior, to Thales was to say that he was an intellectual genius: cf. *Birds* 1009 and Plautus *Bacch.* 122, *Capt.* 274-5.

184. On the use of the *ekkyklēma* here see Dearden, *The Stage of Aristophanes* 65-67; but I differ from him in assuming (i) that the instruments and map of 200-217 are hung on screens at the rear of the trolley and (ii) that the trolley itself functions as a bed in 254ff. Hence the platform itself is occupied only by the students, of whom there need not be more than four.

186. **like the men captured at Pylos**: in 425 Demosthenes and Cleon had defeated the Spartan force occupying Sphacteria, an island adjoining the promontory of Pylos in the western Peloponnese, and taken 292 prisoners of whom about 120 belonged to the Spartan ruling caste (Thuc. 4.38.4). The prisoners were brought to Athens and kept in chains (Thuc. 4.41.1) until peace should be made; when *Clouds* was produced they had been in confinement for nearly two years, and could therefore be expected, like the students, to be showing the effects of inadequate diet and lack of fresh air.

188. **trying to discover**: Greek *zētousin*, which to a scientist means "inquiring into", but which Strepsiades understands in its everyday sense "searching for".

188. **what is under the earth**: speculation about the interior of the earth was something for which philosophers and scientists were often censured, according to Pl. *Apol.* 18b, 19b, 23d; it could be regarded as impious, being an attempt to discover what the gods have concealed from man. Yet Plato puts a lecture on this subject into Socrates' mouth as the last discourse of his life (*Phd.* 108c-115a), though it is made to serve a moral purpose.

188. **bulbs**: strictly, the bulbs of the purse-tassel (*Muscari comosum*), which were commonly eaten; see Thphr. *HP* 7.13.

192. **Tartarus**: the depths of the underworld, below the realm of Hades ([Aesch.] *Prom.* 152-4); but the minds of Socrates' students penetrate deeper yet.

195. **him**: i.e. Socrates.

202. **Geometry**: for geometrical instruments as a comic stage-property cf. *Birds* 999-1009

203. **for measuring land**: this would naturally be the first practical application of geo-

metry to occur to anyone's mind, since it had given the science its name.

203. **cleruchs:** Athenian citizens who were allocated holdings on territory outside Attica which had been appropriated by the Athenian state. Such settlements had been established on various occasions since the late sixth century; the most recent had been set up on Lesbos in 427, after the suppression of the revolt there, when the greater part of the island had been parcelled out among 2700 Athenians selected by lot (Thuc. 3.50.2). Normally cleruchs took over and farmed their holdings; on Lesbos, however, they lived on rent paid by the former owners who continued to work the land.

205. **it's a ... democratic device:** "Strepsiades thinks that 'geometry' is some (magical?) device for distributing all the land in the world gratis to Athenian citizens like himself" (Dover); such a device would be "democratic" because it would enable the poorest Athenian to become economically independent. At 215-6 Strepsiades again confuses science with magic.

208. **I don't see any jurors:** the joke is not only on Strepsiades' failure to appreciate the limited purpose of a map (which is not a picture or a model) but also on the implication that Athenians have such a passion for litigation that an Athens without lawcourts would not be Athens any more. For Athenian litigiousness cf. 494-6, *Knights* 1316-7, *Birds* 40-41, 108-111.

213. **we laid it out:** The Greek verb is the same as that translated "lying stretched out" in the preceding line; there it referred to the shape and position of Euboea, here it bears the sense "render helpless, knock out" (cf. Pl. *Euthd.* 303b, Xen. *Mem.* 3.13.6). The reference is to the suppression of the Euboean revolt of 446 by an Athenian army led by Pericles (Thuc. 1.114).

217. **in that case ... you're going to howl:** it is not the Socratics' fault that the facts of geography cannot be altered; but Strepsiades is very apt to lose his temper when he cannot get his way (57-59, 121-3, 814-5, 1373-5).

219. **the master:** Greek *autos*, "he himself", commonly used to denote the master of a house (Pl. *Prot.* 314d; Men. *Sam.* 256; cf. *Knights* 127, of a slave who is *de facto* ruler of the household) and by Pythagorean philosophers to denote the founder of their school (D.L. 8.46, cf. Cicero *De Natura Deorum* 1.10).

222. **is an isolated short line** consisting of a single iambic *metron*; for such a short line among the normal three-*metron* lines (trimeters) of dialogue cf. *Ach.* 407.

223. **my sweet little Socrates:** affectionate diminutive, as in 80 and 132; the tone is wheedling, cf. *Ach.* 404, *Peace* 382.

223. **thou creature of a day:** Socrates speaks like a god addressing a mortal. The adjective *ephēmeros* "whose life is but a day" belongs primarily to high poetry; cf. Semonides fr. 1.3; Pind. *Pyth.* 8.95; Pind. fr. 157; [Aesch.] *Prom.* 83, 253, 546, 945; Eur. *Or.* 976.

225- **descry ... decry:** the Greek has respectively *periphronō*, which can mean either
226. "contemplate" (the sense intended by Socrates) or "despise", and *huperphro-*

171

neis whose only relevant meaning is "despise".

226. **the gods:** virtually all Greeks, except natural philosophers, regarded the sun as a god.

* 229. **hanging up my mind:** as one might hang a garment on a tree to dry; for according to the contemporary philosopher Diogenes of Apollonia, of whose doctrines 229-234 are a garbled parody, the air which, in his opinion, constitutes the soul and mind of living creatures must be "pure and dry" if intelligent thought is to take place (Diogenes fr. 4 and A19 D-K). On Diogenes and his air-based theory of the universe and of life, see Guthrie, *History of Greek Philosophy* ii 362-381. Of course, one cannot hang up the mind to dry without also hanging up the body that contains it; hence the need for Socrates to have himself hoisted into the air.

229-
230. **the minute particles of my thought:** Diogenes' reason for believing that the soul consisted of air was that "air is composed of minuter particles than any other substance" (Diogenes A20 D-K).

232-
233. **the earth forcibly draws the moisture of thought to itself:** the notion of moisture (*ikmas*) being "drawn" or "attracted" to some solid substance seems to have played a prominent role in Diogenes' physics; thus he uses it to account for magnetism (A33 D-K). But had Diogenes sought to explain the intellectual inferiority of the earthbound by such an attraction, he would have had to posit a flow of moisture into, not out of, the mind, which would prevent it from being "pure and dry"; and in fact he explained the poor intellect of animals by the fact that the air they breathe comes from near the ground (Diogenes A19 D-K). Ar. is concerned only to make Socrates use the language and concepts of current scientific theory, not to make him argue accurately, consistently or intelligibly.

234. **Just the same thing happens to cress:** cress seeds soak up moisture greedily, and thus provide an analogy for the earth "forcibly draw[ing] ... moisture ... to itself".

235. **How do you mean?:** in the Greek this question stands outside the metre, as similar questions do in *Knights* 1346 and *Birds* 416.

241. **having my goods distrained on:** cf. 34-35; here Strepsiades makes his plight seem more alarming by representing as a present fact what, according to the earlier passage, is as yet no more than a threat.

243. **an equine affliction:** cf. 74.

243. **which has been eating me up fearfully:** diseases, particularly those which involved disfigurement of the skin or decay of the flesh, were often said to "devour" the patient (cf. Aesch. *Cho.* 280-1; Soph. *Phil.* 7, 313; Arist. *Poet.* 1458b19-24); here the expression also hints at the great amount of food that horses need, and at the way they have metaphorically devoured Strepsiades' resources.

244. **one of your two Arguments**: see 112-8 with notes.

247- **we don't credit gods here**: lit. "gods aren't *nomisma* for us". Socrates appears
248. to be using *nomisma* in the sense, etymologically impeccable but not otherwise attested, of "something believed in"; Strepsiades, to whom *nomisma*
means "coinage, currency", is completely confused by this unfamiliar usage.
This is the first appearance in the play of the allegation that Socrates does
not believe in (*ou nomizei*) the recognised gods of the community (cf. Pl.
Apol. 23d, 24b).

248. **what currency do you use for oaths?**: Strepsiades seems to have taken Socrates'
last sentence to mean "we do not regard gods as coins", and, in striving to
make sense of this, he has apparently gathered that in the Socratic "religion"
coins, not gods, are the essential element in the taking of an oath. Accordingly
he asks what kind of coins are required to make an oath acceptable; and since
the currency used by a secret society for a religious purpose is likely to be of
an unfamiliar sort, he thinks of the iron currency of Byzantium, one of the
few states (Sparta was another) that still used this metal for monetary purposes (cf. Plato com. fr. 96, Strattis fr. 36).

*252. **the Clouds**: insubstantial, impermanent things, "mist and dew and vapour"
(330), fit deities for those who teach men to obscure reality under a smoke-
screen of rhetoric. No normal Greek would think of worshipping them: they
lacked the prime characteristic of a god, permanence (immortality). Cf. Juve-
nal 14.97 (converts to Judaism "worship nothing but clouds and the divinity
of heaven").

254- A parody of the initiation rites of various mystery-cults (cf. on 140). Enthrone-
262. ment (*thronōsis*) is mentioned by Pl. *Euthd.* 277d in connection with Corybantic
initiation-rites, but Ar. replaces the chair of initiation (*thronos*) with a low bed
(*skimpous*) perhaps to suggest that the Socratics are so poor as not to possess
a chair and/or so ascetic as not to want to use one. The sprinkling of Strepsiades with fine meal (260-2) is paralleled by the smearing of the initiate with
clay and bran in the ritual described by Dem. 18.259.

256. **wreath**: commonly worn when performing rituals of many kinds.

257. **make a sacrifice of me, like Athamas**: Athamas was the father of Phrixus and
Helle, whom their mother Nephele had saved from being sacrificed by sending
them to Colchis on the ram with the golden fleece (though Helle perished on
the way). Subsequently, perhaps to expiate his share in the plot against
Phrixus and Helle by their stepmother Ino (cf. Hdt. 7.197), preparations were
made to sacrifice Athamas himself; the scholia on the present passage report
that in one of the two tragedies by Sophocles that bore his name, Athamas in
one scene was standing by the altar of Zeus, a wreath on his head, about to be
sacrificed, when he was saved by Heracles. The wreath is the sole point of resemblance (and a very slight one) between Athamas' situation then and

Strepsiades' now; but the Clouds (*Nephelai*) make him think of Nephele whom Athamas had wronged, and that recalls to him what must have been a memorable theatrical experience and makes him afraid of becoming another Athamas. Strepsiades is rather easily frightened (cf. 267-8, 293-5, 481, 497, 506-9).

260. **a smooth talker:** Greek *trīmma* "something well rubbed"; the same word, along with *paipalē(ma)* "sieved meal", is used of a clever, subtle orator in *Birds* 431.

260. **a tinkling cymbal:** lit. "a castanet"; cf. 448.

263- Metre: anapaestic tetrameters; the same metre is resumed between (291-7) and
274. after (314ff) the lyric strophe and antistrophe of the chorus, and then continues until 438 when it is followed by an anapaestic *pnīgos* (439-456).

263. **Let the old man speak fair:** the injunction to "speak fair", i.e. to keep silence, was the normal preliminary to any religious rite (cf. *Ach.* 237ff, *Wasps* 868, etc.); it was addressed to all participants and bystanders. The rite now being performed is very unusual in that only one person is present apart from the officiant.

264. **Air:** cf. 225, 230.

264. **who upholdest the floating earth:** Diogenes of Apollonia (A16a D-K) followed Anaxagoras (A42.3) and the much earlier Anaximenes (A20) in holding that the (flat) earth rested on and was supported by a mass of air below.

265. **bright Sky:** Greek *aithēr*, properly the substance — drier, hotter, purer than the air around us — which lies between the region of ordinary air (*āēr*) and the sky, "the bright upper atmosphere of a clear Mediterranean sky" (Guthrie). When the four-element theory was developed, some philosophers regarded *aithēr* as a form of air, some as a form of fire, some as a fifth element distinct from both; and in both philosophical and popular thought the proximity of *aithēr* to heaven, and its remoteness from the region in which mortal creatures move, resulted in its being widely thought of as divine. This notion is particularly common in Euripides, whose characters call *aithēr* "begetter of men and gods" (fr. 839), "head of the gods" (fr. 919), Zeus (fr. 877, 941), and swear oaths by it (fr. 487); Euripides is presented as a worshipper of Aither in *Frogs* 892. The epithet "bright" (*lampros*) for *aithēr* is a favourite with Euripides (e.g. *Hipp.* 178, *Ion* 1445, *Or.* 1087, fr. 443).

265. **thunder-fulminating** implies that thunder and lightning are caused by the Clouds and not by Zeus; see 374-411.

266. **him who thinks on you:** the Greek noun is *phrontistēs*, from which *phrontistērion* "Reflectory" (94 etc.) is derived. It is used in the plural to refer to the Socratics at 456 and 1039. Altogether this and other derivatives of *phrontis* "thought" occur thirty times in *Clouds*, more often than in all Ar.'s other surviving plays combined.

267   **Not yet, not yet:** the literal-minded Strepsiades assumes that if the Clouds come
      in response to Socrates' prayer then it will rain — and he doesn't want to get
      wet.

* 270- **whether ... or ... or ...:** it was common in prayer to list the favourite abodes of the
   273.   god prayed to and ask him, in whichever of these places he might be, to hear-
          ken and come to his worshipper's call; cf. *Iliad* 16.514-6; Aesch. *Eum.* 292-8;
          Frogs 659, 664f. The Clouds, being novel gods, have no traditional abodes;
          but when clouds first appear in the sky they are in the far distance, and accor-
          dingly the first four abodes mentioned for them are in the far north, west,
          south and east respectively. All, too, are explicitly linked with moisture in the
          form of water or snow.

271. **call the Nymphs to a holy dance:** the particular Nymphs in question are presum-
      ably the Oceanides, daughters of Ocean. The Greek word *khoros* may imply
      both dancing and singing, which are the most typical activities of Nymphs of
      all kinds; for the Oceanides in particular, cf. Callimachus, *Hymn to Artemis*
      13, where Artemis asks for sixty Oceanides as *khorītides*.

271; **the garden of father Ocean:** the garden of the Hesperides, in the far west by the
      Pillars of Heracles (cf. Eur. *Hipp.* 742-751). If "father" here and at 278 means
      that Ocean is father of the Clouds, there is an inconsistency with 569-570
      where their father is Aither; but Ocean may be called "father" as begetter of
      innumerable rivers and nymphs (Hes. *Thg.* 337ff; cf. *Iliad* 14.201 "Ocean, ori-
      gin of the gods").

272. **at the mouths of the Nile ... with golden ewers:** this seems to be based, in a gar-
      bled and poeticized form, on a theory of Diogenes of Apollonia (A18 D-K)
      intended to account for the Nile's summer flooding. According to Diogenes
      the sun drew up moisture from land and sea, principally in the hotter south-
      ern regions, and the resulting deficit of water in these regions was corrected
      by an influx, through subterranean channels, of excess water from the north;
      hence northern lands were watered mainly from above (by rain) and southern
      lands mainly from below (by the Nile flood). Ar. concentrates on one part of
      the process, the drawing-up of moisture from the hotter parts of earth and
      sea, clothes it in mythical-poetic language ("golden ewers"), and replaces the
      agency of the Sun (a traditional god) by that of the novel deities, the Clouds.

273. **Lake Maeotis:** the Sea of Azov, north-east of the Crimea.

273. **Mimas:** the mountainous peninsula north of Erythrae in Ionia, facing Chios. For
      a Greek poet to call a mountain "snowy" need mean no more than that snow
      often falls there; cf. Eur. *Ph.* 802, *Ba.* 661-2.

274. **my sacrifice:** Greek *thusīa* normally means an animal sacrifice, but can sometimes
      (e.g. Eur. fr. 912.4) be used of other kinds of offering to the gods; so here it is
      possible that Socrates has burnt incense on the stage-altar before beginning his
      prayer.

* 275-290 = 298-313 Metre: dactylic, with only one brief interruption (287=310). This
choral entrance-song is unique in extant Greek drama in being sung entirely
offstage; the Clouds do not appear until 323-6. The nearest parallel is the song
of the Frogs (*Frogs* 209ff), though the argument for the Frogs' remaining in-
visible to the audience is largely *ex silentio*.

276. **let us rise and make visible:** responding to Socrates' prayer "arise, appear" (266).

278. **deep-roaring:** echoed in "deep thunder" (285), "deep-sounding" (313): the
Greek words are *baruākheos, barubromon, barubromos*. Taking these words
together with the mention of thunder in 292 and 294, one may presume that
low notes predominated in the melody of the ode.

283. **rushing flow:** Greek *keladēmata*, echoed in *keladonta* "sounding" (284) and
eukeladon "melodious" (312).

285 **the unwearying eye of heaven:** the sun. The word rendered "heaven" is *aithēr*:
cf. on 265.

288- **shake off the rainy mist from our immortal form:** seems to mean "make our-
289. selves look like (anthropomorphic) goddesses rather than masses of vapour":
cf. 329-330, 340-355.

292. **awe-inspiring divine thunder:** as the "thunder" is mentioned as something separate from and simultaneous with the song, it is most likely that it was produced
as a "sound-effect" rather than being, as Dover supposes, merely suggested by
the music. The scholia mention a simple device for the purpose, called a *bron-
teion*, which used the noise of pebbles striking metal. Cf. *Birds* 1750-2 and
Soph. *O.C.* 1456ff.

293- **in response ... I want to fart back:** for the resemblance between the noise of
294. thunder and that of breaking wind, cf. 382-394; for breaking wind and/or
defaecating as a symptom of fright, cf. *Knights* 224, *Wasps* 626, 941, *Frogs*
479ff.

296. **goddamned comedians:** Greek *trugodaimones*, a blend of *trugōidoi* "comedians"
and *kakodaimones* "accursed, wretched".

297. **speak fair:** cf. 263.

299. **gleaming:** a favourite laudatory epithet for Athens, derived from Pindar fr. 76;
cf. *Ach.* 637-640, *Knights* 1329.

300-1. **Cecrops:** a legendary king of Athens.

300- **home of fine men:** Greek *euandron*, a term applied to Athens by Athena in
301. Aesch. *Eum.* 1031 and Socrates in Xen. *Mem.* 3.3.12.

* 302- It is startling that the Clouds, whom Socrates believes to be the greatest of gods,
310. praise the Athenians for their pious worship of the traditional gods, who according to Socrates do not exist or have no power. So again in the lyrics of the
parabasis (563-574, 595-606) they sing to eight gods, all but one of whom
belong to the traditional pantheon. Only at the end of the action (1452-62)
is the anomaly explained: the Clouds, though they are indeed goddesses, are

176

not independent powers, opponents or supplanters of Zeus, but allies and agents of Zeus and the traditional gods, and have come to Athens ostensibly to receive Socrates' worship and give him and his pupil their divine aid, but really to make manifest and to punish the impiety of Socrates and the dishonesty of Strepsiades.

302. **the august rites none may speak of**: the Eleusinian mysteries. Contrast the far from august mystery-rites just performed by Socrates (254-262).

*303- **the temple is opened**: this implies that the hall of initiation (*Telestērion*) at Eleu-
304.   sis, like some other sacred buildings (e.g. the temple of Dionysus in the Marshes: [Dem.] 59.76), was kept closed throughout the year and only opened for its special festival.

307. **the Blest Ones**: the gods.

308. **garlanded** refers to the worshippers.

311- Special mention is given to the City Dionysia, the festival at which *Clouds* was
313.   originally produced.

311. **Dionysian**: lit. "Bromian", from *Bromios* "the Noisy One", a common poetic title for Dionysus.

315. **some kind of female heroes**: it looks as though Strepsiades is frightened again (cf. on 257). "Heroes" — that is, the spirits of great men of the past — were believed sometimes to walk the earth, and it was dangerous to encounter them, especially at night, for one might be struck with paralysis (*Birds* 1487-93, with scholia on 1490; Athenaeus 11.461c). Strepsiades fears that these beings, whose sublime music indicates their supernatural status, may have similar powers.

316. **men of idleness**: "idle" is an epithet that his enemies might apply pejoratively to the Socrates of *Clouds*, because, like the types mentioned in 331-3, he makes no genuine, worthwhile contribution to society; here and in 334 the epithet is put into his own mouth as if it were complimentary.

317- **intelligence and discourse ... incisive and repressive power**: Socrates speaks as a
318.   teacher of rhetoric. The seven expressions he uses here are modish names for oratorical skills (cf. *Knights* 1378-80); four of them are abstract nouns ending in the suffix *-sis*, on which see E.W. Handley, *Eranos* 51 (1953) 129-142.

320. **about smoke**: i.e. about matters of no importance.

*323. **Mount Parnes**: the mountain massif on the northern border of Attica. The side-entrances in the Theatre of Dionysus, by one of which the chorus entered, were actually on the east and west, not the north; so the spectator must forget the real direction of Mount Parnes (which in any case could not be seen from the theatre) and accept the direction in which Socrates points as being that of Parnes.

325. **the woods and the hollows**: the Clouds, moving downwards (323), have reached the dells and spurs of the lower slopes of the well-wooded (Euphanes fr.1) mountain.

177

326. **the wing-entrance:** the point at which the side entrance-passage for the chorus debouched into the orchestra. The actor momentarily drops the dramatic fiction; for similar passing references to theatrical reality cf. 1149, 1352, *Ach.* 416, 442-4, *Peace* 174-6, *Birds* 296, Ar.fr. 188, 388.

331. **"experts":** lit. "sophists". Greek *sophistēs* meant originally an expert practitioner of some skill, later especially a professional teacher of advanced branches of knowledge; by Ar.'s time it had already acquired pejorative connotations, and Plato makes Socrates' unphilosophical contemporaries regard "sophist" virtually as a term of abuse (*Prot.* 312a, 314c-e; *Meno* 92a-c).

332. **diviners from Thurii:** this alludes principally to Lampon (*PA* 8996), the seer and expounder of religious law, who had been sent out by Pericles in 444/3 as official founder (*oikistēs*) of the colony of Thurii in south Italy (D.S. 12.10.3; Plut. *Mor.* 802d). He had subsequently returned to Athens, and remained prominent in public life until 414 at least (*IG* i² 76.47; Thuc. 5.19.2; 5.24.1; *Birds* 521, 988). His chief satirizable vice appears to have been love of good food (Cratinus fr. 57-58; Lysippus fr. 6; Callias fr. 14).

* 332. **professors of the medical art:** not medical practitioners (the high public regard for whom is sufficiently evidenced by the enormous salaries paid to doctors holding state appointments) but medical theorists. Contemporary theories of disease placed great emphasis on climate and weather as causal factors; see the Hippocratic treatise *Airs, Waters, Places*, the "constitutions" in *Epidemics*, and Pl. *Symp.* 188a-b; in Pl. *Polit.* 299b-c it is taken for granted that the study of meteorology is as essential to medicine as it is to navigation. Hence it is natural that the Cloud-goddesses should look with favour on medical theorists.

332. **long-haired do-nothings with onyx signet-rings:** one word in the Greek. Both long hair (cf. on 14) and signet-rings, especially jewelled ones (cf. *Eccl.* 632), imply wealth; either the suggestion is being made that some of the "experts" in useless knowledge just mentioned have greatly enriched themselves and are aping the fashions and luxuries of the aristocracy, or else the circle of the Clouds' protégés is being extended to include all who are able to live in comfort without making any contribution to society's welfare.

* 333. **dithyrambic:** lit. "circular", this being the normal dance-formation for this type of chorus. The dithyramb was a choral performance of song and dance, originally in honour of Dionysus; at the City Dionysia, in addition to the competitions in tragedy and in comedy, there were competitions in dithyramb for choruses of boys and of men. Dithyrambic poets had a reputation for meaningless grandiloquence: in *Peace* 828-831 Trygaeus has seen some of their souls seeking inspiration in the upper air, and in *Birds* 1372-1409 the dithyrambist Cinesias thinks he has found his spiritual home in Cloudcuckooville.

335. **edged with twists of radiance:** lit. "with twisted *aiglē*". The meaning of *aiglē* here is uncertain; I take it to mean the gleaming "silver lining" around the

irregular edge of a dark cloud, as apparently in Bacchylides 12.140.

336. **Typhos,** the hundred-headed monster who once fought against Zeus (Hes. *Thg.* 821ff), was father of the storm-winds (ib. 869-880), hence his connection with clouds.

338. **as a reward for that:** probably at the banquet given by a successful *chorēgos* after the performance (cf. *Ach.* 1154-5, *Peace* 1356-7). No doubt Ar. felt that the dithyrambic poets had done very little to deserve such a reward in comparison with those who wrote and produced comedies, " the most difficult thing in the world" according to *Knights* 516.

339. **lovely big ... flesh of thrushes:** in the Greek the line contains four genitive plural forms of the first declension, all of which have the Doric ending *-ān* instead of the Attic *-ōn* in mocking imitation of the dithyrambic style (the series of dith-yrambic quotations in 335-8 had begun and ended with sequences of genitive plurals in *-ān*).

339. **barracuda fish:** the Greek *kestrā* is probably the so-called "European barracuda", *Sphyraena spet*, though it has also been suggested that the word here denotes the pike.

349. **savage:** this seems to have been a popular designation for promiscuous pederasts (cf. Aeschines 1.52).

*349. **the son of Xenophantus** is identified by the scholia as the tragic and dithyrambic poet Hieronymus (*PA* 7556; *TrGF* 31), whose long hair is mentioned in *Ach.* 388-390.

350. **centaurs:** the centaurs of myth were notoriously lecherous, and "centaur" is attested as a term for over-lustful pederasts by Hesychius κ 2225 and schol. Aeschines 1.52.

351. **Simon** (*PA* 12686) is known to us only from comedy, in which he was accused not only of embezzlement as here (cf. Eupolis fr. 218) but also of perjury (*Clouds* 399-400) and, according to the scholia here, of being in debt (pre-sumably to the state; this, if true, would have entailed automatic deprivation of citizen rights). His association in 399-400 with the politicians Cleonymus and Theorus indicates that he also was a politician, and probably, like them, a supporter of Cleon.

352. **wolves:** typical predators.

353-4. **deer:** proverbially timorous from *Iliad* 1.225 onwards.

*353- **Cleonymus the shield-dropper:** Cleonymus (*PA* 8680) was a minor politician,
354.   active from 426 to 415 (*IG* i^2 57.34; 65.5; *SEG* x 73; Andoc. 1.27). He is satirized by Ar. in every extant play from *Acharnians* to *Birds*, at first as an obese glutton (*Ach.* 88; *Knights* 958, 1290-9), but from *Clouds* on mainly for having once run away in battle discarding his shield (cf. *Wasps* 19-23, 822-3; *Peace* 444-6, 673-8, 1295-1304; *Birds* 290, 1473-81). The shield incident therefore probably happened between *Knights* and *Clouds*,

i.e. in 424, and the battle of Delium, when the Athenian army was routed (Thuc. 4.96. 4-5; cf. Pl. *Symp.* 220e-221c), provides a likely occasion. Compare Aeschines' taunting of Demosthenes for having run away at Chaeroneia (Aeschines 3.152, 155, 159, 175-6, etc).

355. **Cleisthenes** (*PA* 8525) was a beardless man, frequently satirized by Ar. as effeminate (*Ach.* 117-121, *Knights* 1373-4, *Thesm.* 574-654, *Frogs* 48-57, etc); in *Thesm.* 571-2 he is at first sight mistaken for a woman.

356. **if you have ever done so for another**: a variant on the common prayer-formula "if you have ever hearkened to me before" (*Thesm.* 1157-8, Sappho fr. 1.5ff), necessitated by the fact that Strepsiades has only just recognized the Clouds as goddesses. Dicaeopolis, treating Euripides almost as a god, appeals to him in similar terms in *Ach.* 405.

358. **CHORUS**: normally in dialogue the chorus is represented by its leader; but here, where Strepsiades has just asked the Clouds to display the power and beauty of their voices, it may be that the lines were chanted by the whole chorus.

* 359. **priest of the subtlest balderdash**: that the Clouds should speak thus of their devotee Socrates would probably surprise the audience no more than that in *Knights* 296, 1252 and *Wasps* 928 Cleon calls himself a thief. Later, however, they will discover that the Clouds really do regard Socrates' teachings as "balderdash" and have come not to help or honour him but to punish him.

361. **Prodicus** of Ceos was a distinguished intellectual, approximately contemporary with Socrates; he is amusingly portrayed in Plato's *Protagoras*. His main field of interest was semantics; he emphasized the importance of the right use of words and especially of distinguishing the meanings of near-synonyms. He also wrote on ethics, the origin of religion, and apparently on human physiology (fr. 4 D-K). Ar. is the only authority who connects him with astronomy or cosmology, but *Birds* 690-2 is fairly solid evidence that Prodicus wrote an account of the origin of the universe. See Guthrie, *History of Greek Philosophy* iii 274-280.

* 361. **his skill and intelligence**: this compliment to Prodicus has sometimes been taken as ironical, but that would spoil the effect of the contrast between him and Socrates. Prodicus, whatever one might think of his linguistic and other studies, was an accomplished literary artist who properly discharged the literary man's duty of promoting the moral improvement of the community (witness his popular allegory *The Choice of Heracles*, paraphrased by Xen. *Mem.* 2.1. 21-34). Socrates wrote nothing, and his moral influence may well have seemed to Ar. purely destructive, concerned as he was more to refute the unsoundly based beliefs of others than to impart positive doctrines of his own.

362. **swagger ... and cast your eyes sideways**: in Pl. *Symp.* 221b Alcibiades is made to quote this line as correctly hitting off Socrates' bearing, with particular reference to the retreat from Delium in 424. For Socrates' expressive glances cf. also Pl. *Phd.* 115c, 116d, 117b.

363. **go barefoot:** cf. 103.

364. **Holy Earth:** Earth (Ge) was one of the oldest and greatest of divine beings; she is sworn by in *Peace* 188, 1117 and *Birds* 194. The double invocation of Ge here and in 366 is a rare phenomenon and suggest that Strepsiades is deeply moved, first by the sound of the Clouds' voices and then by the astonishing suggestion that Zeus is not a god.

365. **all the rest:** everything commonly believed about other gods.

372. **that point:** that it never rains unless there are clouds.

372. **what you were just saying:** that the Clouds, not Zeus, make rain.

374. **that makes me tremble:** cf. 293-5, where the rare verb *tetramainein* "tremble" is used as it is here.

376-378. Socrates' theory of thunder is not known to have been held by any fifth-century philosopher (the statement of D.L. 2.9 that for Anaxagoras thunder was "a collision of clouds" is at variance with all the other evidence for Anaxagoras' views). Many theorists, however, connected the cause of thunder in one way or another with clouds, e.g. Anaxagoras (A84 D-K), Diogenes of Apollonia (A16), Leucippus (A25) and Democritus (A93).

377. **necessity** (*ananke*) "as a cosmological force runs right through Presocratic thought" (Guthrie, *History of Greek Philosophy* iii 100), being especially prominent in Parmenides, Empedocles, Leucippus and Democritus. In Eur. *Tro.* 886 Hecuba prays to the ruling power of the universe "whoever thou be ... whether Zeus, or the Necessity of nature, or the Mind of man".

* 380. **vortex:** Greek *dīnos* "rotation, whirling", a notion that played a crucial role in the atomistic cosmogony of Democritus (fr. 167 D-K, cf. A1 = D.L. 9.45 and A83). See Guthrie, *History of Greek Philosophy* ii 406-413. But in everyday Attic *dīnos* meant a kind of cup, and it is likely, as 1473 shows, that a "statue" of such a cup stood outside the Reflectory, as a statue of Hermes stood (1478) outside Strepsiades' house — implying to Strepsiades' mind that the Socratics worship *Dīnos*, Vortex, as a god. Socrates himself never mentions such a god.

381. **Vortex is now king in his place:** as Cronus overthrew Uranus and Zeus overthrew Cronus, so now Vortex has overthrown Zeus.

386. **soup:** it would be a beef soup, probably with plenty of meat in it; see next note.

386. **the Panathenaea:** the principal festival of Athena, held on the 28th of Hecatombaeon (roughly July). It was marked by lavish public sacrifices of cows, whose meat was distributed to the population (the fourth-century decree *IG* ii² 334 makes regulations for the distribution) and must have provided many with their best meal of the year.

394. **Ah, that's why ... "fart":** most mss. continue this line to Socrates, but L. Woodbury, *Phoenix* 34 (1980) 112-8, has argued cogently that it belongs to Strepsiades. The opening phrase (Greek *taut' ara*) has already been used three times by Strepsiades (319, 335, 353) when Socrates' words have provided him

181

with an "explanation" of some fact the reason for which he had not previously understood. It is true that many contemporary sophists were interested in etymology, but so were ordinary Greeks: consider, at the very beginning of Greek literature, *Odyssey* 19.407-9 and Hes. *Thg.* 195-200, *Works* 2-3. Since *brontē* and *pordē* are only moderately similar, it is possible that the actor pronounced one or both words abnormally to make them sound more alike (e.g. with a very long, strongly trilled [r], which would further suggest that both words were onomatopoeic).

397. **the weapon of Zeus let loose against perjurers**: one who swears falsely by a god stands self-condemned to punishment by that god; and a perjured oath in the name of Zeus will be punished by Zeus with his own special weapon, the thunderbolt.

398. **babbling prelunar idiot**: Greek *bekkeselēne*, an invented compound each of whose two elements implies that Strepsiades has a primitive mentality. The first, *bekke-*, suggests the story told by Hdt. 2.2 (and in variant versions by other authors) of an experiment conducted by an Egyptian king in order to discover the world's oldest language, which seemed to prove that man's earliest word was *bek* or *bekos*; while the second element suggests the epithet *proselēnos* "older than the moon" traditionally applied to the Arcadians (Hippys, *FGrH* 554 F 7; Arist. fr. 591; Ap.Rh. 4.264f) or to the Arcadian hero Pelasgus (*PMG* 985).

* 398. **the age of Cronus**: the time, long ago, before Zeus became king of the gods; a third imputation, then, that Strepsiades' ideas are archaic and outdated. The name of Cronus is used in the same way at 929, 1070 and *Wasps* 1480, and that of his brother Iapetus at 998.

399-400. **Simon or Cleonymus**: cf. 351-4 and notes.

400. **Theorus** is presumably the associate of Cleon who is frequently attacked in Ar.'s other early plays (*PA* 7223; cf *Ach.* 134ff, *Knights* 608, *Wasps* 42-51, 418-9, 599-600, 1236-42).

401. **Sunium**: the south-eastern extremity of Attica. Since the cape had no special connection with Zeus (its temples were of Poseidon and Athena), its mention here is presumably due to one of the temples' actually having been struck by lightning not long before the production of *Clouds*.

401. **"headland of Athens"**: a Homeric phrase (*Odyssey* 3.278) apparently quoted in its Homeric form, with *Athēneōn* "of Athens" rather than Attic *Athēnōn*.

402. **oak trees**: regarded as sacred to Zeus; cf. *Iliad* 5.693, 7.60, schol. *Birds* 480, and the oracular oak at Dodona. For Zeus to destroy an oak by lightning would thus be as stupid an act of self-injury as to damage his own temple.

404-407. Socrates' theory of the thunderbolt, like his theory of thunder (376-8), is different from any attested elsewhere; its component elements derive from Anaximander (A23 D-K) and Anaximenes (A7), who ascribed lightning to the bursting of clouds by wind, and Democritus (A93), who ascribed it to friction between clouds in contact.

405. **by necessity:** cf. 377. Here the phrase seems little more than a scientistic way of saying "naturally" or "inevitably".

408. **the Diasia:** a festival of Zeus Meilichios, held on the 23rd of Anthesterion (roughly February). Since it was an occasion for whole-burnt offerings (Xen. *Anab.* 7.8.4-5) there could be no state-provided sacrificial meal, but evidently there were family parties and (864) presents for the children.

409. **a haggis:** strictly, a large black pudding (filled with blood and fat: cf. *Odyssey* 20.25-27).

411. **spitting blood:** lit. "making a loose bowel-motion".

414. **a good memory:** for the educational importance of this cf. 129, 483, 629-631, 785-790, 854-5.

415. **soul:** Greek *psūkhē* (again in 420); see on 94.

415- **if neither standing ... yearn for your breakfast:** these are admirable qualities, and
416. according to Plato (*Symp.* 219e-220d) Socrates had conspicuously displayed them during the siege of Potidaea in 432-430. Possibly (cf. 362-3) he was felt to be unduly parading his superiority to physical discomforts.

417. **if you abstain from wine:** Socrates was no abstainer (cf. Pl. *Symp.* 214a, 220a, 223c-d); but Ar. is thinking of the training of would-be orators, who often abjured wine (*Knights* 349; Dem. 6.30, 19.46).

417. **physical exercise:** there is no reason why either an orator or a philosopher should abstain from this, particularly if he was to have the physical toughness demanded by 415-6; Socrates himself is said to have still been a keen wrestler in his late thirties (Pl. *Symp.* 217b-c). "Physical exercise" is then probably a surprise substitute, perhaps for "sexual indulgence" or the like, introducing the notion, strictly inconsistent with the rest of the present passage but developed by Ar. elsewhere (987-9, 1002, 1009-19, 1053-4; *Frogs* 1069-71, 1087-98), that the popularity of rhetoric and philosophy has encouraged young Athenians to neglect their physical fitness.

419. **success in action and deliberation:** a highly traditional definition of the ideal of manly excellence, essentially unchanged from Homer (see e.g. *Iliad* 2.202, 18.105-6) to the fifth-century sophist Protagoras(Pl. *Prot.* 318e-319a). However, the addition of "the warfare of the tongue" slants the definition away from the old ideal of the good citizen, brave in battle and wise in counsel, towards the clever speaker who is successful by verbal dexterity regardless of the merits of his case.

420. **to cogitate on a restless bed:** as Strepsiades did in the opening scene of the play and will do again in 698ff.

421. **that can dine off savory:** savory (cf. *Ach.* 254) was and is a bitter herb used for flavouring; as a meal by itself it would, to say the least, be neither agreeable

nor nourishing.

422. **to be forged on your anvil**: another possible rendering is "to serve as an anvil", i.e. to endure any hardship (as an anvil endures great heat and violent blows).

423. **no god but those we recognize**: actually Socrates' pantheon varies somewhat from one passage to another (cf. 264-5, 365, 627), but it never includes any of the gods commonly worshipped.

424. **Void**: Greek *Chaos*, literally "Gape" or "Chasm", which in Hes. *Thg.* 116 is said to have come into being first of all things. In Ar. it seems to mean "empty space" (cf. *Birds* 1218).

424. **the Tongue**: to worship the tongue is to claim that the power of verbal persuasion over men is almost limitless. Euripides in *Frogs* 892 prays, among other novel gods, to "the pivot of the tongue".

430. **by miles and miles**: lit. "by a hundred stades" (about 11 miles).

433. **that's not what I desire**: he does not want to be a politician, only to be able to avoid paying his debts by successfully defending himself in court.

434. **to twist justice**: Greek *strepsodikēsai*; see on 36.

438. **koppa-branded horses**: see on 23.

445- **audacious, glib, daring ...**: all these expressions are often pejorative, and most of
451. them invariably so; that Strepsiades should be *eager* to be called these names implies in him a high degree of shamelessness.

448. **a walking statute-book**: Greek *kurbis*, which properly denoted one of a set of objects on which the laws of Solon were inscribed. The nature of these objects has been much disputed; R.S. Stroud, *The Axones and Kyrbeis of Drakon and Solon* (Berkeley, 1979), argues convincingly that the *kurbeis* stood in the Agora and were triangular bronze pillars, perhaps about five feet high, topped by pyramid-shaped caps. The meaning of the term as it would be applied to Strepsiades is clear enough: "one who knows more about the technicalities of the law than a normal honest citizen might be expected to know".

448. **a tinkling cymbal**: lit. "a castanet" as in 260.

448. **a needle's eye**: Greek *trūmē*, a word that occurs only here; the scholia offer two interpretations, "hole" and "gimlet". The former is preferable on morphological grounds, and is supported by the derivative *trūmaliā* which occurs in *Mark* 10.25. The idea is of a person as elusive as the eye of a needle can be to one attempting to thread it.

448. **a supple rogue**: lit. "the thong of a whip" as in *Knights* 269.

450. **a whipping-post**: Greek *kentrōn*, properly a slave who has been, or ought to be, tortured with a goad.

450. **a twister**: Greek *strophis;* see on 36.

452- **they** each time denotes the Socratics, the Clouds' "ministers" (436).
456.

457-475. Metre: dactylo-epitrite, consisting of various sequences of the units $-\cup\cup-\cup\cup-$ (hemiepes) and $-\cup-$ (cretic) with successive units normally being separated by a link syllable; variations in the pattern, both paralleled in other basically dactylo-epitrite songs, are the purely dactylic line 460-1 (cf. Eur. *Tro.* 803 = 814) and the ithyphallic ($-\cup-\cup--$) 462 (cf. *Knights* 1273 = 1299).

467- **crowds will always be sitting at your door...:** Strepsiades will become, in effect,
475.   a professional lawyer, taking fees to advise clients on the conduct of litigation and perhaps (though this is not explicitly mentioned here) to write speeches for delivery in the courts.

472. **pleadings:** Greek *antigraphai*, formal written statements of charges, defences, or counter-charges.

476- Metre: anapaestic tetrameters. The couplet resembles the normal form of intro-
477.   duction by the chorus-leader to a contestant's speech in an *agōn* (e.g. 959f, 1351f); for such tetrameter introductions to ordinary dialogue scenes in iambic trimeters, cf. *Birds* 637f, *Lys.* 1072f.

480. **artillery:** Greek *mēkhanai* "devices"; Strepsiades understands it (or rather fails to understand it) in the sense "engines of war".

491. **Am I going ... like a dog?:** as at 139, Strepsiades utterly fails to understand simple figurative language.

494. **what do you do if someone strikes you?:** Socrates wants to know if he is in danger of retaliation.

495. **I wait a little, and call people to witness:** an Athenian who was assaulted called out *martūromai* (1297, *Ach.* 926, *Wasps* 1436, etc), appealing to all within earshot to bear witness to the offence. Unlike most people, however, Strepsiades does not utter the cry immediately on being struck; does he wait till his assailant is safely out of the way, and then prove his injury to any witnesses by showing the bruises?

496. **I go to law:** like the typical comic Athenian; see on 208.

497. **lay down your cloak:** it is the last Strepsiades will see of his cloak (856, 1498; cf. 179).

497. **Have I done something wrong?:** timorous as usual, Strepsiades thinks he is to undress in order to be beaten.

499. **to search your house for stolen goods:** a house could be searched by anyone who believed that property belonging to him was being concealed there; but the searcher had first to remove his outer garments, so that he could not bring anything into the house and afterwards claim to have discovered it there. See the model regulations in Pl. *Laws* 954a-b.

503. **essential features:** Greek *phusis* "nature"; but *phusis* can also mean "appear -ance", and Strepsiades understands it in that sense.

504. **I'll look half a corpse:** see on 103 and 104.

506- **give me a honey-cake ... the cave of Trophonius:** the hero Trophonius had a sub-
508. terranean oracular shrine at Lebadeia in Boeotia. Those who descended to
consult the oracle took with them honey-cakes to placate the serpents of the
cavern. See Paus. 9.39 and Philostratus, *Life of Apollonius* 8.19.

508. **going down inside there:** "down" would be appropriate for the cave of Trophonius, but its place in the sentence leads one to expect that it should also be
appropriate for the actual stage situation. Dearden, *The Stage of Aristophanes*
66, takes it as evidence that the *ekkyklēma* trolley, rolled out of the door at
184, has not yet been withdrawn; if the trolley is still out, Strepsiades will
actually have to step *down* off it in order to go inside. When he and Socrates
have both gone in, the trolley will be withdrawn and the door closed.

510- **Parabasis,** consisting of: prelude, 510-7; leader's speech, 518-562; strophe, 563-
626. 574; epirrhema, 575-594; antistrophe, 595-606; antepirrhema, 607-626.

510- Metre: after two anapaestic lines there is a shift to a song-metre based on the
517. iambic ($\cup - \cup -$) and choriambic ($- \cup \cup -$) rhythms.

510. **Go, and good luck to you:** addressed to Strepsiades. For similar leave-taking
formulae cf. *Ach.* 1143, *Knights* 498, *Peace* 729, and 1113 below.

515- **dipping himself in the dye of:** lit. "colouring his nature (*phusis*, see on 503)
516. with". The metaphor is chosen with an eye to the probability that member-
ship of Socrates' school will literally alter Strepsiades' colour; and in fact,
like Chaerephon (504), the other students (103, 120, 186) and later Pheidippides (1112, 1171), he duly acquires a scholastic pallor, or so he says (718).

* 518- Metre: eupolidean, a tetrameter with the following scheme:
562. $\left\{ {\overline{-}\,\overline{\cup} \atop \cup\,-} \right\} - \times \ -\cup\cup- \left\{ {\overline{-}\,\overline{\cup} \atop \cup\,-} \right\} - \times \ -\cup-$

This metre, which seems to have been a moderately common alternative to the
anapaestic tetrameter in the parabases of Old Comedy, is fully discussed by
J.W. Poultney, *AJPh* 100 (1979) 133-144. The present speech, which is a new
one written for the revised version of the play (see Introductory Note), has
replaced a speech in a different metre (so the scholia on 520).

518. **I:** the poet. Ar. likewise speaks in the first person through the mouth of the chorus in *Ach.* 659-664, *Wasps* 1284-91, and *Peace* 759-774 (and of the hero in
Ach. 377-382, 499, 502-3); his normal practice, however, is to let the chorus
speak in their own name and refer to him in the third person, as in *Ach.* 628-
658 and *Knights* 509-550.

519. **Dionysus who nurtured me to manhood:** Dionysus was the patron god of drama;
and Ar. had become a dramatist when barely out of boyhood, and may well
have been preparing himself for this profession much earlier still.

*521- **you** seems to mean here "you Athenians". The only plausible alternative would
523. be that it meant "the international audience at the City Dionysia" as opposed
to the more homogeneous public who attended the Lenaea (cf. *Ach.* 502-8);
but it would then be impossible to explain "in this place" (528), since Dionysian and Lenaean audiences were alike only to be found in one place, the Theatre of Dionysus. Ar. must therefore be claiming to have done the Athenians a
favour by producing *Clouds* first at Athens rather than abroad ("this place" in
528 will then mean "Athens"). The claim is of course preposterous, since Old
Comedy, unlike tragedy and unlike later comedy, was so far as we know never
produced outside Attica; Ar. is perhaps humorously pretending to be an international celebrity who could find an enthusiastic audience almost anywhere
(cf. *Ach.* 646-654, on the high regard in which he is held by the Spartans and
by the king of Persia).

524. **vulgar men:** Cratinus and Ameipsias. For other attacks by Ar. on Cratinus see
Ach. 849-853, *Knights* 400, 531-6 (and contrast *Frogs* 357 written long after
Cratinus' death); on Ameipsias, *Frogs* 14-15. But to Ar. *every* practising com-
ic poet except himself is "vulgar".

527. **the bright ones among you:** or, with A, "you bright ones".

528. **in this place:** in Athens (cf. on 521-3).

528- **my virtuous boy and my buggered boy:** two brothers who, with their father,
529. were the chief characters of Aristophanes' first comedy, *Banqueters*, produced
in 427; this play, like *Clouds,* was much concerned with the contrast between
traditional and modern education. "Buggered" may mean little more than
"immoral, vicious" (cf. 909, 1330), but the product of the new education may
well have actually been presented as effeminate, if it is he who in Ar. fr. 218
is said to be "as smooth-skinned as an eel, with golden ringlets" (for ringleted
hair as a sign of effeminacy cf. *Wasps* 1069-70).

528- **were extremely well spoken of by certain men:** this has usually been taken to
529. allude to the comparative success that *Banqueters* enjoyed when it was produced (it won second prize); but this does not fit the order of exposition: certain men speak well of the play — Ar. gives it to Callistratus to produce — the
public take it to their hearts. The passage has, I believe, been correctly interpreted by S. Halliwell, *CQ* 30 (1980) 42-43, who sees in it "a reference to some
form of patronage"; at any rate it makes sense if we suppose that in 428, before
submitting his first play to the archon in the hope of being "given a chorus",
Ar. showed the script to two or three men of social distinction and literary dis-
cernment, and that they were instrumental in persuading the archon to find a
place in the festival programme for this very young dramatist.

530. **being still unmarried and not yet supposed to give birth:** Ar. is the young mother,
Banqueters the baby. The passage does not prove that in 427 Ar. was legally
debarred by reason of age from acting officially as a producer (*didaskalos*) at

a major dramatic festival; at most it implies that many people would have thought it improper or presumptuous for such a young man to do so. Ar. himself may have shared that feeling; in *Knights* 512ff he says that the reason why he delayed so long before applying for a chorus in his own name was that he thought comic production "the most difficult thing in the world".

531. **exposed the child:** for the exposure of illegitimate children, compare the plot of Menander's *Epitrepontes*; also Eur. *Ion* 344ff, 951ff, and Terence, *Hecyra* 400. A legitimate child, especially a girl, might also be abandoned if the father exercised his right to refuse to rear it; see Men. *Perik.* 810ff; Poseidippus fr. 11; Terence *H.T.* 626ff.

531. **another girl:** this girl represents Callistratus, the official producer of *Banqueters* (*Proleg.* III 38 Koster). Note that Greek *pais*, like English "girl", can sometimes refer to a young married woman (cf. *Lys.* 90, 697) and may well do so here, since (i) it is not very likely that the parents of an unmarried girl would agree to bring up a foundling child she had discovered and (ii) Callistratus must have been old enough to bear the responsibilities of an official producer.

532. **you ... reared it and educated it:** the public took the infant under their wing, as it were, by showing their approval of the play when it was performed.

534. **Electra:** the daughter of Agamemnon and sister of Orestes. In all three surviving tragedies on the theme of Orestes' revenge — Aeschylus' *Choephori*, Sophocles' and Euripides' *Electra* — Orestes offers a lock of his hair as a mourning-tribute at his father's tomb, and the offering is discovered by, or reported to, Electra. Only in Aeschylus' play does Electra herself go to the tomb, find the lock there, and accept it as evidence that her brother has returned from exile; and it is probably of Aeschylus that Ar. is thinking here (indeed Sophocles' and Euripides' plays may well both be later than the revised version of *Clouds*). If he has Aeschylus in mind, he has made an error, since Electra in *Choephori* goes to the tomb, not "seeking" signs of her brother's return, but bringing a drink-offering sent by her mother; the sight of the lock is a complete surprise to her. Ar.'s memory of *Choephori* may be hazy, as his memory of Aeschylus' *Persians* seems to be in *Frogs* 1028-9. The crucial point for him is that the sight of the lock kindled hope in Electra after many years of loneliness and oppression; similarly, the sight of "intelligent spectators" will kindle hope in the breast of Ar.'s personified comedy after its previous disheartening failure.

*537. **Look at the modesty of her nature:** this play, Ar. asserts, avoids the cheap and vulgar laughter-raising devices which other comic dramatists habitually employ; for similar lists of comic clichés Ar. claims to eschew see *Wasps* 57ff, *Peace* 739ff, *Frogs* 1-20. But many of these devices are in fact used later in the play (see notes below).

538- **she hasn't come ... red at the end and thick:** this is not a denial that the male
539. characters in *Clouds* wore the large leather phallus traditional in comedy; it

denies only the use of a particular variety, "red at the end", i.e. circumcised (for which cf. *Ach.* 158-161).

539. **the children:** boys formed an important part of the theatre audience (*Peace* 50, *Eccl.* 1146, Pl. *Gorg.* 502d).

540. **nor has she made fun of men who are bald:** hardly surprising, since Ar. was bald himself (*Knights* 550, *Peace* 767-773).

540. **cordax:** a salacious comic dance associated with drunkenness (cf. 555 and Thphr. *Char.* 6.3).

541. **the one with the leading part:** lit. "the one who speaks the lines".

541-2. **hitting ... with his stick:** but see 1297-1300!

543. **nor ... rush on stage with torches:** but see 1490ff!

543. **nor cry "help, help":** but see 1321 and 1493!

545. **give myself hairs:** Greek *komō*, which means both "give myself airs" and "wear my hair long": Ar. is punning on his own baldness (see on 540). My rendering of the pun is that of E.K. Borthwick, *Eranos* 77 (1979) 166-7.

*546. **nor try ... a second and a third time:** this assertion is audacious even by the standards of the present passage, since it is certain that substantial parts of the revised *Clouds* are taken over virtually unaltered from the original version; and some years earlier, in *Peace* 751-760, Ar. had repeated almost word for word a passage he had used in *Wasps* 1029-37.

549. **Cleon,** son of Cleaenetus, of Ar.'s own deme of Cydathenaeum (*PA* 8674), had been the most influential politician at Athens in the years following the death of Pericles. After the production of Ar.'s *Babylonians* in 426 Cleon had attempted to prosecute Ar. for slandering the state in the presence of foreigners (cf. *Ach.* 377-382, 502-3, 630-2), and from then on, at least, Ar. was his sworn enemy. Cleon was viciously attacked in *Knights*, in the first version of *Clouds* (581-594), and in *Wasps* (see especially the trial scene, 891-1008, where Cleon appears as "the Dog of Cydathenaeum"). Then in the summer of 422 he was killed when commanding the Athenian forces attempting to recapture Amphipolis.

550. **I did not have the hardihood ... when he was down:** not true; Ar. attacked Cleon after his death in *Peace* (47-48, 269-272, 313-320, 647-656, 752-760).

551. **these fellows:** other comic dramatists, such as those presently mentioned.

*551. **Hyperbolus:** son of Antiphanes, of the deme Perithoidae (*PA* 13910), entered politics at an early age (Cratinus fr. 262; Eupolis fr. 238) in the middle 420's, having first brought himself before the public as a prosecutor in the courts (*Ach.* 846-7). He owed his wealth to a lamp-making business (1065; *Knights* 739, 1315; *Peace* 690). After Cleon's death Hyperbolus succeeded to his position as the leading figure in the Assembly (*Peace* 679-692) and the favourite victim of comic satire. Probably in spring 416 (cf. Andrewes on Thuc. 8.73.3) he was banished by ostracism, as the result of a temporary coalition between

Nicias and Alcibiades each of whom would otherwise have been in danger of banishment himself (Plut. *Nic.* 11; *Alc.* 13); in 411 he was murdered by an oligarchic group at Samos.

552. **his mother:** Hyperbolus' mother was a character in Eupolis' *Maricas* (see on 555) and probably also in Hermippus' *Bread-sellers*. Ar. himself attacked her later in *Thesm.* 839-845, not only on her son's account but also for being a money-lender.

*553. **Eupolis,** son of Sosipolis (*PA* 5936), was perhaps the leading comic dramatist of Ar.'s generation after Ar. himself. He made his début in 429 (*Proleg.* III 33 Koster), won his first victory in 426 or earlier (*IG* ii² 2325.126) and won seven victories in all (Suda ε3657). In 421 his *Flatterers* defeated Ar.'s *Peace*. His last datable play is *Demes*, produced probably in 412, of which papyri have preserved substantial fragments (*CGF* 92-94); he is said by the Suda to have perished at sea "at the Hellespont, in the war against the Spartans", very likely at the battle of Cynossema in 411.

553. **Maricas:** the chief character in the play of the same name by Eupolis, produced in 421. Maricas was a barbarian slave and a caricature of Hyperbolus, just as the barbarian slave Paphlagon in *Knights* had been a caricature of Cleon.

*554. **a vile rehash of my Knights:** apart from the basic idea of presenting a disliked politician as a barbarian slave, the fragments of *Maricas* (including those embedded in the papyrus commentary *CGF* 95) do not suggest any very close resemblance between that play and *Knights*. An exception is Eupolis fr. 193, which is virtually identical with *Knights* 188-9; but it cannot be excluded that Quintilian may have confused the two plays. Eupolis countered Ar.'s accusation of plagiarism by claiming (fr. 78) that he had himself had a hand in the composition of *Knights*; on the question what factual basis, if any, this allegation had, see *CQ* 30 (1980) 51-53.

*555. **a drunken old woman:** according to the scholia this character represented Hyperbolus' mother.

555. **cordax:** see on 540.

*556. **Phrynichus** son of Eunomides (*PA* 15006) was a comic dramatist contemporary with Aristophanes and Eupolis. His first production, like that of Eupolis, was in 429 (*Proleg.* III 33-34 Koster), his first victory in 429 or 428 (*IG* ii² 2325. 124); we meet him last in 405, when his play *Muses* took second prize to Ar.'s *Frogs*.

556. **the one the sea-monster tried to devour:** Phrynichus must have written a parody on the story of Andromeda, who was left in bonds on the seashore to be devoured by a monster but was rescued by Perseus (cf. *Thesm.* 1009-1135 which parodies Euripides' play on the subject produced in 412). Phrynichus substituted an ugly, bibulous old woman for the beautiful princess Andromeda, and Eupolis is accused of having plagiarized the character. Ar. when he treated the

theme went one better than Phrynichus: *his* "Andromeda" is an old man!

557. **Hermippus**, son of Lysis (*PA* 5112), was active as a comic dramatist at least from the middle 430s: a fragment of the festival records (*Hesperia* 12 [1943] 1) shows that he won first prize at the City Dionysia in 435. He is not certainly heard of later than the date of the revision of *Clouds*, and may well have died about 417. The play in which he attacked Hyperbolus was *Breadsellers* (*Artopōlides*), presumably produced in 420 or 419.

558. **all the others:** the comic dramatist Plato wrote a play *Hyperbolus*; no doubt there were also other comedies directed in whole or in part at Hyperbolus between 421 and his ostracism, but no specific evidence survives.

559. **my similes about eels:** the reference is to *Knights* 864-7, where Paphlagon (Cleon) is compared to an eel-fisher who fishes best in troubled waters. The plural "similes" is what might be called a plural of aggrievement; the child who says to another "stop pinching my biscuits" has not necessarily had more than one biscuit taken.

*562. **you will be thought ... to have been wise:** for this appeal to the audience to think of the judgement of posterity cf. *Frogs* 705, 736-7.

*563-574 = 595-606 Metre: each stanza divides naturally into four sections, each section addressed to a different god. The first two sections of each stanza are iambo-choriambic (cf. 511-7); the third is dactylic; the fourth begins in iambo-choriambic again and ends with a glyconic $(-\times-\cup\cup-\cup-)$ and a pherecratean $(-\times\cup\cup--)$. Both in metre and in content the song resembles *Knights* 551-564 = 581-594; it is a cletic hymn, in which the chorus invite various deities to come and join their dance. All but one of the deities summoned are traditional ones, and right at the start Zeus is emphatically called king of the gods, contrary to the belief of Socrates (365-381); see on 302-310.

565. **great** (Greek *megas*) appears in every section of this stanza: Zeus is "the great sovereign", Poseidon "great and mighty", the Sky "greatly renowned", and the Sun "a great Power".

566. **the Warden of the Trident:** Poseidon.

567- **him who savagely ... the briny sea:** Poseidon is the god of earthquakes and tidal
568.   waves.

569. **our own greatly renowned father:** see on 271.

570. **the Sky:** Greek *Aithēr*; see on 265.

*570. **who nourishes all living things:** in Empedocles fr. 100 D-K *aithēr* is what animals breathe, and in *trag. adesp.* 112 it "gives breath and nourishment" to all mortal creatures. In *Frogs* 892 Euripides is made to pray to "the *aithēr* on which I feed".

571. **the Charioteer:** the Sun. The Sun's chariot, in which he drives across the sky every day, makes no appearance in Homer (though cf. *Odyssey* 23.243-6) but is a regular attribute of the Sun in later poetry (first in *h.Hom.Dem.* 63, 88 and

Mimnermus fr. 12 West = 5 G-P) and in art from the sixth century.

575-594 = 607-626 Metre: trochaic tetrameters.

576: **us:** the Cloud-goddesses.

580. **we either thunder or rain:** thunder or rain would result in the suspension of the assembly debating the proposed expedition (cf. *Ach.* 169-173) and would thus give time for second thoughts about it; thunder in particular would encourage people to believe that the gods were opposed to the expedition and that it should be abandoned. Note however Eupolis *CGF* 92. 30-32, on the Mantinea expedition of 418: some members of the board of generals made use of an opportune thunderclap to urge that the expedition be cancelled, but an unnamed demagogue persuaded the people to go ahead with it.

581. **tanner:** the wealth of Cleon's family appears to have come from a tanning and shoemaking business; cf. *Knights* 44, 136, 197, 314-321, 369, 449, etc., etc.

581. **Paphlagon:** the name of the character who represents Cleon in *Knights*; it can signify (i) "Bubbler" (cf. *Knights* 919-922) and (ii) "man from Paphlagonia" in northern Asia Minor, implying that Cleon is of barbarian descent.

583. **amid the lightning came the burst of thunder:** a quotation from Sophocles' *Teucer* (fr. 578).

584. **the moon took to forsaking her path:** there was a total eclipse of the moon on 9 October 425. This was some months before the annual election of generals, but after Cleon's success at Pylos most Athenians must have expected that he would be chosen when the time came.

584- **the sun ... said that he wouldn't give you light:** this threat came true: there was
585. an annular eclipse of the sun on 21 March 424 (cf. Thuc. 4.52.1), probably a few weeks after the election (the election was normally held in the seventh prytany period [Arist. *Ath.Pol.* 44.4] which at this time corresponded more or less to February). Any Athenians who thought that the eclipse meant the gods were angry with them for making Cleon a general will have been reinforced in their belief by the earthquake which followed a few days later (Thuc. loc. cit.).

587. **they say:** this popular belief appears again at *Eccl.* 473-5. The scholia narrate the myth associated with it: "When Poseidon and Athena were disputing possession of Attica, and Athena won, Poseidon was so vexed that he cursed the city, saying 'The Athenians will always make the wrong decision'; but Athena, hearing him, added the words ' ... and yet be successful'."

591. **seagull:** this bird was type of voracity and thievishness: cf. *Knights* 956 and Matron, *Attic Dinner* 10-11.

591. **theft** probably here denotes embezzlement of public money; cf. *Knights* 79, 205, 258, 296, 444, 716-8, 826-7, 1031-2, 1218-24.

592. **the stocks:** lit. "the wood", described more fully in *Knights* 1049 as "a wooden frame with five holes" (for feet, hands and head).

595-606. Whereas the strophe invoked gods whose sphere is all the earth, sea and sky, this antistrophe is concerned with four gods who have special associations with particular localities. Compare the way in which the chorus's first song, whose strophe (275-290) surveyed the whole earth, focused in its antistrophe (298-313) on Attica; the present antistrophe, like the earlier one, ends with Dionysus, at whose festival the play is being produced.

595. **Grant me thy presence too:** this seems to be the meaning of Greek *amphi moi aute* in this context; but the phrase is adapted from a stock opening formula for dithyrambs and other hymns in which the words had a totally different meaning and construction, something like "let me also sing of ...". Cf. Terpander fr. 1 Page; *h.Hom.Pan.* 1; Eur. *Tro.* 511; Ar. *CGF* 63.55.

596. **Cynthus:** the highest point (about 385 feet) on Apollo's sacred island of Delos.

598. **blest Lady:** Artemis.

601. **our own native Goddess:** to speak thus of Athena the chorus must drop their role as cloud-goddesses and sing simply as a chorus of Athenian citizens. Cf. *Birds* 789 where a chorus which in general maintains its dramatic role very consistently uses "us" to mean "the performers of comedy".

602. **mistress:** lit. "charioteer"; for the metaphor cf. Simonides epigr. 30 Page, where a boy Olympic wrestling champion is called a "skilful charioteer of wrestling".

602. **aegis:** this attribute of Zeus and Athena, originally imaged as a storm-cloud, had by the fifth century been transformed by popular etymology into a goatskin cloak or cape, and appears as such in archaic and classical representations of Athena. It was Athena's weapon for striking panic into her enemies (*Odyssey* 22.297ff; cf. *Iliad* 5.738-742, 15.308-327).

603-604. **he who haunts Parnassus' rock:** Dionysus was thought to reside at Delphi during the three winter months when Apollo was held to be absent and the oracle was closed; and in alternate years a women's festival with maenadic rites was held in his honour on the heights of Parnassus above Delphi.

604. **pine-torches:** carried by the maenads or their leader, who is partly identified with the god: cf. Eur. *Ba.* 146, 307; Eur. fr. 752.

614. **Selene:** the Greek has not *Selēnē* as in 607 but *Selēnaiē*, a form at home in elevated poetry (e.g. Empedocles fr. 43 D-K) and intentionally incongrouous in the present context.

615-616. **you don't keep the calendar right:** i.e. the Athenian official months are often out of step with the moon. A similar complaint is made in *Peace* 414-5; and Thuc. 4.118.8; 4.119.1; 5.19.1 show that between spring 423 and spring 421 the Spartan calendar gained four days on the Athenian. In Athens at any rate, however, the discrepancies cannot at this period have been large, since the waning moon is a sign to Strepsiades that the official month will soon end and more interest be added to his debts (16-18). The discrepancies were caused by the archon, who had charge of the official calendar, ordering the insertion of intercalary days, most often perhaps in order to postpone a festival which for one reason or another could not be held on its appointed day. The Assembly could give directions to the archon on calendar matters (cf. *IG* i^2 76.53-54); and the mention of Hyperbolus' supposed punishment (623-6) suggest that a decree for an irregular intercalation had recently been passed at his instigation. For a full discussion of the intercalation and suppression of days in the Athenian calendar see W.K. Pritchett, *Ancient Athenian Calendars on Stone* (Berkeley, 1963) 326-348.

617- **the gods are always ... reckoning of the days:** the gods, it is assumed, regulate
619.   their calendar strictly by the cycle of the moon; accordingly they may well expect a festival-sacrifice from the Athenians on a day which the Athenians, owing to intercalations, are not in fact keeping as a festival. The gods apparently do not realize that it is the Athenians who are in error; they lay the blame on the Moon.

620. **you are applying torture:** to slaves giving evidence in legal proceedings.

621. **holding a solemn fast:** fasting in memory of the dead was not to our knowledge a normal Greek custom, but this passage indicates that some people at least practised it. So, perhaps, by inversion, does Soph. *El.* 278ff (Clytaemnestra holds a *feast* each month on the day she killed her husband).

622. **Memnon or Sarpedon:** children of the gods who were killed in the Trojan War. Sarpedon was a son of Zeus and king of the Lycians; he was killed by Patroclus. Memnon was a son of Eos (Dawn), and king of the Ethiopians; he was killed by Achilles.

623. **pouring libations:** at a festal banquet.

623. **Hyperbolus:** see on 551.

624. **this year:** probably 424/3; nothing in the present speech indicates that it was written for the revised version of the play, and its close parallelism with 575-594 (Athenians' ingratitude to the Clouds: their ingratitude to the Moon; punishment of Cleon recommended: punishment of Hyperbolus described) strongly suggests that it belongs to the original version as 575-594 certainly does.

624. **sacred remembrancer:** Greek *hieromnēmon*, the title of the chief Athenian delegate to meetings of the Amphictyonic council, the governing body of a religious league controlling the temples at Thermopylae and (in part) Delphi. The council met twice yearly, in spring and autumn; the incident here mentioned therefore probably took place in autumn 424.

624- **had his garland taken away by us gods:** we do not know what this refers to. Since
625.   magistrates wore garlands as symbols of their office, "to lose one's garland" can mean "to be deprived of office" (cf. *Knights* 1227; [Dem.] 26.5; 58.27; Lycurgus, *Against Leocrates* 122); but deposition from office was the act of men, not gods. Starkie therefore makes the attractive guess that a wind-god

had blown the garland from Hyperbolus' head.

627. **By Respiration, by Void, by Air:** Heraclitus (A16 D-K) and Diogenes of Apollonia (A19) associated intelligence with breath, and it is thus natural enough for Socrates to worship breath; in *Frogs* 893 Euripides is made to pray to his own nostrils. For Void as a Socratic "god" cf. 424, for Air cf. 264.

638. **measures, or words, or rhythms:** the first lesson is to be on the theory of poetry. "Rhythms" refers to the various types of metrical unit on which a verse-form may be based (iambic, dactylic, etc.: cf. 650-1) and "measures" to the numbers of such units that a line can contain (cf.642). But Strepsiades thinks of a kind of measure with which he is more familiar — measures of capacity.

640. **quarts:** the *khoinix* was a little less than a quart or a little more than a litre.

642. **the three-measure or the four-measure:** Socrates means the iambic trimeter, the normal dialogue metre of both comedy and tragedy, and the trochaic tetrameter, frequent in comedy and used in tragedy by Aeschylus, by Euripides in his later work, and occasionally by Sophocles. Arist. *Poet.* 1449a21-27 compares the merits of the two as dialogue metres. Our evidence suggests that when *Clouds* was first produced the use of the trochaic tetrameter in tragedy had recently been revived after a generation of neglect; no instance is known between Aesch. *Ag.* 1450-73 and Soph. *O.T.* 1515ff (Soph. fr. 269c. 21-24 Radt is from *Inachus*, probably a satyr-play).

643. **the gallon measure:** Greek *hēmiekteōn*, a measure of capacity equal to four *khoinikes* (cf. 645). As between the "three-measure" and the "four-measure" Strepsiades will naturally prefer the larger.

647. **perhaps though you might be able:** or, with the ms. tradition, "you'd certainly be very quick", which would be spoken sarcastically.

648. **my daily groats:** cf. on 106.

651. **enoplian ... digital:** the phrase rendered " digital" is *kata daktulon* "by dactyl"; *daktulos* also means "finger", whence Strepsiades' misunderstanding. The precise technical meaning of *enoplios* and *daktulos* in late fifth-century metrics is not known, and Pl. *Rep.* 3.400b, where both are mentioned, is of little help. Since the dactyl is presumably so named from the analogy of the bones of the human finger (long-short-short) dactylic rhythm is likely to have meant for Ar. much the same as what it means for us; but ancient scholarship could not decide (as the scholia show) what Ar. meant by enoplian rhythm, and it is unlikely that modern scholarship will be able to. For a recent discussion and bibliography see R. Pretagostini, *QUCC* n.s. 2 (1979) 119-129.

[653]. This line ("What else, if not this finger here?") and 654 are both responses to the same request by Socrates, and can hardly stand together in the text; and 654 is far the more vigorous of the two. For the plausible theory that the two lines are alternative drafts by Ar. see K.J. Dover, *ICS* 2 (1977) 151-2.

654. **in my boyhood, it was this:** the phrase *kata daktulon* suggests to Strepsiades'

mind *katadaktulismos*, the obscene and contemptuous gesture of extending the middle finger at a person (cf. *Ach.* 444, *Knights* 1381, *Peace* 549).

659. **quadrupeds:** in view of the etymological transparency of Greek *tetrapoda* it is surprising that Socrates makes no objection when Strepsiades includes the fowl in his list. Perhaps to an Attic farmer *tetrapoda* just meant "livestock", and Socrates passes over the error because it is irrelevant to the topic under discussion, gender.

*659. **are properly called masculine:** "properly" (*orthōs*) in a linguistic context will bring to mind the name of Prodicus (cf. on 361) and his interest in the proper use of words (*orthoepeia, orthotēs onomatōn*: cf. Pl. *Euthd.* 277e) An animal "*im*properly called masculine" would be a female animal the noun for which had a typically masculine ending, e.g. a mare (Greek *hippos*, never *hippē*). Another leading sophist, Protagoras, is also known to have concerned himself much with linguistic usage (Pl. *Crat.* 391c) and in particular with grammatical gender; he established the classification of nouns as masculine, feminine and neuter, and is said to have argued that certain feminine nouns "ought" to be masculine (Protagoras A27, A28 D-K).

661. **fowl:** Greek *alektruōn*, the normal word in Attic both for the cock (e.g. 4, *Wasps* 100, *Eccl.* 391) and the hen (e.g. Ar. fr. 18, 185, 186; Theopompus com. fr.9).

666. **"fowless":** Greek *alektruaina*, an invented word formed on the model of *leaina* the feminine of *leōn* "lion", *Lakaina* from *Lakōn* "Laconian", etc.

666. **"fowler":** Greek *alektōr*, a genuine poetic word for "cock" (e.g. Aesch. *Ag.* 1671, *Eum.* 861) not used in ordinary Attic (*Wasps* 1490 is tragic parody; in Cratinus fr. 259 *alektōr* keeps company with the highly poetic verb *kanakhein*).

669. **cardopus:** kneading-tray. The Greek word is feminine despite its typically masculine ending; Socrates argues that, being feminine, it should be made to *sound* feminine by a change in its ending.

673. **just like Cleonymus:** i.e. the ending of *kardopos* is the same as that of men's names such as *Kleōnumos*, which would seem to imply, incorrectly, that *kardopos* is masculine.

675. **Cleonymus never had a cardopus at all:** Strepsiades, unable to understand what Socrates has just been saying, fastens on the one phrase that seems to him to have some meaning, *kardopos Kleōnumōi* "a kneading-tray to Cleonymus", which could be taken to mean " a kneading-tray *belonging* to Cleonymus". He thinks Socrates must have made a mistake: Cleonymus (evidently the politician so often satirized by Ar.: see on 353-4) "never had" a kneading-tray. Why not, and why the past tense? Perhaps the point is that once (before he went into politics?) Cleonymus was so poor that he could not afford a tray to knead barley-cakes, i.e. could not prepare his own food; cf. *Knights* 1290-9 where he is said to have partaken gluttonously of other people's. In the next line the

196

joke moves in another direction.

676. **the kneading he did was done in a round mortar:** the best explanation of this expression is that of Dover (see now *Greek Homosexuality* [London, 1978] 139), that Cleonymus was "rejected by women and reduced to masturbation". The crucial clue is the middle voice of the verb *anematteto*, which ought to mean "kneaded himself up": compare the verb *dephein*, "knead" in the active voice, "masturbate" in the middle. At the time being spoken of, Cleonymus could neither make himself a meal nor procure himself a sex-partner. Dover explains the "round mortar" as a reference to masturbation using two hands rather than one; Strepsiades would probably illustrate the meaning of the metaphor with the help of his own comic phallus.

678. **Sostraté:** probably not a reference to any specific individual, but just a typical woman's name. Ar. uses it three times for fictitious characters (*Wasps* 1397, *Thesm.* 375, *Eccl.* 41).

680. **Cleonymé never had a cardopé:** Strepsiades now realizes, as he thinks, what Socrates was getting at. He has been incorrectly making *kardopos* masculine, "just like Cleonymus": the word for "kneading-tray" is really feminine — and so is Cleonymus. Hence this inquiry, as "enlightenment" dawns, providing the climax of this joke-sequence as Cleonymus is in effect called a woman, in reference no doubt to his cowardice (cf. 353-4). As usual, of course, Strepsiades has misunderstood: Socrates had used the name Cleonymus merely as an example, and had not been thinking of its best-known bearer at all. But Strepsiades is (in Ar.'s view) right about Cleonymus for all that, just as he is right about Amynias in 692.

684. **Lysilla, Philinna, Cleitagora, Demetria:** these are probably just the first four women's names that happen to come into Strepsiades' head. Lysilla (*Thesm.* 375) and Demetria (*PA* 3326a-f, 3327-8) were names borne by Athenian citizen women; Philinna appears later as the name of a courtesan (title of a play by Hegemon) and of a freedwoman (in Menander's *Georgos*); Cleitagora was the subject of a well-known drinking song (*skolion*) quoted in *Wasps* 1245-7.

*686. **Philoxenus**, son of Eryxis, of the deme Diomeia (*PA* 14707), is mentioned several times in comedy as a passive homosexual (*Wasps* 84; Eupolis fr. 235; Phrynichus com. fr. 47). In later writers (starting with Arist. *Eth. Eud.* 1231a17) his name became a byword for gluttony.

686. **Melesias** is unidentifiable; we know that Melesias, son of the politician Thucydides (*PA* 9813), was a person of little ability or merit (Pl. *Laches* 179c, *Meno* 94c-d), but nothing is said about him elsewhere that might call his masculinity into question, and Plato can present him as on friendly terms with the courageous soldier Laches; and the name is not rare at this period.

686. **Amynias** son of Pronapes (*PA* 737) is elsewhere satirized in comedy as a long-haired, boastful man, addicted to gambling, who lived by sponging on rich

friends and bringing malicious prosecutions (*Wasps* 74-76, 466, 1267-70; Cratinus fr. 212 Kock = 213 Edmonds). In 423/2 he was a member of an embassy to Thessaly (*Wasps* 1271-4; Eupolis fr. 209).

687. **those aren't masculine:** Socrates is speaking only of the last two names, "Melesias" and "Amynias": in three of their five case-forms these names have endings indistinguishable from those of women's names like "Demetria", and Socrates, as the example of *kardopos* showed, thinks the gender of a noun ought to be predictable from its ending; so these two names cannot "really" be masculine. But Strepsiades and the audience are bound to take him as meaning something else: that the three men named (including Philoxenus) are better described as women.

690. **come here, Amynia:** Greek *Amūniā*, the vocative case of the man's name *Amūniās*, could theoretically also be the vocative of a woman's name **Amūniā*.

699. **how the bugs are going to take it out on me:** lit. "what a penalty I'm going to pay to the bugs".

700-706. Metre: iambo-choriambic, except for the third line which consists of an iambic metron plus the unit $- \cup - \cup \cup - \cup \cup -$. Comparison with the antistrophe (804-813) shows that the strophe is metrically (and, we may presume, musically) incomplete: it ends at a point where in the antistrophe there is not even a pause. It seems that the song is halted by Strepsiades' cries of pain.

701-704. **twist ... twirl ... jump:** no doubt, thanks to the bugs, Strepsiades is doing all these things, not mentally but physically, as the chorus sing!

708-722. Metre: 708 is bacchiac ($\cup - -$ twice), a very rare metre in comedy used only for special effects, here probably parody of a tragic chorus addressing a suffering hero. Strepsiades' reply begins with two iambic trimeters and then shifts into anapaests, which continue to 722.

710. **Tom Tugs** (rhyming slang for "bugs") renders *Korinthioi* "Corinthians" which may have been a current slang expression for *koreis* "bedbugs"; note that the joke in *Frogs* 433 is based partly on the same punning link between Corinth and bedding.

718-719. **lost my money ... lost my shoes:** possibly parodying Eur. *Hec.* 159-161 "What family, what city have I? Lost is the old man, lost are the children". Strepsiades can hardly really have gone pale in the short time he has been in the school, nor does his son make any comment on his colour when they meet again; perhaps Strepsiades believes that the unnatural pallor of the other students is due not merely to lack of fresh air and exercise but to some magic or miasma in the school's atmosphere (cf. his frightened reluctance to go in, 506-9) and, lacking a mirror, supposes this must have affected him too.

721. **whistling in the dark:** lit. "singing a watchman's song": watchmen may sing or hum to help stay awake, alert and in good spirits (cf. Aesch. *Ag.* 16-17), and singing like a watchman" had apparently come to mean "trying to keep up

one's spirits in a depressing situation".

*730. **lambskins:** the coverlets of the bed, with which Strepsiades covers his head at 727 and 740.

730. **a lovely bit of ... fraudulent ingenuity:** Greek *gnōmēn aposterētrida*, in sense approximately equivalent to *nous aposterētikos* "a defraudative idea" in 728; but the adjectival suffix used here (cf. *aulētris* "flute-girl", *orkhēstris* "dancing-girl") indicates that Strepsiades' mind is beginning to wander from intellectual to sexual thoughts.

733. **Have you managed to het hold of anything?:** i.e. "have you reached any useful conclusions in your thinking?"

734. **I've got hold of my cock:** the thoughts that were invading Stepsiades' mind at 730 (see last note but one) have now taken complete possession, and he is busy masturbating.

740- I have retained the manuscripts' assignment to Socrates of these pieces of tutorial
745.   advice, but there is a good case for assigning them (and the similar advice in 761-3) to the chorus-leader; Socrates would then be offstage (as in 699-722 and 726-730), or absorbed in cogitations of his own, while Strepsiades was thinking out his problems. See M.W. Haslam, *HSCP* 80 (1976) 45-47.

745. **weigh it in the balance:** one of several guesses in the scholia at the meaning of the verb *zugōthrizein*, which occurs nowhere else; another possibility is "lock it up" (from *zugōthron* "bar or handle of a door", a word known to schol. E and to Pollux 10.16).

* 749. **a Thessalian sorceress:** for the famous witches of Thessaly, and their supposed ability to bring the moon down from the sky, cf. Pl. *Gorg.* 513a; Horace *Epod.* 5.45-46; Pliny *N.H.* 30.7 on Menander's comedy *Thettale*. Strepsiades apparently envisages his sorceress as a purchased slave; Thessaly provided numbers of slaves to other parts of Greece through the activities of kidnappers who sold their victims to slave-dealers (*Wealth* 520-1).

751. **case:** Greek *lopheion*, properly a case for storing helmet-crests.

756. **Because money is lent out by the month:** cf. 16-18.

761-3 may be spoken by the chorus-leader rather than by Socrates; see on 740-5.

762. **pay your thoughts out a bit into the air:** cf. 229-230.

763. **like a cockchafer tethered ... with a thread:** this was a children's game, to let a cockchafer-beetle fly on the end of a string attached at its other end to a piece of wood too heavy for the insect to lift; cf. Herodas 12.1 Cunningham.

766. **druggists:** Greek *pharmakon* has a wider meaning than English "drug"; it could denote anything that affected, or was thought to affect, the physical or mental condition of a person who consumed it or to whom it was applied – a medical preparation, a poison, or a magical charm (note that the word translated "sorceress" in 749 is *pharmakis*). Glass may well have been thought to have magical powers because of its rarity, its delicacy, and its power to kindle fire.

768. **glass** was at this date rare and precious in Greece; it is coupled with gold in *Ach.* 74 and Hdt. 2.69.2.

772. **make the writing melt away:** the clerk is assumed to be writing on a waxed tablet; Strepsiades' idea is to destroy the record by concentrating the sun's rays on the wax with the aid of his burning-glass.

775. **get your teeth into:** lit. "snap up", cf. 490.

783. **you're drivelling:** why is Socrates so contemptuous of this "solution", after his approval of Strepsiades' earlier ludicrous suggestions (757, 773)? Those earlier suggestions were logically flawless; their only drawback was that they were impossible in practice. The present one, on the other hand, is perfectly practicable but unsound in theory: it cannot benefit Strepsiades because it would result in there being no Strepsiades to benefit. Socrates' students earn black marks for theoretical incoherence – not for lack of common sense.

788. **that feminine thing that we knead groats in:** he cannot remember the word *kardopos* (669-680) – which in any case is *not* the first thing he was taught about. He remembers this, and other earlier lessons, later on (828, 847-851, 1247-58).

792. **to be a verbal twister:** Greek *glōttostrophein*; see on 36.

797. **a fine upstanding fellow:** Greek *kalos te kāgathos*; see on 101. Strepsiades is not exactly being ironical, since Pheidippides does have many of the qualities that entitled a man to be called *kalos kāgathos*, such as noble descent, good looks and sporting prowess; but he is certainly thinking bitterly of a quality that any *kalos kāgathos* would be expected to possess and Pheidippides does not, namely that of being a dutiful son.

800. **high-flying:** lit. "well-feathered".

800. **the house of Coesyra:** see on 48.

802. **I'll throw him out of the house:** he made the same threat at 123, and it proved empty; will things be any different this time?

804- This is the antistrophe to 700-6 but is three lines longer (see on 700-6). The
813. extra lines, like most of what precedes, are iambo-choriambic.

804- **Do you perceive ... whatever you bid him:** with M. Landfester, *Mnemosyne* 28
807. (1975) 386-7, I take these lines as addressed to Strepsiades and not, as most editors have supposed, to Socrates.

806. **this man:** Socrates (who has no doubt indicated by gesture that he is at least interested in the possibility of taking Pheidippides as a pupil).

810. **lap up as much as you can:** i.e. demand and receive a high fee for Pheidippides' education. Socrates in fact never explicitly names his fee; but 876 (Hyperbolus did learn ... for a talent") is sufficient intimation that he expects a very substantial payment – a prospect that does not perturb Strepsiades in the least ("Don't worry, teach him").

812- **for such things ... otherwise than expected:** Socrates will take this as meaning
813. that Strepsiades' present state of infatuation, in which he is set on having his

son taught rhetoric at any price, may well not last long. But in retrospect, later on, we may see that this utterance was the first of a series, obscure to begin with but later increasingly clear (1113-4, 1303-20), in which the chorus foreshadow the disaster to which Socrates' impiety and Strepsiades' dishonesty are leading.

814. **by Mist:** a variant on the Socratic oath "by Air" (627, 667).

815. **columns:** evidently to have a colonnade in one's house was a mark of great wealth. The house of the very rich Callias had at least two colonnades (Pl. *Prot.* 314e-315c). As yet no fifth-century house with a colonnade has been excavated in the city of Athens, though some have been found in the Attic countryside: see R.E. Wycherley, *The Stones of Athens* (Princeton, 1978) 237-246, who gives references to detailed accounts of particular houses or house-groups.

820- **To think ... so antiquated:** in an amusing reversal of the normal pattern of gen-
821. eration-conflict, it is the father who accuses his son of out-of-date thinking.

824. **be sure not to divulge this to anyone:** Strepsiades treats the "knowledge" he has acquired as a holy secret (cf. 140, 143).

827. **there is no Zeus:** cf. 367.

828. **Vortex is king, having expelled Zeus:** cf. 380-1.

* 830. **the Melian:** thinking of Socrates as one who disbelieves in and scoffs at the traditional gods, Strepsiades confuses him with the notorious atheist Diagoras of Melos, who openly mocked at all religious beliefs and observances and was eventually tried for impiety and condemned to death in his absence (*Birds* 1072-4; [Lys.] 6.17-18). On Diagoras see Guthrie, *History of Greek Philosophy* iii 236-7, and most recently M. Winiarczyk, *Eos* 67 (1979) 191-213, 68 (1980) 51-75.

831. **the footsteps of fleas:** cf. 144-152.

833. **the bile-sickness:** one form of insanity was believed by contemporary doctors to be due to overheating of the brain through an excess of bile (Hippocr. *On the Sacred Disease* 18).

834- **don't slander men of ingenuity and intelligence:** the similarity to 105 ("Be
835. quiet, don't say anything so childish") directs our attention to the fact that Pheidippides' attitude to the Socratics is unchanged since his previous refusal to have anything to do with them, while Strepsiades is even more under their spell now than he was then. In 1464ff these attitudes will be completely reversed — and Pheidippides will call his father mad (1475) for a reason exactly the opposite to that for which he thinks him mad now.

836. **anointed himself:** to keep the skin from drying out in the sun.

837. **gone to a bath-house:** a fee was charged for the use of public bath-houses, but it must have been very small: note that Demos in *Knights* 1061 apparently regards a daily bath as normal. A person who avoided bath-houses to save money

would be either very stingy or extremely ascetic: Strepsiades thinks the Socratics are stingy, but the audience is meant to realize that they are actually ascetic (cf. 415-7, 441-2). Socrates is again "unwashed" in *Birds* 1554-5; and Plato makes one of Socrates' most fervent admirers admit (*Symp.* 174a) that it was rare for Socrates to take a bath.

838. **squander my livelihood by washing yourself**: lit. "wash-away-for-yourself my livelihood". Strepsiades, at home with the smells of the farm (44, 50), considers frequent bathing a pointless extravagance; in the wealthy circles in which Pheidippides moves it is a social necessity.

838. **as if I were dead**: after a funeral the relatives washed themselves to remove the ritual pollution of having been under the same roof as a corpse. Strepsiades seems to be making two points at once: (i) Pheidippides is treating his father's property as his own, as though he had already inherited it; (ii) in Strepsiades' view the only occasion when a thorough wash is really necessary is when it is a religious requirement, as after a funeral.

845. **shall I ... get him adjudged insane**: Pheidippides is thinking of bringing the type of legal action called a *graphē paranoiās*. The object of such an action was to prevent an insane head of a family from dissipating his property (Pl. *Laws* 929d; Arist. *Ath.Pol.* 56.6), and if successful it resulted in the defendant being deprived of all control over the property, though he apparently remained nominal owner of it (Pl. *Laws* 929e; Aeschines 3.251). Plato makes it clear that a dutiful son would be most reluctant to take action of this kind; and according to Xenophon (*Mem.* 1.2.49) one of the allegations made by the accusers of Socrates was that he encouraged sons to do so.

851. **"fowless" ... "fowler"**: cf. 666.

853. **Children of Earth**: he means "stupid clods" (cf. Alexis fr. 108.5); but the expression also suggest the Titans, children of Ge (Earth), who warred against the Olympian gods, and so conveys a hint (unintended by Pheidippides) that the Socratics too are enemies of the gods. For the association between the notions "earth-born" and "enemy of the gods" cf. Eur. *Ba.* 538-544, 995-6.

857. **I've invested it in knowledge**: he is pretending that the loss of the cloak was the necessary price he had to pay for the benefits of a Socratic education.

859. **"for essential purposes", as Pericles would have put it**: when the Spartans invaded Attical in 445, Pericles was said to have given the Spartan king Pleistoanax a bribe of ten talents to withdraw; he entered the amount in the accounts of his generalship as having been spent "for essential purposes" (*eis to deon*) (Plut. *Per.* 22-23). Strepsiades' "essential purpose" is again education.

863. **the first obol of jury pay I received**: in 423 jurors received three obols a day (*Knights* 51, *Wasps* 609), raised a few years before from two obols (schol. *Wasps* 88, schol. *Birds* 1541). There is no need to take the present passage as implying that earlier still the rate had been one obol; the phrase means simply

"the very first money that came to hand".

864. **the Diasia:** see on 408.

869. **doesn't know the ropes and lashings:** lit. "isn't familiar (*tribōn*, see next note) with the hanging gear (*kremasta*)". *Kremasta* was one of the two headings (the other was *xulina*, wooden gear) under which the Athenian naval authorities catalogued the equipment of a warship; it included such items as sails, ropes and anchors. See J.S. Morrison and R.T. Williams, *Greek Oared Ships 900-322 B.C.* (Cambridge, 1968) 289, 294-302. The word "hanging" no doubt reminds us of our first sight of Socrates, suspended in a wicker cage in mid-air (218ff).

870. **Hang you ... weceive a good lashing yourself:** lit. "you yourself would be an old worn cloak (*tribōn*, cf. previous note) if you were hung up". A slave or a prisoner might be hung up or trussed in order to be flogged (cf. Soph. *Ajax* 108-110, *Ant.* 308-9; Herodas 4.78; Terence, *Phormio* 220), and a fuller cleaning clothes would hang them up and beat them; hence the meaning is "You could do with being hung up and beaten as soundly as a fuller beats a dirty cloak". Socrates ignores the insult, but comments (872-3) on Pheidippides' sloppy pronunciation in this sentence, the first he has heard him speak; he particularly mentions the word *kremaio* "you were hung up", in which Pheidippides may perhaps have slurred the sequence *-aio* so that it came out as [æw] or even [æə].

871. **how dare you curse your teacher?:** this admonition will boomerang on Strepsiades at 1467, when Pheidippides, asked to help his father destroy "that villain Chaerephon and Socrates", replies "But I couldn't wrong my teachers".

874. **effective forensic defence . . . persuasion by bombast:** in Greek the three nouns all end in *-sis* (cf. on 317-8).

876. **Hyperbolus did learn them, for a talent:** this conveys to Strepsiades that it will be possible, but very difficult and very expensive, to make an orator of Pheidippides; to the audience, that Hyperbolus was totally devoid of natural oratorical ability; to both alike, that the training Socrates can offer must be a valuable asset, since Hyperbolus was prepared to pay so heavily for it and it has made him such a successful prosecutor and politician. This is the only place in comedy where Socrates is accused of being the "teacher" of a detested political figure, as he was accused at his trial of having "taught" Critias and others (Aeschines 1.173; Xen. *Mem.* 1.2.12-39; cf. Pl. *Apol.* 33a-b). The fee of a talent is twelve times the highest sophist's fee reliably attested (Pl. *Apol.* 20b: Euenus of Paros charges five minas for a course in how to be a good man and citizen; [Pl.] *Alcib. I* 119a, referring to a fee of 100 minas charged by the philosopher Zeno, presumably in the mid-fifth century, is suspect evidence).

878- **At any rate .. you can't think how cleverly:** it is typical of Strepsiades that the
881. evidence he cites of his son's brilliance is such as might have been relevant if

203

Pheidippides were applying for admission to a kindergarten.

880. **figwood:** the mss. have "leather", of which a cart could hardly be made; figwood, being of no value as timber, might well be given to children to play with and make things out of.

883. **whatever that may be:** cf. 113.

887. **I shall not be there:** Socrates offers no explanation of his absence, and the only plausible explanation is theatrical: the actor who played Socrates would also play one of the two Arguments. For other flimsily-motivated exits by characters whose actors are required for other parts, see *Knights* 154, *Wasps* 141, *Peace* 49, *Birds* 847, *Thesm.* 458.

888- As the scholia observe, a choral ode would be expected here; indeed, had the
889. revised play ever been produced, an ode would have been essential to give the Socrates actor time to change his costume (see previous note). In view of the other evidence for the incompleteness of the revision, it is more likely that Ar. had not written this ode at the point when he decided to cut short his work on the play than that it was written and later lost in transmission.

* 889. How were the two Arguments costumed? One scholium says they were brought on "in wicker cages, fighting like cocks", but this is incompatible with much in the text (including the Better Argument's very first words); possibly it is an inference from something said by the chorus in the first version of the play (see Dover's introduction, pp. xc-xci; the baroque metaphors of *Frogs* 814-829 may give an indication of the sort of expression that might be misinterpreted by a commentator). From the text we learn that the Better Argument is represented as an old man (908), and it would be natural to dress him in the costume (or what was believed to be the costume) of the Persian War period (cf. 986), perhaps with a golden cicada as a brooch in his hair (984, cf. *Knights* 1331). The Worse Argument, though somewhat older than Pheidippides (whom he calls "my lad", 1071), is nevertheless young enough to be called a "father-beater" (911); as a hedonist and as an advocate of warm baths (1044-54, cf. 837-8) he evidently shares many of Pheidippides' tastes, and may be assumed to have long, well-groomed hair and be luxuriously dressed.

889-948. Metre: anapaestic.

891. **Go wherever you like:** a quotation from Euripides' *Telephus* (fr. 722), where in the course of a bitter quarrel over whether to sail against Troy Agamemnon said to Menelaus "Go wherever you like; I'm not going to die on account of your Helen."

898 **these fools:** the Better Argument believes that the Athenians have been duped by the sophists and their disciples into accepting their new education and their new morality: cf. 918-9, 925-8.

902. **that Justice simply doesn't exist:** that the words "just" and "unjust" are meaningless. Compare the arguments of the Platonic characters Callicles (*Gorg.*

204

483a-d) and Thrasymachus (*Rep.* 1.343a-344c), who hold in their different ways that the common belief that justice is good and injustice bad is nothing but a fraud perpetrated by the weak among mankind to deter the strong from profiting by their strength. The word rendered "Justice" is not the normal prose word *dikaiosunē* but the mainly poetic *dikē* which is also the name of the goddess of justice (Hes. *Thg.* 902; *Works* 213ff, 256ff).

903. **She dwells with the gods:** Dike (Justice) traditionally "sits by the side of Zeus" (Hes. *Works* 259; Aesch. fr. 530.10 Mette; Soph. *O.C.* 1382). To say that Justice dwells with the gods is in effect to say that the gods are just – a proposition that even Thrasymachus (Pl. *Rep.* 1.352a) cannot quite bring himself to deny, but which the Worse Argument demolishes without a qualm.

904- **how come Zeus ... for imprisoning his father?:** when Zeus had defeated his father
906. Cronus and the Titans in the struggle for mastery of the universe, he confined them all deep below the earth (Hes. *Thg.* 717ff; *Iliad* 8.477-481); since respect for parents was one of the greatest principles of traditional Greek morality, a supporter of this morality who was also a supporter of Zeus was bound to be acutely embarrassed by this story (cf. Aesch. *Eum.* 640ff), unless he took the course of declaring it untrue (Eur. *HF* 1341-6; Pl. *Rep.* 2.378b-c).

907. **Give me a basin:** he affects to want to vomit.

909. **faggot:** not necessarily a literal accusation of passive homosexuality; Greek *katapūgōn* may here, as in 529, be no more than a strong word for "immoral, vicious".

910- **Your words are like roses ... as an honour:** Pheidippides reacts similarly when
914. similarly reviled by his father (1327-30).

911. **father-beater:** the audience will take this as just another piece of wild abuse; but the Worse Argument's teaching will in fact make Pheidippides into a literal father-beater.

912. **you're spangling me with gold:** a garment spangled with gold (*Knights* 968; [Dem.] 50.34; Democritus of Ephesus, *FGrH* 267 F 1) was more beautiful and more valuable than it would otherwise have been; so the Worse Argument is saying "you are painting me in more admirable colours; you are enhancing, not besmirching, my reputation". Cf. *Eccl.* 826 "everyone was gilding [i.e. praising] Euripides".

915. **archaic:** to the modern-minded characters of this play, this is the worst of insults; the Worse Argument repeats it, or variants on it, at 929, 984-5 and 1070, and elsewhere Socrates uses similar terms to Strepsiades (398), Strepsiades to Pheidippides (821) and Pheidippides, after his stay in the Reflectory, to Strepsiades (1357, 1469).

916. **to school:** i.e. to the traditional schools in which music and poetry were taught by the *kitharistēs* (cf. 964-972), physical culture and especially wrestling by the *paidotribēs* (cf. 973-980).

919. **the silly fools** probably denotes the same persons as "the young lads" above.

920. **dirty:** strictly "dry-skinned" because unanointed (cf. 836). Unlike the ascetic Socrates, the Worse Argument is an enthusiastic advocate of the life of luxury and pleasure. Socrates, we might say, is devoted to the study of science, language and rhetoric for its own sake; the Worse Argument, and later Pheidippides, will show the consequences of taking his lessons seriously and putting them into practice.

921. **a beggar:** i.e. neglected and despised, "in the days when [the Better Argument and his] just cause flourished and it was the done thing to be decent" (961-2).

922. **Mysian:** Mysia was a district of north-west Asia Minor, to the south of the Troad.

922. **Telephus:** a king of Mysia, and hero of a play by Euripides (produced in 438) in which he appeared disguised as a beggar. The relevance of mentioning Tele - phus here is not clear: possibly the point is that the Worse Argument, when he was a "beggar", with typical impudence pretended to be a king in disguise.

923- **Pandeletean maxims:** a surprise for "rotten vegetables" (cf. *Ach.* 469) or the like;
924.   sophistries are the Worse Argument's natural diet. Pandeletus is said by the scholia to have been a politician, given to bringing malicious prosecutions; his period of celebrity may have been a decade or so before the production of *Clouds*, since the only other reference to him is in Cratinus' *Cheirons* (fr. 242), a work of the 430s.

923- **a little bag:** mentioned in order further to characterize the Worse Argument as a
924.   beggar: beggars typically carried a bag (*pērā*) in which to keep the scraps they were given (cf. *Odyssey* 13.437-8).

925. **the cleverness:** either the cleverness which enabled him, in his days as a "beggar", to live without working, or the cleverness that has since taken him from rags to riches.

929. **Cronus:** cf. on 398.

941. **I'll concede my opponent that right:** contrast *Knights* 335-341, where Paphlagon and the Sausage-seller nearly come to blows over the question which of them shall speak first. The Worse Argument here speaks as if it were an advantage to be the first speaker; occasionally we find a defendant in court asserting that it is (cf. Dem. 18.7), but the Worse Argument himself well knows that it is better to have the last word. In all formal debates in Ar., except *Wealth* 487-618, the first speaker is the ultimate loser.

949-958 = 1024-33 Metre: iambo-choriambic (cf. 512-7, 563ff, 700-6).

953. **superior:** I translate my tentative conjecture. The reading of the mss., "better when he speaks", conforms metrically neither to the antistrophe (1028) nor to the general rhythm of the song, and I suspect it of being an intrusive gloss.

*957. **my friends:** they leave it vague who they mean, and characters and audience alike will suppose that they mean Socrates, his pupils, and the Worse Argument; but in the end we will find that it was not so, for the Clouds prove to be

206

enemies and punishers of the Socratics. Note, even now, their warm praise of the Better Argument before and after his speech (959, 1024-9), which has no equivalent in what they say to his opponent. Compare the ambiguity of 812-3.

959-1023. Metre: anapaestic tetrameters, ending (from 1009) with an anapaestic *pnī-gos*. The Worse Argument's reply (1034-1104) is in iambic tetrameters, shifting into iambic trimeters at 1085 and ending (from 1089) with an iambic *pnīgos*. The formal debates in *Knights* (761-835, 841-940) and *Frogs* (905-991, 1004-98) are likewise in two metrically contrasting halves (in *Frogs* the iambics precede the anapaests), and in each case the anapaestic metre is assigned to the more dignified (or, in *Knights*, the slightly less undignified) of the two contestants.

966. **not to keep their thighs together**: the scholia indicate that the speaker has in mind the possibility of boys practising self-stimulation by rubbing the genitals with the thighs. The Better Argument has what Dover has called an "obsession with boys' genitals": cf. 973-8, 989, 1014.

967. **"Pallas the terrible, sacker of cities"**: ancient scholars were uncertain whether this song had been composed by Stesichorus of Himera (sixth century) or by Lamprocles of Athens (early fifth century); the evidence of their confusion is assembled by Page in *PMG* under Lamprocles fr. 1. The most plausible solution is that there were two separate songs, by Stesichorus and by Lamprocles, both of which began *Pallada persepolin* "Pallas sacker of cities", and that the one quoted by Ar. is that of Stesichorus: see D. Holwerda, *Mnemosyne* 5 (1952) 231 n.l.

967. **"A strain that sounds afar"**: the poem which began thus (*PMG* 948) was also of disputed authorship; the scholia state that "its author cannot be discovered, for Aristophanes <of Byzantium> found it as a detached fragment in the <Alexandrian> Library, but some say it is by Cydides of Hermione". The name "Cydides" presumably conceals the lyric poet Cydias mentioned by Pl. *Charm.* 155d and Plut. *Mor.* 931e.

*968. **mode**: or "melodic pattern", Greek *harmoniā*. The exact nature of the various *harmoniai* on which Greek music was based (the Dorian, the Mixolydian, etc.) remains disputed; some see them as specific melodic scales, others merely, in Henderson's phrase, as "musical idioms" each of which, however, required a different tuning (the literal meaning of *harmoniā*) of the instrument. For the former view see R.P. Winnington-Ingram in *Grove's Dictionary of Music and Musicians*[5] (1954) s.v. "Greek Music (Ancient)"; for the latter, M.I. Henderson in *The New Oxford History of Music* i (London, 1957) 336-403.

*969- **some convolution ... in the style of Phrynis**: Phrynis was a Mytilenaean cithara-
971.   player, who won first prize in a contest at the Panathenaea of 456; according to [Plut.] *Mor.* 1133b he was the first musician to use modulations and changes of rhythm, and presumably these are the "convolutions" and "twists" complained

of here. Similar language is used of these innovations by Pherecrates fr. 145. 14-18.

* 972. **disfiguring the music:** literally "making the Muses disappear".

* 973- It was normal and accepted at Athens for mature men to be sexually interested in
  980. young males; but it was traditionally considered improper for the latter to do anything positive to attract potential lovers. For this "double standard" cf. Pl. *Symp.* 182d-183d; see Dover, *Greek Homosexuality*, for a full discussion of the relevant social conventions.

973. **to cover themselves with their thighs:** i.e. to endeavour to maintain modesty as far as one can when naked.

974. **the onlookers:** wrestling-schools were places of public resort: cf. on 178.

974. **anything that was – cruel:** i.e. anything that would arouse in the onlookers the torments of unsatisfied desire (cf. Hdt. 5.18.4).

977. **no boy would anoint himself below the navel:** it sounds as though modern youth are being denounced for degenerate luxury (cf. 836 and 920); but then the speaker's tone changes abruptly, and it turns out that he is complaining that an erotico-aesthetic delight he once enjoyed is no longer available.

978. **dewy down:** this expression (lit. "dew and down") has been very variously interpreted; the least unsatisfactory explanation is that of J.J. Henderson, *The Maculate Muse* (New Haven and London, 1975) 145 n.194, who takes it to mean early pubic hair bedewed with sweat. Anointing would remove the sweat.

979. **water down his voice:** i.e. talk in a mincing tone.

981- **radish ... dill ... celery:** not that these are especial delicacies, but the point is that
  982. a boy was not allowed to take even herbs without permission, much less meat or fish or cheese.

* 983. **dainties:** Greek *opsa*, which could refer to almost any food other than cereals and wine; everybody of course ate *opsa* to some extent, but the compound *opsophagos* and its derivatives, one of which is used here, tended to connote *excessive* fondness for tasty and expensive foods; cf. *Peace* 810 and Aeschines 1.42.

983. **to have his legs crossed:** probably refers to standing with one foot crossed over the other – an indolent-looking posture which might well be thought unseemly, especially in the young.

984. **the Dipolieia:** a festival of Zeus, held on the 14th of Scirophorion (roughly June) and notable chiefly for the archaic and bizarre ritual of the Buphonia (see on 985).

* 984. **cicadas:** it had once been fashionable to wear a golden cicada as a brooch in the hair; this ornament seems to have become obsolete shortly after the Persian Wars. Cf. *Knights* 1331, and see A.B. Cook, *Zeus: A Study in Ancient Religion* (Cambridge, 1914-40) iii 250-6 and Gomme on Thuc. 1.6.3.

985. **Cedeides:** a contemporary dithyrambic poet, "very old-fashioned" according to the scholia; *IG* i^2 770 (late fifth century) commemorates one of his victories,

and incidentally allows us to be certain of his name, which mss., papyri and other witnesses between them present in nine different forms.

* 985.   **ritual bovicide:** Greek *Bouphonia* "murder of the ox", the name given to the principal ceremony of the Dipolieia, which was performed as follows: an ox was slaughtered, the slayer ran away, the instrument of death was solemnly tried, condemned, and thrown in the sea; then after the sacrificial feast the ox was stuffed, stood on its feet and yoked to a plough. See H.W. Parke, *Festivals of the Athenians* (London, 1977) 162-7.

987.   **right from the start:** from their earliest boyhood: compare Pheidippides' "five fleeced cloaks" (10), and contrast 964-5.

* 988.   **to dance at the Panathenaea:** for the Panathenaea cf. 386. The reference here is to a dance called the *purrikhē*, regularly performed at the festival, in which the dancers, naked except for a hoplite shield, performed evolutions similar to the movements of a fighting man in defence and attack (cf. Pl. *Laws* 815a; Eur. *Andr.* 1129-36). See E.K. Borthwick, *JHS* 87 (1967) 18-23 and *Hermes* 96 (1968) 63-65; Parke, *Festivals of the Athenians* 36 and Plate 7.

* 989.   **holds his shield in front of his ham:** probably Greek *kōlē*, lit. "ham", means "penis" both here and in 1018, though this meaning is not attested elsewhere. Clearly we are to understand that the boy is holding his shield too low — perhaps from lack of strength or stamina, perhaps because he is unused to public nakedness through not having attended gymnasia and wrestling-schools.

989.   **caring nothing for Tritogeneia:** Tritogeneia was a title of Athena (*Knights* 1189; *Iliad* 4.515), most often taken in antiquity as meaning "born at Lake Tritonis" in Libya (cf. Aesch. *Eum.* 292-3); here, for added solemnity, the genitive case of the name appears in its epic form, ending in *-ēs* instead of *-ās* (cf. 401, 614). Since the *purrikhē* was a religious ritual performed in Athena's honour, to dance it improperly was a gross insult to her.

991.   **to hate the Agora:** old-fashioned people considered it improper for the young to frequent the Agora, the market-place and main public square of Athens: so in *Knights* Demos, "reverting to the old ways", bans from the Agora (1373) all whose beards are not yet grown.

991.   **shun the bath-houses:** cf. 837-8 and 920.

992.   **flare up:** Greek *phlegesthai* implies an intense access of emotion (Soph. *O.C.* 1695), but the emotion need not be outwardly expressed (Pl. *Charm.* 155d). Here the emotion may be shame, anger, or a mixture of the two; whether it stimulates the victim to active retaliation will no doubt depend on whether he has been insulted by an equal or by one of his elders and betters.

995.   < **defile** > **the statue of Honour:** to soil the statue of a deity was to display wanton contempt for that deity (cf. *Frogs* 366); Honour (*Aidōs*) was the power that made one feel "ashamed of what is shameful"; hence "defile the statue of Honour" = "make a wanton display of shamelessness". That the corrupt last

word of the line (in the Greek) must conceal a verb meaning something like "defile" is fairly certain; it is less clear precisely what verb is required.

* 997.   **have an apple thrown at you:** as a love-token: cf. Theocr. 5.88; 6.6-10.

997.   **shattered:** lit. "broken off".

998.   **Iapetus** was an elder brother of Cronus (Hes. *Thg.* 134-7); cf. on 398.

1001.   **the sons of Hippocrates:** Hippocrates, son of Ariphron, of the deme Cholargus (*PA* 7640), was a nephew of the great Pericles. Elected a general for 426/5 (*IG* i^2 324.3) and 424/3, he perished at the battle of Delium late in 424 (Thuc. 4.101.2), leaving three sons, Pericles (*PA* 11810), Telesippus (*PA* 13541) and Demophon (*PA* 3701). These youths were several times ridiculed in comedy as swinish and uneducated (so the scholia here); Eupolis fr. 103 (from *Demes*, produced as late as 412) calls them "abortive children, bleating infants". They appear also to have had misshapen heads, like their great-uncle Pericles (Ar. fr. 112, 557).

* 1001.   **a pap-sucker:** lit. "one who feeds like a baby on blite (*Amaranthus blitum*)", which is a tasteless vegetable; hence "an insipid milksop".

1003.   **outlandish chatter on thorny subjects:** lit. "thistle-outlandish chatter". Cf. *Knights* 1375-80, where youths are said to sit in the Agora discussing the technical merits of orators.

1004.   **sticky, contentious, damnable:** one word in the Greek.

1005.   **the Academy:** the precinct of the god Academus, later the site of Plato's school, which had been laid out as a park by Cimon, probably in the 460s, with a stream, shaded walks, and running-tracks (Plut. *Cim.* 13.8).

1006.   **green:** the mss. have "white", but this might suggest that the reeds were dry, whereas they would certainly be fresh, no doubt from the stream close by (see previous note).

1007.   **green-brier and ... poplar and freedom from cares:** in the Greek "freedom from cares" (*aprāgmosunē*) comes second, not third, in the list. For the mixture of literal and metaphorical "smells" cf. 50-52.

1012-   **a shining breast ... a small prick:** a summary of what were "down to the mid-
1014.   dle of the fifth century the most striking and consistent ingredients of the 'approved' male figure" (Dover, *Greek Homosexuality* 70; on the aesthetics of penis size see *ib.* 125-135), as evidenced by vase paintings and also e.g. by Achaeus *TrGF* 20 F 4, a description of young athletes "gleaming with the bloom of youth on their powerful shoulders". If he keeps to the old ways, Pheidippides is told he will be strong, athletic, handsome and admired.

1017.   **a pale skin:** cf. 103, 186, 503-4, 718.

1018.   **a big ham:** cf, on 989.

1019.   **a long ... winded decree:** the list is given a surprising turn to end with: under the aegis of the Worse Argument, Pheidippides will become an orator and propose verbose decrees in the Assembly.

1022.   **Antimachus** was "satirized in comedy as a good-looking pathic and effemi-
         nate" according to the scholia, which say, rightly or wrongly, that he was
         not the same man as the Antimachus of *Ach.* 1150ff; we know nothing
         else about him.

1024-   **you who perfect yourself in wisdom:** the strongest indication yet that the
1025.   chorus are really opposed to Socrates and all he stands for. The mention
         of "wisdom" (Greek *sophiā*) recalls 954-5, just before the Better Argu-
         ment's speech, when the chorus said "everything is at stake here for Learn-
         ing (*sophiā*)"; it was not then clear whether they meant the old or the new
         learning, but now it is apparent that they meant the old, against which the
         Worse Argument's alternative has no more than a specious plausibility
         (1030-1). Thus when, long before (412), they addressed Strepsiades as "you
         who desire the higher wisdom (*sophiā*) from us" they were deceiving him;
         the Worse Argument will deceive him just as easily.

1024-5. **fair and lofty:** lit. "fair-towered".

1027.   **the bloom of virtue:** Greek *anthos* "flower" and its derivatives were used met-
         aphorically, as here, three times in the Better Argument's speech (962,
         978, 1002), leading up to his idyllic picture of springtime in the Grove of
         Academe (1005-8). He has invested his portrayal of the old education with
         floral beauty and floral fragrance.

1034-1104. For metre see on 959-1023.

1038-   **For it was for just this reason ... justified pleas:** "Worse Argument" is not just
1040.   a label pinned on the speaker by his opponents; he frankly admits, as is fur-
         ther shown by the phrase "the inferior case" (1042), that his opponents'
         cause is morally right and his wrong. Like Thrasymachus in Pl. *Rep.* 1.
         343a-344c, but in defiance of all accepted ethical standards, he does not
         mind if people think him wicked so long as they think him happy and suc-
         cessful.

1040.   **established values:** Greek *nomoi*, here not "laws" (for an Athenian orator
         could not openly ask a jury to disregard the law of the land) but "norms of
         behaviour established by custom" such as the *nomos* that it is disgraceful to
         strike one's father (cf. 1420-6).

1041.   **staters:** the name "stater" was applied to a variety of non-Athenian standard
         coins, mostly of high value: 'thus the Persian gold daric (called a stater by
         e.g. Hdt. 7.28.2) was worth 20 drachmas (Xen. *Anab.* 1.7.18) and the elec-
         trum stater of Cyzicus even more ([Dem.] 34.23-24). "More than ten
         thousand staters" thus suggests something of the same order of magnitude
         as does a "whole load of talents" (lit. "more than many talents") in 1065.

1044   **he won't let you bathe in hot water:** this was implied by 991 ("shun the bath-
         houses"), since it was in public bath-houses that heated water for washing
         was most readily available (hence poor men haunted them in winter simply

211

to keep warm: *Wealth* 952-3).

1046. **they ... make the man who takes them a coward:** so *com. adesp.* 56 speaks of certain persons as "tender from having hot baths and delicate from lying on soft beds".

1047. **held round the waist:** a common wrestling metaphor (*Ach.* 571, *Frogs* 469, *Eccl.* 260) meaning "powerless to fight back", "as good as beaten".

1048. **of the sons of Zeus ...:** again, as in 904-6, the Worse Argument exploits the fact that his opponent believes both in traditional Greek morals and in traditional Greek myths, and that the two were often not obviously compatible.

1051. **Heraclean baths:** a name applied to warm springs such as those at Thermopylae, which were said to have been created by Athena (Peisander fr. 7 Kinkel) or Hephaestus (Ibycus fr. 19 Page) for Heracles to wash in.

1055. **you object to their frequenting the Agora:** cf. 991.

1057. **"agoretes":** in fact the Homeric noun *agorētēs* has nothing to do with market-places; it means "orator". It is used twice of Nestor (*Iliad* 1.248, 4. 293) and also of other wise elders (*Iliad* 3.150, 7.126); but it can be used in a hostile sense of persons who are allegedly clever talkers and nothing more (*Iliad* 2.246, *Odyssey* 20.274).

1058-9. **the tongue ... not right for the young to train:** cf. 931, 1003, 1013, 1018.

1060. **be modest:** Greek *sōphronein*, to know one's place (in relation to the gods or to one's human superiors) and behave accordingly; cognate words appeared at the start of the Better Argument's speech (962), at its climax (1006), and in the choral comment after it (1027).

1060. **two pernicious evils:** modesty, and neglect of "the tongue". The Worse Argument cares nothing for the well-being of society but solely for maximizing the individual's profit and pleasure; to him, a bad action means an action that is bad for the doer of it, and like Thrasymachus (see on 1038-40) he holds that in this sense it is bad to be virtuous.

1063. **Peleus got his knife because of that:** the hero Peleus, when staying with Acastus at Iolcus, resisted the amorous advances of his host's wife Hippolyte (or Astydameia), and she then accused him to her husband of attempting to dishonour her. To punish Peleus Acastus abandoned him unarmed on Mount Pelion to be devoured by wild beasts, but the gods, "pitying him for his chastity" (schol. Pind. *Nem.* 4.57), arranged through Hephaestus that he should be given a knife to defend himself. For Peleus' reputation, based on this story, for self-control (*sōphrosunē*) cf. Pl. *Rep.* 3.391c.

1065. **Hyperbolus from the lamp market:** see on 551 and 876.

1067. **Peleus got to marry Thetis:** according to the best known of several versions of the myth (Pind. *Isthm.* 8.27-53), the sea-goddess Thetis was courted by Zeus and Poseidon until they learned that she was fated to bear a son mightier than his father, whereupon they had her married to Peleus "virtuous and

212

wise of heart ... the most pious man that the plain of Iolcus nurtures". This is one of the very rare cases in Greek myth of a formal marriage between a mortal and a deity.

1067. **virtue**: Greek *sōphronein*.

1068. **she left him and went away**: in the *Iliad* Thetis is sometimes thought of as still living with Peleus (1.396, 18.55-60) but more usually as having returned to her father Nereus' home in the depths of the sea (1.358, 24.80-83). The latter is almost certainly the older version of the tale (for in the common folktale pattern of the man who woos and wins a mermaid, the mermaid always in the end returns to her native element), and it is the version normally assumed in post-Homeric poetry. The motive here assigned for Thetis' departure is the speaker's *ad hoc* invention: the usual story was that Thetis left Peleus in anger because he had spoken abusively to her (Soph. fr. 151) when he surprised her holding the infant Achilles over a fire, not realizing that she was trying to make him immortal (Ap. Rh. 4.866-879).

1068. **wanton**: Greek *hubristēs*, the antithesis of *sōphrōn*, connoting self-indulgence without regard for the rights or dignity of others. Thetis left Peleus not, as tradition asserted, because he treated her with too little respect (see previous note), but because (in bed) he treated her with too *much* respect!

1070. **mauled**: lit. "treated wantonly or violently", implying "the degradation ... of the woman in some way, either by the man's treating her roughly or by making her perform specialized sexual acts" (Henderson, *The Maculate Muse* 159).

1070. **a hulking old Cronus**: lit. "a Cronus-horse". For "Cronus" see on 398; the addition of *-hippos* "horse" may be intended to suggest "a great big Cronus" (cf. *hippokrēmna* "horse-cliffish" i.e. "towering great" *Frogs* 929) or be little more than a means of extending the name to add emphasis and ridicule, as Dicaeopolis does when at *Ach.* 1206 he greets his enemy Lamachus as *Lāmakh-ipp-ion*.

1073. **boys**: i.e. homosexual relationsnips.

1073. **cottabus**: a game which "consisted of throwing wine-lees at a target set in the midst of the diners' couches" (B.A. Sparkes, *Archaeology* 13 [1960] 203) had strong associations with drunken, dissolute and/or erotic behaviour (cf. e.g. *Ach.* 525, Soph. fr. 537).

1073. **good food**: Greek *opsa* (see on 983).

1073. **laughter**: or, with the mss. except R, "giggling".

*1075. **the demands of nature**: for the sophistic opposition between custom or convention (*nomos*) and nature (*phusis*) which often permits or even enjoins conduct that *nomos* would condemn, see Pl. *Gorg.* 482c-484c with Dodds' notes. The authority of *phusis* is not seldom invoked, as by Callicles in *Gorgias* and by "the Athenians" in Thuc. 5.105.2, to justify unbridled

indulgence of the desire to dominate others; here it is made to justify unbridled indulgence of sexual desires, helped perhaps by the fact that one
meaning of *phusis* was "genitals" of either sex (the word is so used on a
fourth-century curse-tablet, *IG* iii [3] 89.a.6).

1076.   **you've had a bit of an affair:** with a married woman; Greek *emoikheusas* from
moikhos "adulterer".

1077.   **you're done for:** an adulterer caught in the act could lawfully be killed by the
husband (cf. Lysias 1).

1078.   **indulge your nature:** see on 1075.

1080-   **Zeus ... is a slave to love and women:** the amours of Zeus, as told in myth,

1081.   were innumerable. Helen uses the same plea to excuse her adultery in Eur.
Tro. 948-950; morally responsible philosophers on the other hand, some-
times denied the truth of the myths in question (Xenophanes fr. 11 D-K;
Eur. *HF* 1341-2; Pl. *Rep.* 390c, 391c-e).

*1083.   **he gets the radish treatment ...:** the law allowed a husband who caught an
adulterer in the act "to treat him in whatever manner he pleased" (Lys.
1.49), and certain physical degradations had become traditional: a large-
rooted radish was thrust up the adulterer's anus (cf. Lucian *Peregr.* 9), his
perineal region was sprinkled with hot ash, and his pubic hair was pulled
out (*Wealth* 168).

1084.   **wide-arsed:** this normally denoted a pathic, one who habitually sumbitted to
buggery (and is so used in 1089ff); the logic of "the radish treatment",
which may be thought of as a symbolic anal rape, was that he who had mis-
used his manhood by adultery should be degraded to the level of those who
deny their manhood by being penetrated instead of penetrating. But the
Worse Argument will maintain that this is no degradation at all; in many
fields the most successful men are pathics or former pathics.

1086.   **You mean ... greater than that?** in effect an answer to the question just put:
"it'll do him the greatest possible harm."

1089.   **advocates:** Greek *sunēgoroi*, persons specially appointed to conduct the prosecution when a trial was ordered by the Council or the Assembly in a case
of public importance (cf. *Ach.* 685; *Knights* 1358; *Wasps* 482; Hyp. *Dem.*
38; Dein. 2.6; [Plut.] *Mor.* 833f). Naturally the best available speakers
would be chosen, so the question is equivalent to "What type of person
provides the leading forensic orators?"

1090.   **From the wide-arsed:** cf. the effeminate *sunēgoros* of *Wasps* 687ff.

1091.   **tragedians:** probably performers rather than poets. The scholia think there
may be particular reference to a tragic actor named Phrynichus, who "was
accused of effeminacy because of the intricacy of his dance-movements".

1093.   **politicians:** the idea that virtually all leading politicians are former male pro-
stitutes recurs several times in Ar. (*Knights* 423-8, 878-880, 1242; *Eccl.*

112-3) and is put in his mouth by Plato (*Symp.* 192a).

1094- **do you realize that you were talking nonsense?**: since "wide-arsedness" is evi-
1095. dently the key to success in oratory, acting or politics, how can it be considered harmful?

*1102. **Here, you buggers ... I'm deserting to your camp**: it is uncertain who is being
addressed, and what is the point of the speaker's discarding his cloak; see
most recently L.M. Stone, *CP* 75 (1980) 321-2. The most satisfactory inter-
preatation, in my view, is that by "you buggers" the speaker is referring to
the "wide-arsed" products of the new education the Reflectory offers, of
whom his opponent has been the spokesman, and that he now desires to
receive this education himself in the hope of winning success and wealth as
an orator. He surrenders his cloak in token of his desire to become a student (cf. 497-500).

1105. **WORSE ARGUMENT**: the mss. give 1105-6 and 1111 to Socrates, but this
would require either a fifth actor or a lightning change of mask and costume; note that throughout the debate the question at issue has been taken
to be whether Pheidippides shall be taught by the Better or the Worse Argument (see especially 929-938), and Socrates has never been mentioned.

1108. **give him a sharp edge**: Strepsiades speaks as if he were a soldier placing an
order for a sword; cf. 1160 where he sings of his son's "two-edged tongue".
The metaphor is helped by the fact that *stoma* "mouth" could be used to
mean "edge of a weapon".

1113- A rudimentary second parabasis, consisting of a brief prelude and a single
1130. epirrhema. According to one scholium (in Vb3 and Vs1) five lines of lyric
are "missing" before 1115; as the writer refers to his commentary on the
first version of *Clouds*, it is likely that the five lines were deleted by Ar. in
the process of revising the play.

1113-4 Metre: an iambic dimeter followed by an ithyphallic (for which see on 457-
475).

*1115-30 Metre: trochaic tetrameters.

1115. **the judges**: the judges of the dramatic competition. Similar advice is given to
the judges by the chorus of *Birds* (1102-17) and of *Eccl.* (1154-62).

1115-6. **do this chorus a service**: i.e. award first prize to the play.

1125. **sling-shots**: hailstones.

1126. **making bricks**: the bricks would be sun-dried, and therefore would be ruined
if it rained before they were ready.

1129. **we shall rain the whole night long**: this would spoil the procession escorting
the bride to her new home, and in particular extinguish the torches that
accompanied it, obviously an evil omen for the marriage.

1130. **even to find himself in Egypt**: Egypt was thought of as very remote (in Pind.
Isthm. 2.41-42 and Eur. *Andr.* 650-1 it is coupled with Phasis at the far end

215

of the Black Sea) and the Egyptians as born liars and cheats (Aesch. fr. 373 Nauck = 726 Mette; Ar. *Thesm.* 920-2; Pl. *Laws* 747c); hence no Greek would normally wish to be in Egypt. But at least Egypt had no rain!

1131. We may now be supposed to assume that several days have passed since Pheidippides entered the school. At 17 the moon had apparently just entered "its twenties"; now it is the twenty-sixth of the month. Similar time-lapses are required in *Birds* (at some point between 1261 and 1494, to give time for the gods to be starved into seeking peace), in *Lysistrata* (between 613 and 706, and between 1013 and 1072), and in *Wealth* (after 626, when Wealth is taken to spend a night in the sanctuary of Asclepius).

1131. **twenty-sixth ... twenty-ninth:** lit. "fifth, fourth, third, then second". The last days of an Athenian month, after the 20th (later 21st), were counted backwards and called ninth, eighth, seventh, etc., "of the waning month" (*phthinontos*); the "second *phthinontos*" was thus the penultimate day of the month. The last day of the month had a special name, *henē kai neā* "Old-and-New" (1134). A month had either 29 or 30 days; in a short month one of the *phthinontos* dates was omitted, but it is disputed which the omitted date was; see most recently J.A. Walsh, *ZPE* 41 (1981) 107-124 and W.K. Pritchett, *ib.* 145-8.

1134. **Old-and-New Day:** the last day of the month, so called perhaps because in theory (i.e. if the month were exactly in step with the moon) it was the day when there was no moon, and so in a sense stood between the old and the new month. It was (1180, 1196-7) the day fixed for the lodging of deposits by intending litigants (see next note); hence Strepsiades' dread of it.

*1136. **lodge a deposit:** in most private and some public lawsuits the plaintiff, and probably also the defendant, had to lodge a deposit (*prutaneia*) with the magistrate who would preside over the case. The money went to the state (*Wasps* 659), but when the case had been decided the successful party could recover the amount of his deposit from his opponent. Once a deposit has been lodged against Strepsiades he will have little hope of avoiding trial, since if the creditor withdraws his claim he will lose his deposit. See Harrison, *The Law of Athens II: Procedure* 92-94, 220.

1139-
1140. **they say they'll never accept that kind of payment:** or "they say that at that rate they're never going to be paid".

1145. **Boy ... boy, boy:** cf. 132; this time Socrates answers the door himself, thus avoiding a repetition of the earlier scene.

1145. **Greeting, Strepsiades:** lit. "I greet (*aspazomai*) Strepsiades", the addressee being named in the third person; the use of this form of greeting, instead of the normal *khaire*, may have had a tinge of snobbery and preciosity (cf. *Birds* 1377, *Wealth* 1042, and especially *Wealth* 322-4).

1146. **please accept this:** we cannot tell what the present was, except that the Greek

216

word for it was masculine; the scholia, referring to 669, suggest a sack (*thūlakos*) of barley groats.

1150. **Almighty Fraud**: lit. "Fraud, queen of all (*pambasileia*)". Having been induced to exchange his allegiance to Zeus the King (*basileus*, 2) for allegiance to the Clouds (*pambasileiai*, 357), Strepsiades has made it plain that he will worship any Power that will enable him to evade his debts: hence it is only natural that he should invoke Fraud as a deity.

*1154-
1170. A monody (solo song) and lyric dialogue, their metre and most of their diction modelled on current tragedy (cf. e.g. Eur. *Hec.* 154-215). At two points specific tragic sources are known: the first line and a half are taken verbatim from a tragedy named *Peleus*, either that of Sophocles (fr. 491) or that of Euripides (fr. 623), while 1165-6 are a slightly modified version of Eur. *Hec.* 171-4. As in many tragic monodies, there are frequent changes of metre: 1154-7 are iambic, 1158-9 dactylic, 1160 spondaic, 1161 again iambic, while from 1162 to 1170 anapaestic and dochmiac rhythms alternate.

1156. **the interest on your interest**: the Greek phrase could also mean "your children's children", and thus plays on common formulae of blessing and curse such as that used in *Birds* 730.

1169. **him**: Greek *sphe* is common in tragedy as an accusative pronoun of the third person singular and plural, though in comedy its only other appearance is in an oracle (in hexameters) at *Knights* 1020. It is at home here in the paratragic context, and makes Socrates' two utterances in this exchange metrically identical; I assume that it was corrupted in *n* and supplanted by an explanatory gloss in RV.

1171. **the colour of your skin**: Pheidippides now has the pallor of an indoor-living student. It is likely that the actor changed his mask.

1172-
1173. **traversive and contradictive**: the two Greek adjectives both end in -*ikos*, like the string of laudatory adjectives applied to the oratory of Phaeax in *Knights* 1378-80; one of them, *exarnētikos* "traversive, good at making denials", occurs only here. The use of -*ikos* adjectives was becoming popular in the 420s among sophists, philosphers and rhetoricians and those whom they influenced: see C.W. Peppler, *AJPh* 31 (1910) 428-444.

1173. **that national look**: for it is typically Athenian to be litigious and argumentative (cf. 496, 1220-1, *Birds* 39-41).

1174. **blooms** echoes the flower imagery of the Better Argument's speech (see on 1027); but what blooms on Pheidippides' face is not youthful health (1002) but flowers of rhetoric.

1174. **"what-do-you-mean?"**: this is the question of a cross-examiner pouncing aggressively on an opponent's feeble answer to a previous question (cf. *Wasps* 1378, Pl. *Apol.* 24e); thus Strepsiades means "you have the look of a powerful cross-examiner".

1175.	**committing felony**: Greek *kakourgounta*; strictly, committing one of those offences (such as theft, robbery and kidnapping) which made the offender liable in certain circumstances to summary arrest (*apagōgē*). See Harrison, *The Law of Athens II: Procedure* 223-5.
1179-1195.	Pheidippides' argument is based on the pretence that *henē kai neā* "Old-and-New" — in reality a current expression familiar to everybody — is an archaism to be found only in the laws and requiring interpetation. His exegesis runs thus: The law says that defendants in certain classes of case shall be summoned to appear before the appropriate magistrate on *henē kai neā*. Now *henē kai neā* cannot be the name of a single day, since to call a day, or anything else, "old and new" is to contradict oneself. The expression must then denote two days, *henē* and *neā*, of which the latter is evidently the New Moon, the first day of the month, and *henē* the day preceding it; and it was the intention of the legislator that plaintiff and defendant should meet at the magistrate's office on both these days. The first meeting was provided for to give the parties an opportunity to settle out of court; if this failed, the case would be submitted to the magistrate on the following day and the deposits paid. Under this system a man with a bad case who refused to settle might very well "feel a bit uneasy on the morning of the New Moon" (1195), for he had passed the point of no return: if he appeared before the magistrate, he would almost certainly be brought to trial, and if he lost would forfeit his deposit, and have to refund his opponent's, in addition to paying the sum sued for; if he did not appear he would lose the case by default. But this whole alleged system is based on nothing but Pheidippides' misinterpretation of *henē kai neā*. Presumably, if Strepsiades' creditors were to take him to court, Pheidippides would argue that as the presiding magistrate had accepted the plaintiffs' deposits on the wrong day (the last of the month instead of the first) the suits were null and void.
1185.	**that's the practice**: viz. for the deposits to be lodged on the last of the month.
1186.	**they**: most people. The magistrates know better, but have their own reasons for letting the practice continue (1196-1200).
1187.	**Solon**, archon in 594/3, had promulgated (either then or later) the code which thereafter, except in regard to homicide, was the basis of Athenian law. In the fifth and fourth centuries Athenians tended to ascribe all their corpus of permanent law to Solon, even though some of it was certainly of much later origin: Andoc. 1.95 actually describes as "the law of Solon" an enactment which he proceeds to quote and whose prescript dates it to summer 410.
1187.	**a friend of the people**: Athens was a democracy, Athenian law was the law of Solon, therefore Solon must have been a democrat; and so, in defiance of the evidence of Solon's own poetry, most Athenians of the fifth and fourth

centuries held him to have been (cf. Isocr. 7.16, Dem. 18.6).

1192. **my good fellow:** Greek ō *mele*, a form of address which appears elsewhere in this play at 33 and 1338, and twenty-three times altogether in Ar.; it can be used by any free person (male or female) to any other person regardless of status or relationship, and its usual function seems to be to say to the person addressed "I am enlightening you on an important point which you would be aware of already if you had been reasonably intelligent".

1197. **Old-and-New Day:** Strepsiades, following his son's example, called this day "Old Day" at 1192, but now he backslides and uses the term with which he is familiar.

1198. **the Tasters:** Greek *protenthai*. Our scanty evidence about the persons so designated (see Athenaeus 4.171c-e) indicates that they performed a religious function of an unknown nature on the day before the festival of the Apaturia, and were jestingly accused of taking advantage of their position to steal the best parts of the festal meal; hence the verb *protentheuein*, used in 1200, comes to mean "take food, money, etc., before the proper time".

1201. **ripe for fleecing by:** lit. "gain for", i.e. "source of profit for".

1203. **earthenware:** lit. "jars".

1205. **I ought to sing a song of praise:** C.W. Macleod, *Phoenix* 35 (1981) 142-4, notes that it is common for the chorus towards the end of an Aristophanic play to congratulate the hero on the happiness he has attained (e.g. *Ach.* 836-859, *Peace* 856-864, *Birds* 1720ff); here there is no one to utter the congratulations but Strepsiades himself, for the chorus know, as the audience soon will, that his happiness is illusory.

1206-13. Metre: the first line is ionic (∪∪ – – ∪∪ –); the rest of the song is in lyric iambics.

1206. **Strepsiades:** by what he imagines is a legitimate poetic licence, Strepsiades transfers his name from the first to the third declension, making its vocative case *Strepsiades* instead of the correct *Strepsiadē*.

1212-
1213. **I want to ... feast you:** this announces the offstage feast which normally occurs towards the end of an Aristophanic comedy, and which may be accompanied, as here, by the arrival of unwelcome visitors who are quickly sent packing: cf. *Ach.* 959-end, *Peace* 1039-1315. The play thus appears, deceptively, to be approaching a happy ending.

1216. **to refuse unblushingly** implies that in fact the speaker felt, when Strepsiades asked him for a loan, that he could not decently refuse. He is, then, not a professional moneylender but an acquaintance and fellow-demesman (1219) of Strepsiades who had enough spare cash to be able to make an advance; and the passage is evidence that if one was asked for a loan by a personal acquaintance, and one had the money to meet the request, it was not done to refuse. Compare in Lysias 19.25-26 the evident embarrassment of Aristophanes (not the dramatist, but an admiral and diplomat) at having to refuse a loan because he had nothing to lend: he felt it necessary to swear on oath that he was himself in debt.

1217-1218. **dragging you here .. over money that's mine:** a man ought to be able to manage his own affairs without troubling others to help him; but if he has to take a dispute to law this is impossible, since even before the case comes to court he needs a witness to prove that the defendant has been duly summoned.

1219. **I'm going to make an enemy of a fellow-demesman:** not that it was unheard-of for fellow-demesmen to be personal enemies (consider Ar. and Cleon, or Euxitheus, speaker of Dem. 57, and his opponent Eubulides); but it might well be unpleasant, particularly when, as apparently here (cf. 1322), the two were also near neighbours. Cf. Dover, *Greek Popular Morality* 277.

1220-1221. **never ... shall I disgrace my country:** the familiar joke on Athenian litigious-ness (see on 1173).

1224. **twelve minas:** this is the same sum named by Strepsiades at 21, and according-ly the scholia and many editors give this creditor the name Pasias mentioned there. This is possible, but nothing depends on it, and we cannot tell if the same transaction is being referred to in both places or not: the horse, to buy which the twelve minas were borrowed, is described in 23 by its brand, but here by its colour.

1225. **dark-grey:** lit. "starling-coloured".

1226. **who ... loathes everything to do with horses:** true but irrelevant, since Strep-siades bought the horse unwillingly on his wife's and son's insistence. In his encounters with the creditors Strepsiades is able to use sophisms of his own devising as well as what he has learnt from Socrates: cf. 1279-95.

1229. **invincible:** Greek *akatablētos*, lit. "un-knock-down-able"; there may be an allusion to a book by the sophist Protagoras which bore the alternative titles *Knock-down Arguments* (*Kataballontes Logoi*) and *Truth*.

1230. **because of that:** because Pheidippides has now been taught Wrongful Argu-ment.

1233. **in whatever place I may require:** the awe attaching to an oath was greater if it was taken in a sacred place, where a god was present to hear it; hence a per-son exacting an oath might specify the place where it was to be taken (cf. Lys. 32. 13).

1236. **Then may ruin ... for your shamelessness:** in a society that takes oaths as ser-iously as the Athenians did, the man who is prepared to perjure himself without fear or shame is at a tremendous advantage. The creditor had chal-lenged Strepsiades to swear to his denial, in the confident expectation that the challenge would not be taken up; at an eventual trial, the jury would be told of Strepsiades' evasion and invited to infer that his denial was false. But to Strepsiades an oath by the traditional gods is a meaningless form of words, and his cheerful acceptance of the challenge leaves the creditor almost helpless and reduces him to impotent cursing.

237.   **This could do with being rubbed down with salt**: salt was used for curing hides; the creditor's paunch is to be used as a wine-skin (cf. *Ach.* 1002).

238.   **four gallons**: lit. "six *khoes*", a *khous* being a unit of liquid measure, rather more than three litres or rather less than six pints.

248.   **cardopus**: cf. 669-680.

255.   **I'll be lodging a deposit**: see on 1136.

260-   **It wasn't by any chance ... that gave tongue?**: when an utterance was so start-
1261. ling in tone or content as to make it hard to believe that it could have been spoken by any human being, it might be said that "some god must have spoken it" (cf. Pl. *Euthd.* 291a). In this case Strepsiades supposes that the god in question may be one of those who figured in the tragedies of Carcinus (see next note); presumably a play of his had included a scene in which a god uttered laments.

1261. **Carcinus**, son of Xenotimus, of the deme Thoricus (*PA* 8254; *TrGF* 21), was a tragic dramatist of some distinction; he is known to have won first prize at the City Dionysia of 446 (*IG* ii^2 2318.81). In 431 he was one of the ten generals, and with two colleagues commanded a naval expedition around the Peloponnese (Thuc. 2.23.2; 25; 30; cf. *IG* i^2 296.30-40); this seems to have earned him the nickname "Lord of the Seas" (*Thalattios*: *Wasps* 1519, Plato com. fr. 134). His three sons were celebrated dancers (*Wasps* 1500-37, *Peace* 781-796); one of them, Xenocles, was himself a tragic dramatist.

1262. **you** is plural in the Greek. In the dramatic situation, the speaker may be addressing himself to (imaginary) curious bystanders as well as to Strepsiades; in performance, however, this "you", like the "you all" of 1226, would probably be directed mainly at the audience — who are equally eager to know who this man may be.

1263. **go away by yourself**: i.e. keep well away from me and everyone else — as if ill-luck, like religious pollution, were contagious. Cf. *Ach.* 1019.

1264- **"O cruel deity ... how thou hast ruined me!"**: quoted, with slight modifica-
1265. tion, from the tragedy *Licymnius* by Carcinus' son Xenocles (fr.2). The speaker in the tragedy was Alcmene, the mother of Heracles, after her half-brother Licymnius had been killed by Heracles' son Tle(m)polemus. Some versions of the myth (e.g. schol. *Iliad* 2.662) say that this killing was accidental; others (e.g. schol. Pind. *Olymp.* 7.49a and 54) that it was deliberate, the result of a quarrel over "certain honours and rulerships"; all agree that the weapon was of wood, a stick or a club. It is not clear what version Xenocles followed or invented, nor what Athena had to do with the matter. There is no positive reason to suppose that a chariot accident figured in Xenocles' play; the words "that smashed my chariot-rail" are Ar.'s words (so the scholia), not Xenocles'.

1266. **Tlempolemus:** c.f. previous note. For the Attic form of the name, preserved by R here, see Threatte i 490.

1267-
1270. **tell your son ... the money he borrowed:** this shows that whether or not the first creditor is to be identified with the Pasias of 21-23, the second creditor is not the Amynias of 31, who did not, one would gather from the text there, lend Pheidippides money but *sold* him or his father some racing equipment.

1271. **you really are in a bad way:** he means that the creditor's remarks show that the accident has deprived him of his reason; the creditor, misunderstanding, takes him to be expressing sympathy.

1273. **as if you'd fallen off a donkey:** it was a popular witticism to say, of a person who appeared to be talking or acting irrationally, "he must have fallen off a donkey"; the expression may well owe its origin to a pun on *ap' onou* "off a donkey" and *apo nou* "out of his mind" (cf. *aponoia* "madness"). See Pl. *Laws* 701c, and for a comic variant of the phrase *Wasps* 1370.

1276. **I think your brain has kind of had a shaking:** cf. Hippocr. *Coan Prognoses* 489 (vol. 5 p. 696 Littré): "Those whose brain is shaken and damaged by blows or otherwise fall down forthwith, lose the power of speech, can neither see nor hear, and generally die."

1279-
1280. **it is always new water every time:** this would be the naive popular view (cf. 373).

1280-
1281. **the sun draws up ... the same water:** this, in one form or another, was the normal scientific view, held for example by Anaximander (A11 D-K), Xenophanes (fr. 30), and the author of the Hippocratic treatise *Airs, Waters, Places* (8).

1289. **by the effluxion ... 1294 with the influx:** Greek *huporreontos ... epirreontōn*, highlighting the alleged analogy between the flow of rivers, which does not enlarge the sea, and the flow of time, which ought not to enlarge a debt.

1292. **against the laws of nature:** Greek *ou dikaion*, literally "unjust". It was common for philosophers to use the word *dikē* "justice" to denote the framework of natural law or the balance of opposing forces in the natural world: thus Anaximander (fr. 1 D-K) had said that the constituents of the universe "make amends and payment to one another for their injustice according to the ordering of Time", Heraclitus (fr. 94) that "the sun will not transgress the limits of his course; if he does, the Erinyes, assistants of Dike, will find him out", and Parmenides (fr. 1.14) that Dike holds the keys of the gates of Night and Day. A similar usage is occasionally found in other writings, e.g. Thuc. 4.62.3 "vengeance does not prosper *dikaiōs*" = "there is no law of nature that vengeance must prosper". Here the creditor's use of *dikaion* in this sense enables Strepsiades to argue, by way of the analogy indicated in the last note, that it is "unjust" in the *other, moral* sense to demand

222

interest on a loan.

1294-1295. **what business have you ... sum of money bigger?**: this is the earliest known attempt to prove that usury is contrary to nature. Aristotle (*Politics* 1258b2-8) reaches the same conclusion on the ground that money was invented as a medium of exchange, not a source of income in itself.

1297. **Witness!**: an appeal to anyone present or within earshot to bear witness that the utterer is being assaulted: cf. 495, *Ach.* 926, *Wasps* 1436, *Birds* 1031.

1298. **branded nag**: Greek *samphorās* (see on 23 and 122): Strepsiades pretends that the horse-loving creditor is a horse. The same cry is uttered at *Knights* 603 by an equine boatswain addressing equine rowers.

*1299. **wanton outrage**: Greek *hubris*, contemptuous disregard of the rights or dignity of others, which was a legal offence for which the penalty was unlimited. On the concept of *hubris* see N.R.E. Fisher, *Greece and Rome* 23 (1976) 177-193, and his forthcoming book *Hybris*.

*1300. **thoroughbred**: lit. "trace-horse". A trace-horse (*seirāphoros*) was one of the two outer horses of a chariot-team of four (the inner ones were "yoke-horses", cf. 122). In a race the right-hand trace-horse had to provide exceptional bursts of energy when rounding the turning-post (cf. Soph. *El.* 721-2), and these horses were accordingly better fed than others (Aesch. *Ag.* 1640-1); hence the use of *seirāphoros* here probably suggests the notion "pampered".

1303-10 = 1311-20 Metre: mainly iambic, though in one section beginning at 1308 = 1316 the rhythm becomes trochaic. Towards the end of the stanza the strophic correspondence is not exact, the antistrophe having an extra cretic (–ᵕ–), at the start of 1318, compared with the strophe; such omission of a metrical element in strophe or antistrophe is not uncommon in Ar. (see A.M. Dale, *The Lyric Metres of Greek Drama*[2] [Cambridge, 1968] 207).

1308-1309. **this sophist**: Strepsiades is meant; the chorus ironically pretend to agree with his deluded belief that he is one of "the intellectuals", "those who know better" (1202, 1207, 1241, 1249-58, 1283-4).

1309-1310. **< recoil from > the villainy**: I translate my tentative conjecture (see apparatus; the transmitted text, which is unmetrical and tautological, would mean "suffer some evil as punishment for the villainy".

1322. **fellow-demesmen** indicates that Strepsiades' house is to be thought of as situated in his own deme of Cicynna, since if he were in the city there would be unlikely to be many other Cicynnians living close by. See further on 138.

1325-1333. Note Strepsiades' insistent repetition of the words "villain" (*miaros*) and "strike your father" (verbal phrase *ton patera tuptein*, noun *patraloiās*). So certain is he that Pheidippides' conduct is monstrous that, faced with the latter's calm assumption that he has done nothing wrong, he can but reiterate his certainty. It has never occurred to him to examine the grounds for the traditional rule, and not till 1430 is he able to argue at all effec-

223

1327.   **felon:** Greek *toikhōrukhos*, literally "burglar", but used as a generalized term of abuse as in *Wealth* 909 and 1411.

1330.   **tank-arsed:** a more colourful synonym of *katapūgōn* "pathic" (cf. on 909), here used, as *katapūgōn* often is, to mean merely "vicious, immoral". The noun *lakkos*, here translated "tank", strictly denotes any natural or dug-out hollow, with a broad opening, adapted for holding liquids; it is the broad opening (cf. "wide-arsed" 1084) that is the point of comparison.

1330.   **shower me with more of these roses:** cf. 910-2.

1336. · **choose which of the two Arguments** ...: not that there is any doubt which of them Strepsiades will choose, since he is certain to defend the "Better", i.e. traditional, viewpoint; the point is that Pheidippides himself is prepared, like Protagoras (see on 112-5), to argue with equal persuasiveness for or against any proposition. If, *per impossibile*, Strepsiades wished to maintain that his son did right to assault him, Pheidippides would be ready to argue that he did wrong. He is not interested in what is true or false, only in what an audience can be persuaded to believe.

1345-50 = 1391-6 Metre: each stanza consists of three units, each unit comprising an iambic trimeter and a reizianum ($\times - \cup\cup - -$), except that in 1350, by a licence of strophic responsion occasionally found elsewhere in comedy, what should be a reizianum takes instead the form $\times - \cup - - -$. See Dale, *Lyric Metres*[2] 56-57, 65-66, 89-91, 189.

1347.   **something:** as the chorus know perfectly well, what Pheidippides is relying on is his ability, acquired in the Reflectory, to "make the worse argument the better".

1351-90 Metre: iambic tetrameters, ending (from 1386) in an iambic *pnīgos*. After the choral antistrophe, 1397-1451 (except 1415, an iambic trimeter parodied from Euripides) is in the same metre, the *pnīgos* beginning at 1445.

1352.   **tell the chorus:** the dramatic fiction is momentarily forgotten, and the chorus-leader speaks like " a producer telling an actor what to do next" (Dover); see on 326.

1352.   **you'll do that anyway:** Ar. may here be making fun of a convention of Old Comedy, whereby each division of an *agōn* is formally introduced by a couplet from the chorus-leader inviting one party to the debate to put his case: "why do we have to ask you to speak? you're impatient to speak anyway." So in *Peace* 1017-22 he makes fun of the convention whereby the preliminary rituals of sacrifice could be performed before the audience but the actual slaughter could not.

1356.   **Simonides** of Ceos, who lived c.556-468, was the leading lyric poet of his day until the rise of Pindar.

*1356.   **"How Sir Ram was shorn":** the opening lines of the song (Simonides fr. 2

Page) are preserved in the scholia:

Sir Ram was shorn, and no wonder either,
when he came to the splendid precinct of Zeus
with its fine trees.

The song was a victory-ode for a wrestler who had defeated Crius ("Ram")
of Aegina at the Nemean games. D.L. Page, *JHS* 71 (1951) 140-2, plausibly
identifies this Crius with Crius son of Polycritus, who in the late 490s was
one of the two most powerful men on Aegina (Hdt. 6.50; 6.73.2); the song
may date from twenty years or so earlier, when Crius was a young man.

*1358. **like a woman grinding hulled barley:** compare the women's work-song *PMG*
869 "Grind, mill, grind; for Pittacus also used to grind, when he was king
of great Mytilene."

1365. **to take a myrtle-branch:** it was customary to hold a bay- or myrtle- branch
when singing at a symposium, if one was not accompanying oneself on an
instrument: so the scholia (quoting Dicaearchus fr. 44 Müller = 89 Wehrli),
and cf. Ar. fr. 430 "He began singing 'The Tale of Admetus' with a myrtle-
branch". Pheidippides refuses to sing, but he is asked at least to hold the
myrtle-branch during his recitation, as a concession to tradition.

1367. **full of noise ... a creator of mountainous words:** the same things are said about
Aeschylus in *Frogs* by the chorus (818-825) and by Euripides (837-9, 908-
940, 945, 1056-8).

1371. **loosed off:** the mss. have "sang", which even if (as is very doubtful) it could
be used of reciting a speech would be inappropriate here where singing and
speaking have just been contrasted. Borthwick's conjecture, for which see
CR 21 (1971) 318-320, would mean "began"; but though *agein* and its
compunds may mean "begin" in relation to singing, wailing, instrumental
performance, or dancing, there is no clear case of their being so used in relation to spoken utterance. I prefer HKE "loosed off, let fly with", of which
HICE "sang" would be an easy visual corruption made still easier by the
mention of singing in 1355-60.

1371. **a speech:** probably the prologue of Euripides' *Aeolus,* in which the audience
were told of the incest of Macareus and Canace, son and daughter of Aeolus, and the birth and concealment of their child. See T.B.L. Webster, *The
Tragedies of Euripides* (London, 1967) 157-160. The incest is mentioned
in *Frogs* 1081 as an example of the immorality of Euripidean tragedy.

1372. **heaven forfend:** lit. "O Averter of Evil", an appeal to a god (Heracles, according to the scholia) to avert any dangerous consequences that might result
from speaking of so dreadful an act. So in *Knights* 1307 a ship is made
to appeal to Apollo the Averter (Apotropaios) that the words just uttered

may be prevented from coming true and Hyperbolus not be allowed to command a fleet against Carthage.

1372. **his sister by the same mother:** note that a brother and sister not born of the same mother were actually permitted to marry by Athenian law (cf. e.g. Dem. 57.20).

1378. **a genius:** Strepsiades may have been intending to continue "... at vulgarity, immorality and atheism" or the like, just as his son had begun "I regard Aeschylus as supreme among poets" and then continued with a string of derogatory expressions (1366-7). But he is first pulled up by the difficulty of finding a form of address that adequately expresses his loathing for Pheidippides, and then on second thoughts decides it would be prudent to say no more.

*1380. **I who brought you up ...:** no doubt most poorer Athenian fathers helped with the children, but the idea of Strepsiades' doing these jobs himself is hardly consistent with what we have been told of the social standing of his wife. In real life she would certainly have insisted on her son's being looked after by a full-time slave nurse.

*1382. **bru:** evidently a nursery word meaning "a drink"; presumably the source of the verb *brullein* "have a feed" used in *Knights* 1126.

1383. **mamma** meant "food"; there was a derived verb *mammān* or *mammiān* "eat (like an infant)", occasionally used in comedy (Callias com. fr. 29), whose compound *blitomammās* is the word rendered "pap-sucker" at 1001 above.

1384. **kakka:** cf. *kakkē* "faeces" (*Peace* 162) and *kakkōnion* "potty".

1385. **carry you out of doors:** the insanitary implications of this are confirmed by Eccl. 321-2: Blepyrus, who has come out of his house to defaecate, remarks "Anywhere's a good place at night; after all, no one will see me".

1387-
1388. **you couldn't ... carry me out of doors:** not that Strepsiades would be likely to take kindly to such a role-reversal if Pheidippides had attempted it; cf. *Wasps* 1442-50, where Philocleon, who has been getting drunk and making a nuisance of himself, is carried kicking and screaming into his house by his exasperated son.

1396. **not a chickpea:** English more usually says "not a fig" (cf. *Peace* 1223) or "not a bean". The skin of the elderly will be worthless because they can look forward to getting "a regular hiding" and having the skin flogged off their backs.

1400. **custom:** Greek *nomoi*; see on 1075, and compare the Worse Argument's claim that he is "the first who conceived the notion of arguing in contradiction to established values (*nomoi*) and justified pleas" (1039-40).

1404. **ideas, arguments and cogitations:** the same three nouns (Greek *gnōmē*, *logos*, *merimna*) appear together in the prelude sung by the chorus before the debate of the two Arguments (951-2).

1407. **a four-horse team:** as opposed to the "chariot-and-pair" which Pheidippides had kept before he entered the school (15). Only the very rich could keep a team of four: the wealth of the elder Miltiades is sufficiently indicated by saying (Hdt. 6.35.1) that he was "of a four-horse-rearing house".

1408. **I shall go on ... you made me break off:** he speaks to his father as if brushing aside an interrupter at a public meeting.

1412. **that is what being benevolent ... means:** from the agreed premise that Strepsiades' benevolence towards his son was sometimes expressed in beating him, Pheidippides illegitimately infers that all benevolence is always so expressed, and, by a further illegitimate conversion, that all beatings are expressions of benevolence.

1413- **How can it be right ... a free man born:** Pheidippides ignores, as he does
1414.   throughout his argument, the difference between children and adults. The corporal chastisement of children by their parents, as also by their teachers (cf. 972), was lawful and common. An adult son, however, was permitted to take legal proceedings against his father, e.g. for insanity (cf. 845) or for homicide (Pl. *Euthyphro* 3e-4e), and it is not likely that his father could strike him with guaranteed impunity.

1415. **"The children howl; do you think the father shouldn't?":** a parody of Eur. *Alc.* 691. Alcestis has saved the life of her husband Admetus by voluntarily dying in his stead; Admetus, bitterly distressed at her loss, criticizes his own father Pheres savagely for not offering to sacrifice the brief remainder of his life, and Pheres retorts "You enjoy seeing the light of day; do you think your father doesn't?" The same line is quoted verbatim in *Thesm.* 194.

1417. **the old are in a second childhood:** a proverbial saying, also quoted or alluded to by Aesch. *Ag.* 74-82, *Eum.* 38, Soph. fr. 487.3, Cratinus fr. 24, Theopompus com. fr. 69, and Pl. *Laws* 646a.

1419. **it is less natural that they should do wrong:** "natural" renders Greek *dikaion* (cf. on 1292); Pheidippides is equivocating with the moral sense of *dikaion* and thus insinuating that a wrongful act is more heinous if committed by an older person. His argument is in any case hardly consistent with 1417: if old age is a second childhood, and if offences by children ought to be treated leniently, then surely offences by old people ought to be treated leniently too.

1420. **nowhere is it the law:** the wide variations in the *nomoi* of different peoples, Greek and non-Greek, were a topic of interest to many fifth-century Greeks, as Herodotus amply testifies; but there is no sign that they knew of, or thought they knew of, any society in which violence against parents was not reprehensible.

1421-2. **wasn't it a man ... to accept it?:** Pheidippides holds the social-contract theory

227

in its historicist form, according to which the *nomoi* that make an ordered society possible were consciously created at a definite time in the past, before which human life had been anarchic. This theory may have been held by Protagoras (who presents it in a mythologized form in Pl. *Prot.* 322a-d), was certainly held by Critias (fr. 25 D-K = 19 Snell), and is presented by Glaucon in Pl. *Rep.* 2.358e-359b as the view of a vaguely specified "they". See Guthrie, *History of Greek Philosophy* iii 135-147.

1423. **Is it then any less open to me ...?:** a reasonable answer might be "you are free to seek to persuade a majority to change the law, but not to take the law into your own hands as you have done".

1425- **we ... them:** Pheidippides speaks as if on behalf of the whole younger genera-
1426. tion ("we"), making as it were a treaty with their elders ("them").

1425- **we wipe from the record:** the new law is not to operate retrospectively; bea-
1426. tings administered before its enactment may not be avenged. Such clauses against retrospective application appear from time to time in fifth-century laws and decrees, notably in the law and oaths introduced on the restoration of Athenian democracy in 403 (Andoc. 1.86-91) and in the law-code of Gortyn (e.g. v 7-9, vi 24-25, ix 16-17). Similarly when the Athenians made an alliance with the Bottiaeans after a long period of hostility, both sides swore "I will bear no grudges on account of past events" (*IG* i^2 90.15-16, 20-21). Contrariwise, the law of Dracon allowing a person guilty of unintentional homicide to be pardoned by the victim's relatives specifically stated that it was to apply even to homicides committed before the date of the law ([Dem.] 43.57).

1427. **consider fowls and those other animals:** for the belief that a cockerel will fight against its father, cf. *Birds* 757-9, 1343-52. Pheidippides might have found it difficult to give examples of other animals that did likewise: with his sweeping and misleading generalization compare that made by the Worse Argument in 1056-7.

1432. **my good man:** Greek ō tān, a form of address which normally involves an assumption of superiority on the part of the speaker (at least in Ar.'s time; Menander uses it somewhat differently) and is hardly consistent with proper respect for one's father, though Bdelycleon uses it when educating his father in the social graces at *Wasps* 1161. See *CQ* 27 (1977) 273.

1432. **nor would Socrates think it was:** Pheidippides evidently cannot think how to justify his claim that his animal analogy is valid and his father's is not, and instead takes refuge in an appeal to authority. Strepsiades (and Ar. too) has put his finger on a weakness in the arguments of those who appeal to *phusis* to overthrow *nomos* (see on 1075): they invoke *phusis* only when it suits them to do so, and have no objective criterion to determine when appeal to *phusis* is valid and when not.

1433. **in that case**: if you think it right for a person who has been beaten to be compensated for his sufferings (1423-9). The argument which begins here is left incomplete, being interrupted at 1435 and not resumed. Completed, it would run thus: Pheidippides already, under the existing law, has the right to such compensation, at the expense of his own future offspring, whom he can beat with impunity; under his new law he will not dare to beat his son for fear of being beaten himself in his old age; so in the long run he will lose by the change.

1437-
1439.   For a character turning to and addressing the audience explicitly in the middle of a scene, cf. 1201; *Peace* 887, 1115; *Lys.* 1220. The present passage, however, is weak both dramatically and theatrically, and would not be missed if it were absent. Possibly it was written not to stand before, but to be an alternative to, 1440-51, and to lead up directly to 1452: Strepsiades begins to realize that his beating at his son's hands is the natural consequence and penalty of his wrong action in getting his son taught the Worse Argument, admits his error, and at once rounds on the Clouds on whose advice (794-6) he committed it. For other doublets which may similarly originate from alternative drafts cf. 653-4, 1173-6, *Frogs* 1252-60, 1437-53; see K.J. Dover, *ICS* 2 (1977) 150-6.

1443.   **I'll beat mother**: not that he has the slightest grudge against her; he makes this proposal solely to gratify the henpecked Strepsiades — but it has the reverse effect.

1444.   **a ... greater piece of wickedness**: although in general the father-beater and the mother-beater are coupled together as if equally heinous, still Athenian law and custom regarded the bond between child and mother as closer in some respects than that between child and father. Thus brother and sister born of the same mother, even though of different fathers, could not marry (cf. on 1372); and whereas a son could be released under certain circumstances from the duty of maintaining his natural father in old age (e.g. if his father had failed to teach him a trade, or if he had been adopted into another family: see Plut. *Sol.* 22.1 and A.R.W. Harrison, *The Law of Athens I: Family and Property* [Oxford, 1968] 93-4), we know of no circumstances that could release him from the duty of maintaining his natural mother (even adoption made no difference: Isaeus 7.25).

1449.   **the Barathron**: a rocky gully a short way outside the city, close to the northern Long Wall, into which condemned criminals were sometimes thrown (cf. *Knights* 1362; *Frogs* 574; *Wealth* 431, 1109; Hdt. 7.133; Xen. *Hell.* 1.7.20; Pl. *Gorg.* 516d-e; for the location, Pl. *Rep.* 4.439e and W. Judeich, *Topographie von Athen* [Munich, 1931] 140).

1452-
1464.   Throughout the dialogue between Strepsiades and the chorus-leader the rhythm is close to that of tragedy, except that Porson's Law is not observed.

There is no evidence that any specific scene of tragedy is being imitated or parodied; rather the rhythm of these lines is made to harmonize with their content, the revelation that Strepsiades' suffering is a just and divinely-ordained punishment for his own wickedness.

1455.   **because you turned:** Greek *strepsās*, playing on Strepsiades' name: see on 36.

1458-   **This is what we always do ... to fear the gods:** when a mortal has sinful inten-
1461.   tions, the gods may by temptation induce him to translate those intentions into action and suffer the disastrous consequences. This doctrine is perhaps most fully set out by the chorus of Aeschylus' *Agamemnon* (369-402), with particular reference to the destruction of Paris by the agency of "Temptation, unbearable child of premeditating Ruin"; compare also Aesch. *Pers.* 742 (of the ruin of Persia caused by Xerxes) "when a man is determined the god lends a hand".

1464.   **my dear, dear boy:** he has not addressed Pheidippides thus since 110, and then it was from a selfish motive; but at this moment he feels genuine affection for his son as a fellow-victim (1466).

1465-   **murder:** the Greek word need mean no more than "ruin", but it will appear
1466.   that Strepsiades' hatred of Socrates and his associates now knows no limits: when he fires their house he seems quite unconcerned whether they live or die. Cf.1499.

1465-   **that villain Chaerephon and Socrates:** it sounds almost as though Chaerephon
1466.   were the senior partner. Either, as Dover suggests, we have here an unrevised phrase reflecting an earlier state of the play in which Chaerephon had a more prominent role than he does in the play we have, or else Chaerephon is being called a villain for reasons independent of his association with Socrates, e.g. because he was allegedly a thief and informer (see on 104).

1466.   **who have cheated both you and me:** they have cheated Pheidippides by robbing him of his good name. To say that a man had struck his father was an insult that ranked with calling him a murderer or a coward (Lys. 10.6-9) — an insult that Pheidippides now will not be able to avenge or have punished, because it is true.

1467.   **I couldn't wrong my teachers:** Strepsiades' rebuke of 871 recoils on him, as Pheidippides shows that he has replaced the old unwritten law "honour thy father" with a new law "honour thy teacher".

1468.   **of Zeus Paternal stand in awe:** probably a quotation from an unknown tragedy. Zeus Patroos was not officially worshipped by the Athenians (Pl. *Euthd.* 302b-d), though an Attic pot of about 400 B.C., found at Myrmecium on the Strait of Kerch, bears the inscription "of Zeus Patroos" (*SEG* xxvii 437); but Zeus was worshipped under this title in many Greek states, and it occurs in Attic tragedy (Aesch. fr. 162 Nauck = 278a Mette; Soph. *Tr.* 288, 753). In our passage the title is understood to mean "protector of

230

the sanctity of fatherhood" as in Eur. *El.* 671; Xen. *Hell.* 2.4.21; Pl. *Laws* 881d.

1469- **Listen to that ... Is there any Zeus?:** again Pheidippides throws Strepsiades'
1470. own words back at him (cf. 818-821).

1471. **Vortex is king, having expelled Zeus:** Strepsiades' words at 828.

1473. **vortex-cup:** Greek *dīnos*, a cup or bowl with a rounded bottom (supported on wheels, according to schol. *Wasps* 618). Evidently an image of a *dīnos* stands outside the Reflectory, and it was its presence that led Strepsiades to believe that the Socratics worshipped Dinos (Vortex) as a god (see on 380).

1475. I take it that Pheidippides here goes into his father's house; but M. Nussbaum, *YCS* 26 (1980) 78, raises the possibility that he goes into the school and perhaps perishes in the ensuing conflagration. This cannot be disproved, but it is most unlikely that Strepsiades would set fire to the school knowing his son was inside.

1478. **Hermes:** the images of Hermes, which stood at many points in the streets of Athens, consisted of a square pillar with a phallus and with the top of the pillar carved to represent the god's head. One of these evidently stands before Strepsiades' house, as its non-theistic counterpart the *dīnos* stands before the Reflectory.

*1484- **set fire to the house of these prattlers:** the idea of the conflagration with which
1485. *Clouds* ends can be traced to three different sources — one in comedy, one in tragedy, and one in real life.
(i) It is common for a torch or torches to appear, for one reason or another, towards the end of an Aristophanic comedy — usually the torches of a bridal or other procession, as at the end of *Peace*, *Birds* and *Frogs*, or of nocturnal revellers as in *Wasps* (1331), *Ecclesiazusae* (978, 1150), and probably also *Acharnians* though there the text does not mention them; *Wealth* has both a reveller's torch (1041, 1052ff) and processional torches (1194). Here this symbol of Dionysiac joy has been turned into a weapon of destruction. Cf. C.P. Segal, *Arethusa* 2 (1969) 156.
(ii) In Euripides' *Hecuba*, the smoking ruins of Troy are kept constantly before the spectators' minds, and there may have been visible smoke rising from backstage (Hecuba points to it at 823). In his later *Trojan Women* the city is set on fire at the end of the play (1256ff). Compare also the funeral pyre of Capaneus in Eur. *Supp.* 980-1030.
(iii) At Croton in Italy, probably in the mid fifth century, enemies of the Pythagorean school of philosophy set a house on fire while the Pythagoreans were holding a meeting in it, and all but two of those in the house were killed (Iamblichus, *Life of Pythagoras* 249).

1485. **Xanthias:** also the name of a slave in *Acharnians*, *Wasps*, *Birds* and *Frogs*; it means "golden-haired".

231

1489.   **until you bring the house down on them:** in the Greek this line closely echoes 1460 in sound, as is noted by A. Köhnken, *Hermes* 108 (1980) 165 n.39. This may be an indication that just as it was the gods, through Pheidippides, who punished Strepsiades, so it is they, through Strepsiades, who will punish Socrates and his pupils; and Strepsiades' last words in the play (1506-9) suggest that this is the view he takes.

1497.   **CHAEREPHON:** no ms. makes Chaerephon the speaker here or at 1499, but several give him 1505, and if he speaks 1505 it is more likely that he has also spoken before than that (as we should otherwise have to assume) Ar. intended to use a fifth actor. It cannot be proved that Chaerephon speaks at all; but since he was the best known of Socrates' associates and had been frequently mentioned earlier in the play, and since his appearance made him a natural target for caricature (see on 104), it is unlikely that Ar. missed the opportunity to satirize him here. The satire may be directed mainly at his alleged distaste for fresh air (cf. 198-9) which was thought responsible for his pallor: unlike the other members of the school who speak (1495, 1502) he does not address Strepsiades directly – which suggests that he is still inside and cannot see the man on the roof -- and this is confirmed by 1505 which shows that he has then still to escape. He would almost prefer to burn, it is implied, rather than go outdoors.

1498.   **whose cloak you stole:** cf. 497-500, 856-7. The "you" is plural.

1503.   **I walk the air and descry the sun:** he mockingly repeats what Socrates said to him at 225.

1506.   **your:** plural, referring to the Socratics collectively, or perhaps (adopting the readings of E^{ac} in this and the next line) dual, referring to Socrates and Chaerephon.

1506.   **wantonly flouting:** lit. "committing *hubris* against"; see on 1299.

1507.   **seat:** Greek *hedrā* means both "position" (e.g. of a heavenly body) and "rump" (of human or animal); and the Moon could be thought of either as a celestial luminary or as an anthropomorphic goddess (cf. 607-626). Hence there is here not only an accusation of impiety, but also an insinuation of indecency.

1508.   **hit them, pelt them:** for similar cries cf. *Ach.* 280-3, [Eur.] *Rhesus* 675-6, Xen. *Anab.* 5.7.21.

1509.   **remembering how they wronged the gods:** in the Greek this line contains a distinct echo of 1461 (see Köhnken, cited on 1489).

1510-1. Metre: anapaestic.

1510-   **Lead the way out ... dancing for today:** for this perfunctory tailpiece cf.
1511.   *Thesm.* 1227-31; in that play, as in this, the hero's scheme for escaping from his troubles has been a failure.